MILLENNIALS TALKING MEDIA

TALKING MEDIA

Creating Intertextual Identities in
Everyday Conversation

Sylvia Sierra

OXFORD
UNIVERSITY PRESS

OXFORD
UNIVERSITY PRESS

Oxford University Press is a department of the University of Oxford. It furthers
the University's objective of excellence in research, scholarship, and education
by publishing worldwide. Oxford is a registered trade mark of Oxford University
Press in the UK and certain other countries.

Published in the United States of America by Oxford University Press
198 Madison Avenue, New York, NY 10016, United States of America.

Library of Congress Cataloging-in-Publication Data
Names: Sierra, Sylvia, author.
Title: Millennials talking media : creating
intertextual identities in everyday conversation / Sylvia Sierra.
Description: New York : Oxford University Press, 2021. |
Includes bibliographical references and index.
Identifiers: LCCN 2021013373 (print) | LCCN 2021013374 (ebook) |
ISBN 9780190931117 (hardback) | ISBN 9780190931124 (paperback) |
ISBN 9780190931148 (epub)
Subjects: LCSH: Generation Y—Communication—United States. |
Interpersonal communication—United States. | Intertextuality. |
Discourse analysis—Social aspects—United States. |
Stereotypes (Social psychology) in mass media. | Mass media and language—United States.
Classification: LCC P96.G4472 U675 2021 (print) | LCC P96.G4472 (ebook) |
DDC 302.23084/2—dc23
LC record available at https://lccn.loc.gov/2021013373
LC ebook record available at https://lccn.loc.gov/2021013374

DOI: 10.1093/oso/9780190931117.001.0001

1 3 5 7 9 8 6 4 2

Paperback printed by Marquis, Canada
Hardback printed by Bridgeport National Bindery, Inc., United States of America

For my family

Contents

Figures

Figures

Acknowledgments

This book on media references among friends, and ultimately on friendship, would not have been possible without the recorded talk of my friends. I thank them for their willingness to participate in my research, their conversations, their feedback, and the encouragement that they endlessly provided. Analyzing their talk closely has only made me appreciate their friendship, intellect, and senses of humor even more. I am especially grateful to "Paula" for her creativity in creating the inspired mural that became the cover art for this book, and for granting permission to use it for the cover. I also want to thank my friend and photographer Alex Au for taking the high-quality photograph of the mural on short notice, skillfully creating a makeshift photo studio on the spot. Recorded conversations with my friend Maggie Smith did not make it into the book, but I just want to thank her for always being there and supporting me throughout this process.

This book also would not have been possible without Heidi Hamilton. Her scholarship and mentorship have been instrumental in my growth as a researcher. As my academic advisor, professor, and chair of my dissertation committee, she guided me throughout my research trajectory, tirelessly supporting and encouraging me at every turn. I could not be more grateful to her for inspiring me to study both intertextuality and epistemics and for providing input on my work at many stages. I am also extremely grateful to Deborah Tannen and Cynthia Gordon, for their teaching, support, guidance, and feedback during my graduate studies and afterwards. Deborah Tannen taught me so much about research, writing, and speaking about my work that it is difficult to fully express how much of an impact she has had on my scholarly development. Her support in many aspects of my professional life has been invaluable. Cynthia Gordon generously became involved in the early stages of this study, and greatly influenced my understanding of framing in discourse. She has also supported my research, writing, presentations, and every other area of my professional life. I also thank Alla Tovares for being one of the original sources of inspiration for this study, as well as for reading drafts, providing feedback, and meeting with me to discuss data.

Many other teachers have supported me and have had an impact on my development as a scholar, including Anna De Fina, Jennifer Nycz, Natalie Schilling, and Jennifer Sclafani. In addition, I never would have pursued graduate studies without the formative influence of my professors in linguistics at the University of Mary Washington: Paul Fallon, Judith Parker, and, especially, my advisor Christina Kakava, for initially inspiring me to pursue linguistics and for guiding me towards this fulfilling career path. In addition, I thank the graduate professors in the Master of Education program at the same institution, particularly Patricia Reynolds and Jo Tyler, who kept me engaged in linguistics, and supported and encouraged me to pursue doctoral studies. I am very appreciative for thoughtful discussions on my work from my friends and fellow doctoral students Marta Baffy, Daniel Ginsberg, Nazir Harb, Hillary Harner, Didem Ikizoğlu, Joshua Kraut, and Aisulu Kulbayeva. I am also grateful to participants of the Interaction Lab at our university for their engagement with my work.

Various conference presentation audience members provided me with important feedback on different parts of specific analyses that went into this book, for which I thank them. I give special thanks to Stephen DiDomenico for reading and providing comments on one of the chapters of this book, as well as Jenny Cheshire for her comments on earlier versions of two chapters. I am also grateful to Valeria Sinkeviciute for inviting me to present some of my analysis as part of a panel she organized at the International Pragmatics Association in 2017, and for subsequently organizing a special issue in the *Journal of Pragmatics* which published an article based on this work. She and Anne Bezuidenhout provided helpful suggestions on that part of my analysis, along with Jessi Grieser who generously read the article, as well as the two anonymous reviewers. Remy Attig, Dominique Canning, Gwynne Mapes, Lavanya Murali, and Hanwool Choe also read some excerpts and provided feedback in the final stages of finishing the book.

I also thank my department chair, Charles Morris, and my colleagues at Syracuse University for supporting me in my research through travel grants, research grants, course releases, a research leave, and many other forms of support. I owe special thanks to Richard Buttny, Diane Grimes, Lyndsay Michalik Gratch, and Whitney Phillips for their conversations on my work. My students at Syracuse University have also provided me with insight on particular excerpts of my data and analyses. I am also extremely thankful to the three anonymous reviewers for their comments on my manuscript, as well as other anonymous reviewers who have provided me with suggestions on different chapters of this work when it was submitted to different journals. And of course this book would not have been possible without the knowledgeable team at Oxford University Press. I am grateful to Hallie Stebbins, who initially saw promise in my manuscript and worked hard to see that I got meaningful feedback from quality reviewers. My editor Meredith Keffer oversaw most of the process after that point, and I thank her for patiently answering all of my questions and working out important details with me. I also owe gratitude to the copy editor of this book, Christina Jelinek, along with the project manager from Newgen, Rajakumari Ganessin, for her consistent communication and answering my many questions leading up to publication, as well as the production editor at OUP, Leslie Johnson, OUP editorial assistant Macey Fairchild, project manager at Newgen Ashita Shah, and the indexer.

I also thank my graduate student and research assistant Michael Camele for their assistance in formatting the manuscript and much of the work that went before it, as well as for their feedback on my writing. My undergraduate students and research assistants Katherine Vestal and Nittika Mehra also provided me with assistance in the earlier stages of the research that went into this book, and Morgan Salomon assisted me with the final stages of copy editing. Along with Morgan, I thank my other undergraduate RAs Nicolette Angelotti, Julia Desch, Jessica Infante, and Hannah Hamermesh for their assistance with social media accounts for the book. I also appreciate the engagement with my work via Twitter from scholars and students all over the world.

Finally, my family has been a constant source of encouragement. My mother, Joanna Ingraham, inspired me with her fortitude and determination and always encouraged me in my interests. My father, Edward Sierra, has also been a pillar of support throughout my life, providing endless enthusiasm and advice, including lessons on "personality," and following my professional life as if it were a reality TV show. I also thank my step-parents, Mark Ingraham and Judith Sierra, for their steadfast support, along with my five brothers: Joseph Michniowski, Mark Ingraham Jr., Paul Z. Ingraham, Hayden Sierra, and Mason Sierra. My Grandmommy, Amelia Barzelatto, never ends a phone call without telling me how proud of me she is. My aunt, Rhonda McKendrick, and my uncle, Paul Michniowski, have also supported me throughout my life. I am also so grateful to the Simonson family for their love and support. Finally, I am immeasurably grateful to my partner/participant "Dave," not only for his assistance with some of the more quantitative details of my study and streamlining the transcription process, but also for his feedback on my work, steadfast encouragement, endless support, intellectual discussions, letting me read the entire manuscript aloud to him at the final stages, and his endless "sunshine and love" (it's a reference).

1
Introduction

Intertextual Media References in Millennial
Friend Discourse

"Sounds like a bad *Oregon Trail* trip!": Embarking on a Research Journey

On an autumn evening in 2014, I sat bundled by a dwindling fire in the wilderness of the Potomac River's Elm Island, with a mild head injury, when I came up with the idea for this book. As a 27-year-old graduate student in sociolinguistics, I had been recording everyday conversations among my friends and me, with their knowledge and consent, for a little over a month. My near-constant companion and a frequent participant in these conversations was Dave,[1] a fellow graduate student the same age as me whose fashion sense somewhat resembled the pirate Jack Sparrow in Disney's *Pirates of the Caribbean* film series (2003–2017). Dave and I had left the mainland, and I my digital audio recorder, to embark on a camping trip with two of Dave's housemates, Todd and Paula. Todd, an easy-going David Tennant *Doctor Who* (2005–2010) look-alike had been Dave's roommate in college. The two had started living together again soon after Dave started graduate school and Todd started working as a software developer in the same geographic region. They had two other housemates, living communally in a house of four somewhat like the Millennial characters in the American television show *The Big Bang Theory* (2007–2019). Paula, along with Dave and I, was a graduate student in linguistics. She was a couple years older than us and in appearance reminded me of the character Princess Buttercup in the film *The Princess Bride* (1987); she had a brilliant sense of humor with a special skill in crafting clever puns. Dave had introduced Todd to Paula at a house party, and Paula had later moved into Dave and Todd's house, to be with Todd.

The plan for our double-date camping trip was to meet up with a fifth wheel, Todd's childhood best friend, Aaron, on a shore of the Potomac River.

---

[1] All participants in this study (except me) have been given pseudonyms.

Millennials Talking Media. Sylvia Sierra, Oxford University Press. © Oxford University Press 2021.
DOI: 10.1093/oso/9780190931117.003.0001

Aaron, a pony-tailed Eagle Scout pursuing a doctorate in mathematics, would instruct us in rowing a canoe and kayaks down the Potomac River to an island where we would spend the evening camping. At the beginning of our adventure, Aaron had insisted on flipping each of us novices over in a kayak as practice for the potentiality of it capsizing in the rapids. When it was my turn for this initiation ritual, I hit my head hard on the inside of the overturned kayak as I scrambled to the surface. By christening it thus, the trip was doomed to be an amphibious calamity. But, as it happens, the trip not only marked the crystallization of my research topic; the disastrous misadventure would also become a popular topic itself in many of the conversations I would record afterwards.

With my head injury, I rowed the canoe with a shovel while Aaron used the single paddle he had brought. Meanwhile, Dave, Todd, and Paula navigated a mile and a half through the rough river and over its rapids in three stubborn kayaks to safely disembark on the island. Aaron had insisted that we bring more beer than water in our shovel-paddled canoe. Like the Pilgrims on the Mayflower, we ran out of water first. I woke up in the middle of the night to Aaron belching loudly. He then began to writhe and vomit in the tent that we were all sharing. I dived out of the tent head first as Dave chucked out our sleeping bags. We relocated near the red coals of the campfire, trying to forget what we had just experienced by refocusing our attention on the island's clear evening view of the stars as we settled down for a second time.

Despite the day's distractions, I had been preoccupied with choosing a topic to write about as a final paper for a course seminar. As I gazed at the stars, I started thinking about a book chapter we had just read in class by sociolinguist Alla Tovares (2012), on how a family played along with the TV quiz show *Who Wants to Be a Millionaire* and then referred to it in their later conversations. I suddenly realized that while Dave and his housemates did not watch much TV back on the mainland, they frequently played video games. Not only did they play video games, but they so identified with gaming as an activity that in the front sitting room of their square two-story brick house, Paula had painted a large mural on the wall depicting all the housemates[2] as video game characters, along with Paula and Todd's two Bengal cats (Hydra and Liam) (Figure 1.1). I began to wonder if the video games the housemates played and identified with so much made their way into their everyday talk. I then remembered a conversation that I had recorded for my seminar where Dave, Paula, and I had been commiserating about receiving our university stipend checks late, and I joked, "We have been paid by 'Arstotzka.'" Arstotzka is a fictitious dystopian country in a video game we had all played recently, called *Papers, Please* (Pope 2013). Dave's housemates picked up on my reference to

---

[2] The central figure in the mural represents a former housemate who had moved out prior to my study.

Figure 1.1 Paula's mural of the housemates as video game characters

the video game and began to repeat other words from it, making our banal real-life experience into a kind of playful game.

Another key video game reference had its genesis on this camping trip. A few weeks after having survived the trip, I recorded a conversation at a Northern Virginia diner where Dave and I told his childhood friend, Alan, the story of me hitting my head on the kayak. I told Alan how I had "hopped into a kayak first" and "hit my head" while smiling and laughing as I admitted that I "felt kind of dizzy." At this, Alan laughingly cried out "Oh!" and exclaimed, "Sounds like a bad *Oregon Trail* trip!" Alan, Dave, and I all remembered playing the video game *The Oregon Trail* (Rawitsch, Heinemann, & Dillenberger 1985) in elementary school in the mid-1990s on Apple desktop computers. In this video game, the player is a 19th-century wagon leader guiding a party of settlers on the Oregon Trail, and river crossings and injuries are both part of the game. Here, Alan's childhood memories of playing *The Oregon Trail* allowed him to become involved in a story years later about my individual experience of an injury on a camping trip that involved navigating a river.

A few weeks later, I recorded another conversation at Dave's house. Dave, Todd, Paula, and I were telling Jeff, their fourth housemate and Todd's co-worker, a bearded George Costanza from *Seinfeld* (1989–1998) look-alike who did not go on the camping trip, about what he missed. Paula and I expressed our astonishment at how pony-tailed Aaron had shamelessly vomited in the tent that we were all sharing, when Jeff astutely observed, "Long hair don't care." This phrase was text for a popular *internet meme*—a text created, circulated, and transformed by participants online (Phillips & Milner 2017). Thus, this legendary camping trip was the departure point for my fascination with how speakers use shared knowledge of media references to navigate unpleasant experiences in conversation, such as talk about a head injury, getting paid late, and vomiting in a tent.

Purpose of This Book

In this book, I examine everyday interactions to explore how groups of American Millennial friends in their late 20s reference *prior texts* (Becker 1995) by repeating words, phrases, and phonetic features from both popular "old" media such as films, TV shows, and songs as well as "new" media like video games, internet memes, and YouTube videos. I explore how, while these friends use these media references for fun, they also often use them to carry out complex interactional work, ultimately constructing different individual identities while simultaneously reinforcing group identities based on shared knowledge and experience. I investigate how *intertextuality* (Kristeva 1980), or the repetition of texts, is important in creating social connection and group solidarity. More specifically, I show how media intertextuality serves as a resource for overcoming interactional hurdles and bringing friends together.

The study of intertextuality emerged out of a blend of philosophy, literary theory and criticism, and semiotics. Intertextuality in interaction has been increasingly explored in discourse analysis and sociolinguistics, linguistic anthropology, communication, and related fields. Gordon (2009) has shown that intertextuality and *framing*, an interdisciplinary theory of how people expect, perceive, and construct their experiences, are intrinsically intertwined. I contribute to the dialogue on the cognitive and interactional processes of intertextuality and framing by arguing that intertextuality, and thus framing, depend on the management of *epistemics*, a conversation analytical theory of knowledge management that has been applied widely but largely independently. The analyses I present in this book thus have two primary goals: (1) to understand the form and function of media intertextuality in Millennial friend conversations, specifically relating to how these friends use media references to construct themselves as a social group; and (2) to demonstrate how intertextual media references are used as epistemic resources to manage framing, ultimately contributing to group solidarity and friendship. I also examine the ways in which this group's repertoire of media references affects not just how they manage interaction, but also the stereotypes, othering, and views of the world that they sometimes reproduce via some of these references.

Thus, this is fundamentally a study about friends and how and why they reference media. I examine conversations among Millennial friends primarily from an interactional sociolinguistic perspective to investigate how individuals use media references in everyday social interactions to create and maintain friendships—to share inside jokes and craft a group's culture. More specifically, I analyze talk primarily from five naturally occurring conversations among nine friends and myself. These five conversations were recorded across the span of one year (2014-2015) and contain over 140 media references. In chapter 5 I also draw on conversations that were not audio-recorded, but that I observed and reconstructed in my notes afterwards.

This study is specifically about friends who are members of the Millennial generation. For my understanding of the Millennial generation, I draw on generational theory as developed by those who coined the term *Millennial*: historians William Strauss and Neil Howe. However, Strauss-Howe generational theory has generated controversy. While many have praised the authors for their ambition, insights, and accessibility, the theory has also been criticized by several historians and some political scientists and journalists as being overly deterministic, non-falsifiable, and unsupported by rigorous evidence. Keeping this controversy in mind and acknowledging that generations are analytical constructs, I draw on facts presented in Strauss-Howe generational theory that are relevant to my study of Millennial friends, while leaving aside any overgeneralizations and predictions they make about the Millennial generation. I do so with the understanding that their work is the most thorough investigation so far carried out on this topic. I also draw on other related sociological work about Millennials, as well as scholarship on the representation of Millennials in media.

Millennials are generally considered to be those born roughly between 1981 and 1996. They follow Generation X, precede Generation Z, and are the children of Baby Boomers or Generation X members, while some older members may have parents from the Silent Generation. Shaputis (2004) additionally labeled Millennials as the Peter Pan generation, because of their tendency to delay some traditional social rites of passage into adulthood for longer periods than previous generations. For instance, some Millennials live with their parents for longer than previous generations; they also appear to marry later in life. Palmer (2007) regards the high cost of housing and rising price of higher education as some of the factors driving the supposed escape to Neverland. Indeed, at the time of my study, Dave and his housemates lived in a group house in large part due to the high cost of housing and the expense of the higher education that Dave and Paula were pursuing. In addition, The Great Recession, which began in 2007, meant that many Millennials not only graduated college with debt, but they did so with few well-paying job prospects, despite being the most educated generation in American history at that time. Kaklamanidou and Tally (2014:5) even go as far as to state that "downward mobility is a defining feature of [Millennials]." Many of my Millennial friends and I enrolled in higher education in part due to the lack of appealing job prospects we encountered with only undergraduate college degrees. In turn, Dave and his friends created a communal living situation due to economic necessity. The mural from Figure 1.1 is actually on a 2x4 drywall "wall" that the housemates built to create an extra "bedroom" and thus drive the rent of the house down; Dave lived in what had been designed as the dining room of the house. The household's living arrangement relates to Hills' (2006:2) assertion that for Millennials, "forming kin-like relationships with your friends reinvents the family."

In addition to entering adulthood during a time of economic decline, Millennials are generally also marked by their growing up during the Information Age. They are the first generation to come of age with computers in many of their homes, and are overall relatively comfortable in their usage of digital technologies and social media. Indeed, Prensky (2001:1) coined the term *digital natives* to describe many Millennials as "native speakers of the digital language of computers, video games and the internet," having grown up experiencing digital technology. At the same time, it is important to acknowledge that digital inequalities and uneven distribution of internet access exist, and thus there might be intra-generational variation in Millennials' digital practices or competencies (Spilioti 2015). For instance, Watkins (2018) discusses a *mobile paradox*, wherein Black and Latino youth are earlier adopters of mobile technologies and are more active on their mobile devices than white youth, while also not having broadband internet access on home computers. Still, many Millennials came of age during a time when the internet became intertwined with the entertainment industry. Like Dave, his housemates, and myself, many Millennials do not own TVs, instead engaging with TV shows, films, YouTube videos, video games, music, and internet memes using computers, smartphones, and tablets which connect to the internet. As Kaklamanidou and Tally (2014:4) put it, many Millennials are thus "exposed to a steady diet of media." However, as Gerhardt (2012:18) observes, media consumers "do not simply 'use' media in the sense that one uses a toaster to toast bread." While recent work has examined how Millennials use new media, social media, and participate in digital discourse (e.g., Thurlow & Mroczek 2011; Georgakopoulou & Spilioti 2015; Burgess et al. 2017), I add to our understanding of Millennials' media usage by examining how Millennials actually embed both old and new media texts in their everyday face-to-face talk.

Thus, my book is also a study of media appropriation among certain Millennial friends; specifically, how the friends in my study quote a vast array of both old and new media in the form of inside jokes, a phenomenon which characterizes many of their conversations. This study is about how these Millennial friends signal to each other that they are referencing media by repeating words, phrases, melodies, and accents that they have heard or seen, how they mutually engage with references, and in what situations and moments in conversation they do this referencing. In exploring media references among these Millennial friends, I highlight the role of media intertextuality in two fundamental human processes—sharing cultural knowledge and constructing group identity.

Knowledge, Framing, and Identity

Knowledge: Intertextuality and Epistemics

While references to video games like *The Oregon Trail* might be unique to those in the Millennial generation who grew up playing this game, generally speaking, references that demonstrate knowledge about media of some kind in conversation are widespread. Scholars across disciplines have explored the practice of referencing known texts and, more broadly, the insertion of prior texts in new contexts. Literary theorist M.M. Bakhtin's concept of *dialogicality* (1981, 1984, 1986) describes how each word uttered is "half ours and half someone else's" (1981:345), bringing previous utterances, experiences, and meanings with it. Literary critic Julia Kristeva (1980 [1967], 1986) expands on Bakhtin's work and calls the process whereby speakers and hearers re-appropriate language *intertextuality*, in which "any text is constructed as a mosaic of quotations; any text is the absorption and transformation of another" (Kristeva 1986:37). A colorful mosaic of well-known quotations is on full display when people repeat media texts in their everyday interactions.

With his focus on repetition of "prior texts," linguist A.L. Becker (1994) uses the word *languaging* to describe the active, repetitive process of language use, which "can be understood as taking old texts from memory and reshaping them into present contexts" (Becker 1994:166). Thus, intertextuality is relevant not only in literature and written texts, but also in spoken language. In an early discourse analytic study of intertextuality, Tannen (2007

[1989]) highlights how repetition is prominent both within and across individual conversations, also arguing that repetition creates connection between interlocutors. This is related to Becker's observation that "social groups seem to be bound primarily by a shared repertoire of prior texts" (1994:165). Thus, repetition of prior texts is not only a fundamental characteristic of conversations, but it also serves the social function of bonding around shared cultural knowledge.

This social bonding function of repetition is paramount to people trying to construct and maintain friendships. Friends can connect over shared memories and experiences in a conversation where they repeat phrases from *The Oregon Trail,* if all of them remember playing the video game. Indeed, Becker had also posited that, "apparently free conversation is a replay of remembered texts—from TV news, radio talk, The New York Times . . ." (cited in Tannen 1989/2007:55). While Becker hinted at the possibilities of prior media texts embedded within everyday conversation, he left this observation open for future researchers to examine with empirical data. One of the earliest scholars to research this topic is Schlobinski (1995), who observes German youth making references to TV quiz shows, films, comics, and music lyrics to create diverse youthful speaking styles, and also cites Wachau's (1989) investigation of a group of teenage girls and their expressions lifted from advertising and music. Widely referenced in the more recent literature on this topic is Spitulnik's (1996) study, which examines the medium of radio in Zambia to study how phrases and discourse styles from radio broadcasts are recycled and reanimated in everyday conversation. She argues that public accessibility of radio, detachability of media fragments, and people's active engagement with radio allow public words "to have lives of their own yet also be fibers of connection across various social situations and contexts" (161), playing a major role in the creation and integration of communities. Spitulnik's analysis reveals the intertextual process through which public radio texts function as reference points for the circulation of discourse, providing insights into the intertextual relations between media texts and everyday talk.

Media texts have been fruitfully examined as part of children's talk inside and outside of classrooms. Indeed, Dyson (2003) finds that primary school students share a "common sociocultural landscape" in which they reference televised sports media, cartoons, and music for meaning making, learning, and social affiliation. Similarly, Lytra (2007) examines how Greek schoolchildren embed snippets of songs, fragments of talk from comedy shows, singing routines from variety shows, and chants from football matches to play and form social identities. Maybin (2003) also finds that students use snippets of popular songs to play in the classroom while displaying and experimenting with different institutional identities. In addition, Rampton's seminal (1995) study examines adolescents' singing of popular music specifically as a linguistic resource used for social or ethnic "crossing" with voices not their own in British multiethnic classrooms (see also Rampton 2006). Exploring instances of Bollywood film dialogue interwoven into conversation among desi teens, Shankar (2004) finds that this practice allows teens to enact humor, flirting, conflict, and other types of talk. Poveda (2011) additionally examines how a group of Latin American students in a multicultural high school in Madrid appropriate the label *India* (American native) from a historical novel for verbal play among peers. Examining how lack of knowledge about media texts can be a source of exclusion for ESL students, Duff (2002) analyzes prevalent talk about pop culture, primarily relating to television, in a Canadian high school. These studies, many of them focusing on multiethnic and polylinguistic settings, show that speakers appropriate older forms of media like songs, novels, TV, and film starting from a young age and continuing through adolescence for a variety of interactional functions.

In an early large-scale study focusing specifically on media references, Albada and Godbold (2001) analyze survey data of U.S. college students' use of media references in interaction, and find that films are quoted more often than TV shows, that media references often occur in multi-turn exchanges, and that they are perceived as creating increased pleasure and affiliation among interactants. In another early study on media references to film and TV shows, Scollo (2007) examines their structures in social interaction among family, friends, and students, as well as on TV, finding that they typically include a trigger, a reference, and a response. She also finds that media references are performed for the humor, pleasure, play, shared identity, and bonds that they create.

Most of the recent research on media texts in talk has focused on television and film media. Many studies suggest that television texts in particular are part of the cultural repertoire (e.g., Bryce & Leichter 1983; Lull 1990; Spigel 1992, 2001; Bryant & Bryant 2001). Tovares (2006, 2007, 2012) has published a body of work analyzing how television texts function in everyday interaction among family and friends. She demonstrates that family and friends creatively repeat television texts to express thoughts and feelings, create involvement and alignments, discuss private issues without getting personal, entertain one another, educate and socialize children, discuss their differences in attitudes and values, and construct certain identities (as knowledgeable). Tovares' studies on TV talk in family interaction show that repeating media texts is not a passive process, but rather is active and creative, and can be used to serve a variety of functions among friends and families. Further examining the functions of referencing media in family talk, Beers Fägersten (2012) analyzes what she calls *intertextual quotation* of television, videos, and movies, finding that it is primarily a playful act, ratified by repetition and laughter, and that it serves three functions: reflecting evaluative stance towards ongoing conversation, establishing interactive alignment, and strategically rekeying or reframing interaction for the purpose of conflict resolution. Kelley (2013) additionally analyzes how gay men reference camp film and TV to mitigate delicate matters, construct and perform identity, and establish community and bonding. Thus, these studies demonstrate that a variety of TV and film texts can be actively repurposed to serve specific functions, ultimately binding speakers together as a cohesive social group. Building on prior work regarding media texts in interaction, in Sierra (2016) I examine how friends in their late twenties—the same participants as in this larger study—creatively appropriate texts from video games they have played to resolve knowledge-related problems in their interactions, which is ultimately conducive to group identity construction as "nerds" with shared video game–playing experiences.

There is a burgeoning body of work adjacent to research on the creative appropriation of media texts in conversation that focuses on related forms of everyday linguistic creativity (e.g., Crystal 1998; Cook 2000; Jones 2012, 2016; Thurlow 2012). This kind of creativity includes joking and all types of verbal play, such as repetition (Carter 2015; Toolan 2012) and hybridity or blending (Vásquez & Creel 2017). Linguistic creativity often derives from "linking previously unrelated ideas, concepts or elements into new patterns" (Jones 2012:6). Relatedly, in our current media landscape, "Creativity mediated through new technologies [results from] processes of combining existing resources to create new meanings" (Jones 2012:168). This type of creativity thus often involves the repurposing of existing media texts in new discourse contexts. While many of the studies of linguistic creativity examine it against the backdrop of more traditional media (such as literature and film) and new technology including online discourse as creative texts, there is also an increasing interest in everyday language creativity (as explored in Carter 2016). In the present study, I contribute to research on media appropriation and linguistic creativity by showing how knowledge of shared old and new media texts are used as creative linguistic resources in the everyday conversations of Millennial friends.

Many of the aforementioned studies on intertextuality and linguistic creativity recognize the role of knowledge in creating new meanings and identities in interaction. In his work on constructing group identity via humor, Norrick (1989:120) describes why knowledge makes creative intertextual jokes conducive to creating involvement and solidarity: "Complementary exhibition of shared knowledge, particularly when it involves some specialized or arcane source, attests to common interests and encourages mutual involvement." Knowledge management—also known more formally as *epistemics*—is thus important in intertextuality. While the importance of knowledge itself has been recognized in studies of intertextuality in interaction, none draw explicitly on contemporary theorizing on epistemics in discourse.

However, epistemics in interaction has been thoroughly studied in recent years within the subfield of conversation analysis (CA) within sociology. As Heritage (2013) explains, epistemics in CA "focuses on the knowledge claims that interactants assert, contest and defend in and through turns-at-talk and sequences of interaction" (370). Thus, the study of epistemics in CA explicitly focuses on the role and importance of knowledge in interaction. The key foundational work in this area is Raymond and Heritage's (2006) study, in which they demonstrate that epistemic claims in talk are central to management and maintenance of social relations. In fact, Heritage (2012) further proposes that an *epistemic engine* drives sequences of talk, so that any imbalance in epistemic status among interlocutors, expressed through verbalized epistemic stances, results in a sequence where speakers attempt to equalize the imbalance.

Thus, Heritage (2013:386) argues that this work on epistemics in conversation demonstrates that "the organization of social action itself is profoundly intertwined with epistemic considerations." Heritage (2013) also suggests that in addition to the management of epistemic positions driving talk forward, epistemic management may be involved in topic shift, and may be implicated in the closure of sequences, topics, and conversations. Heritage (2013) points to future directions for research in epistemics. The first of these is to consider the multidimensionality of epistemic status, captured by a "topographical map" metaphor (Schütz 1946), which embraces complexity resulting from different epistemic resources and standpoints. Heritage also indicates the need to look beyond individual and dyadic interactions by considering epistemic ecologies.

van Dijk (2013, 2014) takes a broad approach to epistemics, suggesting that it is especially worthwhile to study ". . . on the one hand because most of human knowledge is acquired and shaped by discourse, and on the other hand because language use, in general, and the production and understanding of discourse, in particular, are impossible without the activation of massive amounts of knowledge of the world" (2014:5). Thus, van Dijk highlights the crucial importance of knowledge and our ability to analyze its role in discourse. van Dijk is most interested in *social knowledge* which he defines as "the shared beliefs of an epistemic community, justified by contextually, historically and culturally variable (epistemic) criteria of reliability" (2014:21). In my study, it is precisely social knowledge about media, shared by the epistemic community of Millennial friends, that is my main focus.

Heeding van Dijk's (2013:498) call for *epistemic discourse analysis*—or "the systematic and explicit study of the ways knowledge is interactively 'managed' (activated, expressed, presupposed, implied, conveyed, construed, etc.) in the structures and strategies of text and talk"—I expand on what previous studies have mentioned regarding the importance of knowledge in intertextual processes and merge this area with work on epistemics. I develop a framework to show how intertextuality is not only interconnected with framing, but how intertextual references can also be understood as contributing to epistemic management. I argue that acknowledging both intertextual and epistemic processes simultaneously allows us to better understand knowledge, relationships, and identity construction.

Framing

As social groups reshape prior texts in everyday conversation, they also create new frames. Bateson (1972) originally introduced the concept of *frame* to describe how people interpret what is going on in interaction (joking, arguing, commiserating, etc.). He conceptualizes every frame as having an underlying *metamessage* which conveys to participants how they should interpret the message. Goffman (1974) expands on frame analysis, describing the occurrence of laminated or layered frames, meaning that multiple activities are happening at once. Leaving the door open for future research, Goffman writes, "Every possible kind of layering must be expected" (1974:157). He also introduces the term *keying* to characterize the tone of the interaction, which he saw as central to frame analysis, and describes how keying could also be subject to rekeying—a change in tone. Goffman's work was, for the most part, based on his own observations and theoretical in nature, and he left the particulars to be worked out by future generations of interactional researchers.

Tannen and Wallat's (1993) analysis expands on framing in interaction, outlining how speakers manage frames moment by moment through linguistic and paralinguistic means. They define *interactive frame* as "a definition of what is going on in interaction, without which no utterance (or movement or gesture) could be interpreted" (Tannen & Wallat 1993:59). This focus on how framing is managed in interaction is crucial to understanding the importance of framing in everyday life. Tannen and Wallet also describe *knowledge schemas* as "participants' expectations about people, objects, events and settings in the world" (1987/1993:60), which are based on prior experiences and inform shifting between interactive frames. Tannen and Wallat's work is instrumental in clarifying how Goffman's frames function in conversation, as well as in developing an interactional, linguistic approach to framing which prioritizes the role of knowledge in making sense of the world.

Addressing the details of framing, especially how frames are layered or what Goffman (1974) calls *laminated* in discourse, Gordon (2002, 2008, 2009) argues that intertextuality and frames are fundamentally linked. Gordon's (2009) analysis builds on Tannen's (1989/2007) work on repetition in discourse, with an emphasis on how intertextuality is used to construct the family as a social group with a shared set of prior texts, while also accomplishing different kinds of framing. Gordon shows how intertextually reshaping a family member's words enables speakers to laminate frames. Like Gordon, Tannen (2006) examines intertextuality in family discourse, analyzing how a couple's arguments are reframed and rekeyed over the course of one day. She defines *reframing* as "a change in what the discussion is about" and builds on Goffman's (1974) work on *key* to define *rekeying* as "a change in the tone or tenor of an interaction" (Tannen 2006:601). This focus on how intertextuality contributes to rekeying and reframing further illustrates how intertextuality and framing are intertwined.

These empirically based findings on framing demonstrate that speakers must draw on pre-existing *knowledge schemas* (Tannen 1993) in order to shift interactive frames fluidly and purposefully. As Gordon (2009) has demonstrated that intertextuality and framing are inextricably intertwined, I suggest that intertextuality is also an important site of epistemic management, and that both are implicated in framing. By analyzing intertextual references as epistemic resources, I anchor my attention on the shared knowledge and experiences required to manage frames, and in doing so show how these processes are constitutive of various individual and group identities.

Identity

Previous work on how identity is not a purely internal phenomenon and is socially constructed in interaction serves as a framework for my own analysis of identity among Millennial friends. The construction of group identity relies on some form of consensus across individuals in a social group that they are similar, or that they have a shared identity based on *adequation* (Bucholtz &

Hall 2005). Bamberg (2011) describes similarity/difference as a dilemma that involves "the establishment of a synchronic connection between sameness and difference (between self and other)" (1). Bucholtz and Hall (2004) stress that these are active processes that are interactionally achieved by speakers. Similar to how families may form a "familylect" (Søndergaard 1991), or a family's particular way of speaking, groups of friends also use shared prior texts, as Gordon (2009) has shown for families, to constitute a bound social group with its own culture. In this study, I analyze intertextual media references in everyday conversation as a specific kind of shared prior text that friends can draw on to express their shared cultural knowledge and thereby reinforce their shared identity.

Goffman (1959) describes the *presentation of self* as the core of social interaction, and theorizes that in interaction people are always concerned about preserving *face*—the positive social value one constructs for oneself. Importantly, Goffman views face not as something internal to the individual, but a facet of social life that is constructed and managed through taking up different kinds of footings, creating alignments to ourselves and others, as well as to utterances. This conceptualization of self as external has been influential in subsequent studies of identity, since such studies have evolved to view self as actively constructed through discourse, instead of an a priori, internal phenomenon (e.g., Ochs 1993; Bucholtz & Hall 2005). Such work has demonstrated that identity is actively constructed through everyday practices, which has influenced the linguistic understanding of identity as constructed via discourse.

Many researchers have used stance as a way to approach identity construction in discourse (e.g., Biber & Finegan 1989; Ochs 1993; Kärkkäinen 2006; Englebretson 2007; Du Bois 2007; Bucholtz 2009; Coupland & Coupland 2009; Jaffe 2009). Ochs (1993:288) defines *stance* as "a social act that reveals one's epistemic attitudes, such as how certain or uncertain a speaker is about something, and displays of affective attitudes, such as intensity of emotion or kind of emotion about some referent or proposition." Based on one's sense of the act and stance meanings encoded by linguistic constructions, analysts can examine a speaker's social identity construction. Ochs emphasizes that there is no strict mapping of certain acts and stances onto certain identities, and that people may use different kinds of acts and stances to construct themselves variably within some particular social status or social relationship (1993:289). Thus Ochs encourages a social constructivist approach to identity, where researchers should ask, "What kind of social identity is a person attempting to construct in performing this kind of verbal act or in verbally expressing this kind of stance?"

Du Bois (2007) focuses on two types of stance: affective (regarding emotion) and epistemic (regarding knowledge). For my study, epistemic stance is particularly relevant, as speakers make intertextual media references that also indicate an epistemic claim. As described earlier in the discussion of the CA work on epistemics, the exploration of epistemic stance in identity is taken up by Raymond and Heritage (2006), who define the epistemics of social relations as "methods for managing rights to identity-bound knowledge in self-other relations" (678). Through the negotiation of epistemic stances, speakers express differing epistemic statuses in regards to their rights to assess epistemic territories, making relevant and managing self-other relationships and interactional identities (see also Schiffrin 1996; Gordon 2007).

In sum, identity construction has been shown to be analyzable as it is actively constituted via discourse, and the examination of stance has proved to be a productive site for analyzing identity construction. Most relevant to my study is epistemic stance, or the expression of knowledge that can craft a distinct identity. Gordon (2006), Hamilton (1996), and Tannen (2006) suggest the importance of examining identity construction as it occurs across interactions (i.e., intertextually). By bringing together intertextuality, epistemics, and framing, I argue that knowledge-based identity construction can be more fully analyzed and understood.

Media References in Millennial Friends' Talk Study Methodology

Exploring Millennial Friends' Talk

Ethnographies of naturally occurring talk among friends has primarily focused on friendships among children and adolescents.[3] In addition to M. Goodwin's 2006 study of schoolgirls' games, Hewitt (1986) analyzes interracial adolescent friendships. Bucholtz's 1999 work on "nerd girls" examines high school girls' friendships, while her 2009 work explores friendships among boys in high school. Mendoza-Denton (2008) contributes to this body of work with her study of high school Latina girls involved with gangs. Much of the canonical CA work (e.g., Sacks' lectures published in 1992; Sacks 1999; see also Schegloff 1989) has also focused on "mundane data," which frequently has consisted of friends' talk. This body of work has provided important insights into how friendships are formed and managed prior to adulthood, but adult friendships

---

[3] M. Goodwin (2006) provides a comprehensive overview of much of this work.

have been under-studied. Even when adult friendships have been the focus of research, women friends specifically seem to have received the most attention (e.g., Coates 1989, 1996, 1997, 1998, 2000; Hunt 2005; Raymond & Heritage 2006; Tannen 2017; Tovares 2006). Tannen's (1984/2005) study appears to be an exception in studying an adult mixed-gender friend group.

As Tannen writes, "Recording a conversation among friends that would have taken place anyway makes available for study patterns of language use that do not emerge among strangers, such as playful routines, irony and allusion, reference to familiar jokes, and unstated assumptions" (1984/2005:43–44). Indeed, the occurrence of playful routines, irony and allusion, and reference to familiar jokes are a primary focus of my analysis of mixed-gender Millennial adult friends' talk through the examination of intertextual media references. The unstated assumptions of the speakers relate to their knowledge management; these ultimately contribute to their shared group identity construction based on similarity in interaction. Furthermore, the fact that these friends were a relatively homogenous group means that in large part they had similar habits of media consumption. As children of the Millennial generation, they had seen many of the same American films and TV shows and played the same video games. As adults who came of age during the digital revolution, they all spent a good deal of time online, viewed many of the same YouTube videos, saw the same internet memes, and thus had similar epistemic access to prior media texts; thus their conversations, which are rife with intertextual media references, lend themselves to the study of the phenomenon and how the deployment of these interactional resources contributed to shared identity construction.

Following in the tradition of sociolinguists such as Hamilton (1994/2005), Schiffrin (1987), and Tannen (1984/2005), my participation in the conversations I recorded had distinct advantages, such as allowing me to know as much as possible about the conversational setting and the participants' relationships with each other. If I had questions about the participants or some stretch of talk, I asked my participants for their insights, in a kind of "playback" (e.g., as conducted by Labov & Fanshel 1977 and Tannen 1984/2005) or through follow-up emails during my analysis. Using a small and unobtrusive digital recorder, or sometimes my mobile phone, ensured that I could easily record long stretches of conversations in various settings. I recorded conversations at fairly frequent intervals with Dave's and my friends, primarily on or around the weekends, and typically at Dave's house and in restaurants. In addition to Dave's housemates and their friends, I also recorded conversations with my friends in the absence of Dave, which took place on a university campus.

I ceased recording once I had started conducting playback interviews and realized that, to some extent, the participants and therefore the data were somewhat "tainted," since the participants became aware at this point of my research interests, which had developed to include how the study of intertextual media references in everyday talk could illuminate my earlier interests in epistemics and identity construction. Therefore, in some of the later conversations I recorded, which I do not draw from in this study, participants sometimes would say things like, "This would be great for your research" or "That's a reference!" and I even caught myself asking on occasion, "Is that a reference to something?"

Collecting and Analyzing Data: Identifying Intertextual Media References

At the beginning of data collection, I did not have a clear objective in collecting a particular kind of talk. I simply started recording conversations in which I was a participant, with the hope that something interesting would reveal itself. This is how I began to record many conversations that I was later able to choose from for this study. As I described at the outset of this book, Tovares' (2012) analysis of how TV shows served as intertextual resources in family conversations inspired my noticing how Dave's housemates frequently used knowledge about video game texts as intertextual resources in their conversations. Once I had struck upon the idea of analyzing video game references in the conversations I had recorded, I then began to notice when the housemates used video game references when I was not recording. I started to supplement my recorded data with notes about conversations where video game texts seemed to function the same way as the initial instances I had recorded, checking with Dave (since he was present in many of the interactions) to try to maintain accuracy in recalling the details.

After my initial analysis of excerpts of talk that included references to video games, which focused on the larger theoretical issues of video game intertextuality, framing, epistemics, and group identity construction (see Sierra 2016), I became interested in media intertextuality in conversation more broadly, such as media references to books, songs, TV shows, movies, video games, and internet memes. A question that I had only partially begun to answer in my original, more theoretically oriented analysis emerged that seemed to be important in demonstrating how intertextual processes work in talk more generally: How do speakers signal that they are making an intertextual reference in talk, and how do listeners show mutual engagement with such references? In order to explore this next phase of the study, I needed to draw on much more data than the two original video game examples I had analyzed. I ultimately chose to focus on five recorded conversations of approximately seven hours of talk among nine of my friends and me (10 participants total). I selected these out of my larger set of 40 conversations containing 45 hours and 24 minutes of talk among 26 participants that I had recorded across the span of one year, in 2014–2015. I selected these five conversations due to the relatively high concentration of media references they contained. In these conversations, I identified media references as words, phrases, or phonetic qualities (such as those related to the performance of stylized accents or singing) that could be traced back to a specific media text.

The Conversations and the Millennial Friends

I first returned to my original two conversations of focus, transcribing and annotating additional media references, along with relevant details such as the type of media reference, the specific source text, who made the reference, etc. As described at the outset of this book, the first recorded conversation of one hour and nine minutes of casual talk among Dave, his housemates, and me in their kitchen/dining room on a Saturday night had stood out for its rich use of references to the video game *Papers, Please.* About a month later, I had recorded the one hour and 34-minute conversation between Dave and his close friend from his school days, Alan, and me eating dinner at a diner in Northern Virginia. About 50 minutes into this conversation, when Dave and I began to tell Alan about our recent disastrous camping trip, Alan and Dave made references to the video game *The Oregon Trail.*

Next, I worked through a 34-minute conversation among the housemates, Dave, and me, again in the kitchen/dining room of their house. This conversation contained a lively extended sequence where Dave and his housemates referenced the song "Belle" from the 1991 Disney film *Beauty and the Beast* with new lyrics about Paula drinking gin and tonic. Besides this sequence, the 34-minute conversation was a treasure trove of media references, containing more than two references per minute, for a total of 85 references.

The fourth conversation I worked through was chosen for a similar reason to the third; it contained an extended media referencing sequence, specifically during part of the conversation when Jeff brought his relatively new girlfriend Dee over, and the housemates and a friend of Todd's began to ironically reference related internet memes about the importance of "leg day," or a day devoted exclusively to exercising the lower body. Focusing specifically on that sequence, I annotated, transcribed, and added the references to memes to my data set. I did not annotate or transcribe the rest of this conversation since the majority of it contained Todd and his friend quietly painting board game miniatures while watching and occasionally commenting on a YouTube video.

Finally, after reviewing the examples I had collected so far, I realized that the conversations I had been working with did not strike a gender balance; the overwhelming majority of the media references were made by men, yet I sensed from my own experience and observation that women were just as likely to make media references as men in conversation. One possible explanation for women making fewer media references in the conversations I had recorded is that more than half of the recorded participants were always men, which may have caused the women to talk less overall (see Duncan & Fiske 1977; Karpowitz & Mendelberg 2014). Therefore, I decided to include a one hour and eleven-minute recorded conversation among three other women doctoral students and me, which took place in a graduate student lounge on a Friday afternoon. The participants in this conversation are Holly, one of my closest friends at the time and quite the comedian; an older graduate student, Myriam, who often occupied the graduate lounge, and, briefly, Tiffany. Holly and I were not close to Myriam and Tiffany but we were friendly with them. This conversation is memorable because in it, Holly and I make six references to the 1993 film *Groundhog Day*, starring Bill Murray, which we had recently watched together. I annotated, transcribed, and added those six and four other examples of media references made by these women and me to my data set. In the end, this gave me a total of 148 media references across five conversations; 86 from men and 62 from women. The counts of media references depended on my ability to recognize each reference as a participant and analyst, and playback interviews were also very useful in that other speakers occasionally pointed out a reference that I had not recognized. As mentioned earlier, I also took notes on conversations that I observed but which were not recorded, and these appear occasionally in this book.

The 10 American friends whose recorded conversations I examine are similar in some important ways. Almost all were Millennials in their late 20s, except for Miriam, who was in her late 30s and a member of Generation X; this has some interesting consequences in conversations where the other Millennial students make media references in her presence (see chapter 3). They all grew up in a broad spectrum of American middle-class homes; some grew up with less, some with more. None of the friends were openly LGBTQ-identifying at the time that I recorded their conversations. None of them had been married, and none had children. They all lived in the metropolitan Washington, DC, area. Many of these participants lived rather comfortably given the economic era they grew up in and the fact that many were temporarily graduate students living for 4–8 years on modest fellowship stipends in the expensive DC area. Almost all of them had bachelor's degrees (with the exception of Alan, who had some college education), and just over half were in a PhD program in linguistics at a prestigious East Coast university (Dave, Paula, Holly, Miriam, Tiffany, and I). Their relatively high level of education and some of the individuals' explicit interest in language might factor into their frequent engagement in and enjoyment of witty banter involving media references. The recorded participants speak different American English dialects, with Mainstream U.S. English being the most salient in the recorded contexts. They demonstrate through their media references that they engaged largely with U.S. media.

Despite their broad similarities, these Millennial friends are also of course unique individuals. In analyzing the recordings, I discovered how each of them has their own conversational style (Tannen 1984/2005), their own use of humor and way of laughing, and their own level of comfort with performing accents and singing when making media references. There is also ethnic diversity among them and many are second-generation Americans, as would be expected in one of the most diverse American generations ever, only eclipsed by Generation Z. Tiffany is African American, Alan is a second-generation Chinese American, John is a second-generation Japanese American, and Miriam is a second-generation American of ethnically Jewish Middle Eastern heritage. Jeff is a second-generation Egyptian European American and I am a second-generation Polish American with Hispanic heritage. Along with Jeff and me, all other recorded participants are white European Americans.

It is paramount to keep in mind the similarities and differences among the Millennial friends in this study, especially since my analysis of their interactions is not intended to and cannot represent those of all Millennials or all 20-somethings at any given point in time. I simply present a qualitative case-study analysis of a set of these particular Millennial individuals' conversations, with a focus on the conversations that occurred at Dave's house with his housemates. These are the very friends whose camping trip adventure and whose conversations afterwards about the trip inspired my thinking about media intertextuality: my romantic partner and fellow linguistics graduate student Dave, his close friend and housemate, Todd, Dave's and my linguistics colleague and Todd's significant other, Paula, and Todd's co-worker, Jeff.

I focus on these housemates as participants for a few reasons. Exploring one friend group's (and one house's) discourse in depth allows me to provide a *thick description* (Geertz 1973), in something akin to an ethnography, of this *thick community* (Blommaert & De Fina 2017; Blommaert &

Varis 2015), bound as the participants are in shared nationality, race, and so-cial class. Related also to methodological considerations, as Dave's partner, I had easy and frequent access to conversations with him and his housemates. Furthermore, their conversations turned out to be a rich data set for a study of media references. Paula and Jeff had improv comedy experience, while Paula had also done some stand-up comedy, and the two were playful, humorous, and made an abundance of media references in the conversations I recorded. A drawback of the focus on this one thick community is that since all the housemates are white middle-class Americans, the analysis might overrepre-sent these kinds of speakers and their communicative practices. Throughout the book, I highlight salient moments of whiteness in terms of what kind of media is referenced and how the references are performed.

As I have mentioned, I myself did not know at the time I recorded these conversations that I would focus on media references for this study. But again, once I became interested in video game references that night camping on the island, I started examining references to internet memes and other kinds of media. Howe and Strauss (2000) observe that the teen trend in most types of media use was down (with the exception of computer use) among Millennials in 2000. Yet one of the characteristics that make my data set unique, and which I believe is distinctive of the Millennial generation more broadly, is the vast array of media, both old (books, songs, TV shows, films,) and new (video games, internet memes, YouTube videos) that these friends reference in their daily interactions. In presenting an in-depth examination of the discourse of these friends, I locate, describe, and offer analytical interpretations of media references in conversation by integrating theoretical perspectives of intertex-tuality, framing, and epistemics. In doing so, I also contribute to the ongoing exploration in linguistics, communication, and related fields of how social groups and identities are created through talk, and the role that media plays in these processes.

Issues with Analyzing These Millennial Friends' Talk

As I mentioned previously, one of the advantages of the data collection for this study was my own participation in the conversations I recorded, as has been found by other interactional sociolinguists. My participation allowed me to know as much as possible not only about the sequencing and structure of the talk, but also about the conversational setting, the participants' backgrounds, and their relationships with each other. When I had questions about the participants or some stretch of talk, I asked my friends for their insights during playback interviews or through follow-up emails during my analysis. In addition to this advantage, the conversations I recorded originally among my friends and me turned out to be a rich source of data for studying my primary research interests: knowledge management and identity construction.

A question that has been raised by some audience members at talks and workshops on this study has concerned the role of the *Observer's Paradox* (Labov 1972) in my data collection. That is, how did the fact that the conversations were being recorded, and that I was in my role as "researcher" along with my role as "friend," affect the participants' behavior? Can we consider the participants' conversations to genuinely be "naturalistic"? My general answer to this question is that speakers usually seemed to "be themselves" even with the recorder on, especially after a few minutes of engaging in conversation with each other. While this was generally the case, I do have the sense that two of Dave's housemates, Jeff and Paula, may have taken on more performative behavior than they would have otherwise. It is difficult to say this with certainty, however, because the two of them are always quick with jokes and laughter, both having been trained in improv comedy. However, it is possible that they "dialed it up" even a little more than usual when they knew the recorder was on. It is also possible that this was the case for other participants. The primary evidence that Jeff in particular operated in more of a *performative manner* (Schilling 2013) was his frequent references to the recorder itself throughout my data collection, saying things like "Let the record show . . . ," addressing the recorder formally as "Recorder," and saying things like "This is for science." As Schilling (2013) acknowledges, "The data are always potentially subject to effects of the research situation . . . as for example with a participant who talks into the audio recorder in an obviously performative manner" (127). However, Gordon (2013) has shown that the Observer's Paradox is not a problem per se, and she analyzes how speakers use a tape recorder as a resource for individual identity construction. In my data, Jeff's frequent playful remarks about the presence of the recorder can similarly be seen as relevant to his own identity display as a humorous and playful person.

A potential drawback to the method of recording and analyzing one's friends' talk is that doing a critical analysis of such conversations can be fraught. This project was initially about the micro-level interactional work being done by my friends and me—examining how we signal media references, respond to them, and create epistemic play frame shifts with them. It was only after my doctoral dissertation was complete that I started examining the conversations from a more critical perspective, turning my attention to issues of race, gender, and sexuality that surface in some of the media references. It was through the process of these analyses that I started to experience the impact of personal and relational face risks involved in critically analyzing one's friends' discourse practices as racist, sexist, or homophobic. On the one hand, I started to understand why interactional sociolinguistic studies, often consisting of data among the researcher's friends or family, do not often approach this territory. I certainly did not set out to expose my friends to critique, and at times it was difficult to discuss my analysis with them afterwards. On the other hand, I realized that my recordings of everyday conversation among my friends had much to offer in terms of understanding the ideological implications of media references in talk. As such, in the critical analyses of this book, I attempt to focus on the discourse practices of the individuals, rather than on the individuals themselves. The fact that we sometimes unthinkingly reproduce media stereotypes via playful media references demonstrates that these tropes are so pervasive and insidious that they permeate everyday discourse. In turn, those media-embedded ideologies are recirculated and reinforced in our daily social interactions. Returning to the benefits of this methodological approach, in playback interviews and other conversations, my friends and I had critical discussions of some of the more salient stereotypes that emerged in our conversations. These discussions generally resulted in a heightened awareness about the problematic nature of repeating certain media tropes in our conversations. There is a case demonstration of this phenomenon in chapter 4.

Finally, another interesting phenomenon occurred within me as a participant-observer where, after the second conversation I decided to analyze, I became aware of and even hypersensitive to the occurrence of media references in conversation, and this possibly affected my spoken behavior when they occurred. This is most noticeable to me in the last three recordings of this study where I often simply laugh or do not say anything during speaker's intertextual media references, instead of taking a more active participation role (although my participation in such references had never been as active as that of speakers like Jeff and Paula). However, I do not think that my limited active participation hindered my friends from engaging in extended intertextual media reference play in their conversations, as should be clearly evident in the examples presented in this book.

Preview of the Chapters

Chapters 2 and 3 focus on how intertextual media references are phonetically signaled in conversation and how participants mutually engage in such references. Chapter 2 focuses on how media references are signaled in the river of talk through prosodic, paralinguistic, and phonetic features in everyday conversation, building on Gumperz's (1977, 1982) work on *contextualization cues*. These cues can be thought of as "oars" in the river of talk.

Chapter 3 moves from the signaling mechanisms of intertextual media references to examining the corresponding process: listener engagement with media references. I analyze four different ways through which listeners engage with media references in my data set when they hear them. I pay special attention to participation in play around the media references as a way of engaging with references. In both chapters 2 and 3 I comment on the media-embedded stereotypes and identity work being done through the signaling of and engagement with media references where it is relevant. In these two chapters, I also begin to preview the second half of the book's focus on how the media references are used to shift both the knowledge required to participate and the *frames*, or activity of talk, as a remedy to knowledge imbalances and interactional dilemmas.

Chapters 4 and 5 move from focusing on "how" people make media references to "why" they make them: what interactional functions do they serve, beyond simple affiliation? Chapter 4 focuses on how media references often serve to resolve interactional dilemmas that arise when speakers have different knowledge territories about topics of talk. Focusing on references to internet memes, I show how making these references often constructs lighthearted *play frames* (Bateson 1972; Goffman 1974) while also shifting *epistemics*, or the knowledge required to participate in the conversation. I call these combinatorial conversational moves *epistemic frame shifts*: shifts in both the epistemic territory of talk as well as in the frame. I also focus on the stereotypes embedded within memes and how those ultimately are reinforced in these references. I show how referencing memes is ultimately conducive to constructing shared group identity in interaction.

Chapter 5 further investigates how speakers use media references as resources to manage epistemic imbalances and interactional dilemmas, creating epistemic frame shifts and constructing shared group identities in interaction. In this chapter I focus on references to video games that friends have played together in the past. I show how epistemic frame shifts facilitate different group members' involvement in conversation and assist them in being active in constructing their identities as individuals, friends, and members of a specific epistemic ecology. Additionally, here I illuminate frame lamination and show how embedded frames can occur within overlapping frames of talk, causing speakers to become even more enmeshed in their overlapping video game frame experiences. Finally, I examine some of the stereotypes and ideologies embedded within the video games and how those are reproduced in referencing the games.

Chapter 6 includes a brief summary and discussion of the key findings of this study and how they contribute to our understanding of media, knowledge, and identity in everyday interaction. I also provide insights from this study and discuss how knowing more about media references and the interactional work they do has affected my personal life and conversations, and the takeaways for readers.

2
"One of us"
Signaling Media References

The simple phrase "I'll be back" is recognizable to many English speakers
as Arnold Schwarzenegger's catchphrase, originally used in the hugely successful and critically acclaimed American science fiction film *The Terminator*
(1984). This phrase is even more recognizable (and fun) if it is said with an
approximation of Schwarzenegger's Austrian accent and in a lowered pitch; by
using these cues, a speaker can signal that this phrase is in fact a reference to a
particular media text instead of just a common everyday declaration. This example illustrates how the vast majority of the media references in my data are
signaled, in part, via repetition of a recognizable word or phrase from a media
source, but they are also often accompanied by other phonetic cues (as well
as via embodied facial expressions and gestures). In fact, most of the media
references in the conversations that I recorded combine two to five of these
different cues. References to purely text-based media, such as certain internet
memes or video games, are more likely to be signaled with fewer phonetic
cues, while references to auditory media like TV shows, movies, and songs
are more likely to use more. In referencing a song from a movie—for example,
"Belle" from Disney's animated film *Beauty and the Beast* (1991)—a speaker
can potentially use a foreign accent, different pitches, singing, and other phonetic cues. For the most part, I focus on contextualization cues one at a time in
this chapter, but these cues are often combined in conversations.

In this chapter, I focus on how media references are signaled in the speech
stream through phonetic, prosodic, and paralinguistic features in everyday
conversation. While scholars have explored the interactional importance of
media intertextuality in relational and identity work in conversation, there
has been little research on how people signal media references. Yet, after listening to the plethora of media references my friends and I made in five of
our conversations following our voyage down the Potomac river, it became
apparent that speakers must somehow signal that they are making media
references in the ongoing flow of talk. While I am also interested in the interactional functions of media references (see Sierra 2016), I believe scholarship could benefit from understanding how such references are signaled

Millennials Talking Media. Sylvia Sierra, Oxford University Press. © Oxford University Press 2021.
DOI: 10.1093/oso/9780190931117.003.0002

when they are introduced into talk. These cues can be thought of as "oars" used to navigate the course of talk. I build on Gumperz's (1977, 1982) work on *contextualization cues*, the mechanisms through which certain meanings are phonetically signaled in talk, and apply this concept specifically to media references. By describing the linguistic features that accompany the insertion of media references into the river of talk, this chapter lays out the basics of how speakers make media references. I argue that the signaling of media references allows speakers to engage with them and participate in playful intertextual processes in talk. In this chapter, I also begin to point out how signaling playful media references often (but not always) serves to negotiate epistemic, or knowledge, imbalances as well as interactional dilemmas, or awkward and unpleasant moments in interaction; this will be explored in more detail in chapter 4 and chapter 5. I also analyze additional playback interview data I collected, in which I asked the participants for their insights regarding the media references they made. Lastly, I weave in analyses of the identity work being constructed with the media references, as well as the media stereotypes that are repeated in some of them. To summarize, many of the examples in this chapter begin with an epistemic imbalance and interactional dilemma, are smoothed over by media references signaled with contextualization cues, and ultimately accomplish various kinds of identity work.

Contextualization Cues

Gumperz (1977, 1982, 1992) developed the concept of a conversational *meta-signaling system* (1977:192) in which contextualization cues are defined as "any aspect of the surface form of utterances which, when mapped onto message content, can be shown to be functional in the signaling of interpretative frames" (1977:199). In other words, cues such as pitch, intonation, rhythm, loudness, and nonverbal cues (like gestures, facial expressions, eye gaze, etc.) carry contextual meaning, and when combined with utterances, they signal to listeners how messages ought to be interpreted. Contextualization cues can thus signal how the frame, or the activity of talk, ought to be interpreted (is it serious? playful?). Contextualization cues are crucial in talk because they allow for what Gumperz calls *conversational inference*: the process of interpreting meaning, in which conversational participants are able to immediately assess interlocutors' intentions, and on which they form responses (1977:191). Since speakers in my data are obviously able to somehow interpret intertextual media references and the playful frames that accompany them, in this chapter I explore how contextualization cues are used to signal media references.

Gumperz briefly analyzes a sequence of talk that includes what could be considered playful intertextual references, describing some of the more common contextualization cues. Some of these same cues also signal media references in my data. Presenting an interaction observed on an airplane where a male passenger walks down the aisle saying, as he passes by two women passengers, "Tickets, please! Tickets, please!" Gumperz explains how this is recognizable as a playful intertextual joke, referencing "an announcement, or . . . a stock phrase associated with travel situations," due to the combination of higher pitch, loudness, and staccato rhythm (1977:198). When one of the women responds by play-admonishing her friend, "I TOLD you to leave him at home," Gumperz observes that the stress on "told" marks her statement as another intertextual stock utterance. The man's playful response, "Step to the rear of the bus, please," is also said with a higher pitch, loudness, and a particular intonation, making it recognizable as an intertextual reference to what a bus attendant might say (Gumperz 1977:198). Thus, this early work on contextualization cues hints at their relevance for signaling playful intertextuality, since in this case they are described as signaling culturally known "stock" phrases. In addition, Gumperz also acknowledges that other signaling mechanisms can function as contextualization cues, including specific words or sounds, idiomatic or formulaic expressions such as interjections, frozen sequences, and code-switching (1977:199).

Gumperz's work on contextualization cues has been followed up with more empirical studies. Here I review some of these empirical studies that have examined specifically how both the reported speech of others (a form of intertextuality) and play are signaled in interaction. While many studies have focused on the use of quotatives such as *go* or *be like* in intertextually voicing others in American English interaction (Blyth et al. 1990; Buchstaller & D'Arcy 2009; D'Arcy 2017; Romaine & Lange 1991; Tannen 1986/2011; Yule & Mathis, 1992), Mathis & Yule (1994) bring attention to the use of "zero quotatives" where direct speech is reported with neither a reporting verb nor an attributed speaker. In some of the zero quotative cases that Mathis & Yule (1994) examine, paralinguistic modulation of voice quality is what signals reported speech. They make a connection between this practice in everyday conversation and "intonational quotation marks" which Bakhtin (1981) identified in the analysis of literary text. Specifically, they find that breathy voice, harsh voice, nasal voice, creaky voice, falsetto, loudness, and shifts in pitch are all used to signal reported speech in zero quotatives.

Similarly, in Tannen's (1989/2007) work on repetition, she shows how breathy voice, loudness, distinct intonation patterns, and other paralinguistic features are all used to indicate distinct voices in a single oral narrative. Couper-Kuhlen (1996, 1999) and Günther (1999) both observe that noticeable shifts in pitch, loudness, tempo, voice quality, intonation, and rhythmic pattern signal another "voice," also referred to as "reported dialogues," or "reported speech." Shifts in pitch in particular have been well researched as indicators of reported speech (e.g., Hirschberg & Grosz 1992; Jansen et al. 2001; Fletcher 2005; De Decker 2013; Jones 2016), although these studies have not examined the roles that speaker baseline pitch and the pitch of those being quoted plays in these shifts, which I will address in this chapter. Finally, Park (2009) shows that in addition to a change in voice quality, smile voice and laughter can also be used when quoting a non-present third party. These studies highlight the phonetic work that speakers do to indicate that they are intertextually quoting other voices in their speech.

As for signaling play in interaction, Glenn and Knapp (1987) find that "unusual paralinguistic features such as marked changes in pitch, intonation, volume, or accent" can cue play. The fact that these features are "unusual," or "marked," make them stand out in conversation, thus signaling that something different is happening (in this case, play). Both Tannen and Wallat (1993) and Gordon (2002, 2008, 2009) show that high-pitched voice specifically indicates play and non-literal meanings, in both institutional and familial settings, respectively. High-pitched voice is also used in teasing (Straehle 1993), a more specific type of play, along with cues such as intonation, stress, and vowel and voice quality, such as nasality (215). Additionally, Bowman (1978) finds that laughter, smiling, explicit verbal statements (e.g., "Let's just play!"), nonverbal exaggerated and/or repeated movements, and decreased social distance between participants are cues for initiating and maintaining play. In sum, pitch, intonation, and loudness are the most common cues observed that are used to signal both intertextuality and play in interaction, with more specific features like accent, nasality, and breathy voice being used in particular instances. Numerous scholars have identified how various linguistic and paralinguistic features cue the animation of intertextual speech and play. I extend this work by examining the specific features used to signal intertextual playful media references.

Almost all of the media references in my data set (141/148; 95%) are zero quotatives and are signaled instead with contextualization cues. The fact that most of these references do not involve quotatives (such as 'be like,' 'like' and 'say') underscores that they are understood to be shared texts, with no need for a quotative. Indeed, D'Arcy (2012) writes that the null form, (along with *be like* and *go*) favors quotes with *mimetic encoding*, defined by Buchstaller (2008:23) as "quotes that contain sounds or voice and gestural effects." My data is in line with this finding, showing that zero quotatives make use of other audible contextualization cues. It is extremely unusual for a reference to not be signaled with any contextualization cues. Only three references in over 140 had no identifiable contextualization cue associated with them. In two of these cases, the initial use of the reference did not succeed in garnering any listener response, but when the reference was repeated by the same speaker at a later time with at least one contextualization cue, listeners *did* recognize the references and they responded to them. This provides strong evidence that contextualization cues do extra work to highlight media references for listeners, thus making these cues worth further exploration.

In this chapter, I begin by describing the most common features used to signal media references in my conversational data, including a variety of phonetic, prosodic, and paralinguistic contextualization cues similar to the ones that have previously been found to signal intertextuality and play. For each contextualization cue that I discuss, I provide representative examples of how the feature is used to signal media references from conversations among Millennial friends. I discuss why these contextualization cues are crucial for interlocutors to "get" media references. The examples I present to illuminate each contextualization cue in this chapter are references to audio–video media such as movies, TV shows, and YouTube videos.

Five Ways Media References Are Signaled in Talk

"Not that there's anything WRONG with that": Word Stress and Intonation

Out of all the options available to speakers when making media references, the most common contextualization cue used to signal these references in my data is word stress (123/148; 83%), consisting in different instances of vowel lengthening, loudness, and a pitch accent, or raised pitch (see Bolinger 1958 and Zsiga 2012). Word stress acts as a contextualization cue, highlighting a media reference in the speech stream for interlocutors. A listener might hear this word stress within the media reference itself, or in a word preceding the media reference.

In the following conversation, my partner Dave's two housemates, Paula and Jeff, have been talking with me in their kitchen/dining area. I was there visiting Dave, who was also in the same graduate program in linguistics as

Paula and me. This is the earliest recording in my data set, and was recorded before I knew that I would be studying media references. Ironically, Paula and I had actually been discussing the difficulty in defining the word *intertextuality*, since I was taking a seminar on the topic at the time, and she was writing a paper for a class that involved the concept. So there is some knowledge imbalance here: I was in a seminar on intertextuality, Paula was trying to grasp the concept on her own, and Jeff was not a graduate student in linguistics and had very little epistemic access to the topic. This epistemic imbalance creates a (minor) awkward interactional dilemma. At this juncture, Jeff initiates a playful frame of talk. I participate in the play frame by signaling a playful intertextual media reference with marked stress; this continues the play frame and shifts the knowledge required to participate in it—instead of epistemic access to what the word *intertextuality* means, now the epistemic territory becomes a film. (In this excerpt, like those that follow, the media references most relevant to the analysis are indicated with arrows and the combination of quotation marks and underlining.)

(1)

1	Paula	Cuz I- Again, I keep thinking that I know what it means.
2	Sylvia	I know, [it's really confusing.
3	Jeff	[Wow, we're all using words that we don't know what they →
4		mean.
5	Sylvia	Ha[hahaha.
6	Paula	[Hahahaha!...Hahaha.
7 ⇨	Sylvia	"You keep using that ∧wo:rd; I don't think you know [what it means."
8	Paula	[I-
9		I [think that's true, cuz I'm just like-
10 ⇨	Jeff	[<Spanish accent, low pitch> "I don't think it ∧mea:ns what you →
11		[think it[means."
12	Sylvia	[Haha.
13	Paula	[I think in my head I'm like, i(h)t's just a fancy word →
14		for allusion.

In lines 1 and 2, Paula and I comment on the epistemic struggle of defining *intertextuality*. Jeff also chimes in on the dilemma and further indicates that one exists here by saying "Wow, we're all using words that we don't know what they mean" (lines 3–4). This observation "triggers" my semi-active consciousness (Chafe 1994), reminding me of a line from a film: "You keep using that word; I don't think you know what it means" (line 7). Here I am referencing the dialogue of the Spanish character Inigo Montoya (played by Jewish American actor Mandy Patinkin) in the American fantasy adventure comedy film *The Princess Bride* (1987) in response to another character, Vizzini. At one point in the film, Inigo comments on Vizzini's repeated use of the word *inconceivable*, saying, "You keep using that word; I do not think it means what you think it means." The only cue I use to signal this playful reference in this conversation is the emphatic stress on "word." Both the lexical content of the reference and this word stress make the reference recognizable for Jeff, although I was actually misquoting the film. Nonetheless, he is able to pick up on the reference as is demonstrated when he repairs it in lines 10–11. He uses a lowered pitch and performs a Spanish accent by deploying some salient markers of a stylized Spanish variety, saying, "I don't think it means what you think it means." While Jeff and I are both referencing this film as a social bonding mechanism—one which reaffirms our identities as friends of the American Millennial generation who grew up watching this popular movie in the 1990s—Jeff does some additional identity work here to "outperform" me with his accent production. By performing this accent, he reproduces the accent from the film, which might function as "voicing the other" (Bakhtin 1984), in this case Spanish speakers. This Spanish accent performance in turn contrastively highlights Jeff's typical accent and identity as that of an American English speaker. I focus specifically on stylized accent performances in media references like this one and their implications later in this chapter.

On a more fundamental level, this example illustrates how the use of stress highlights the media reference for the listener. It may be the case that, often, the word stress actually matches the original text being quoted. In the source text for this reference, Inigo places slight stress on "word" and both instances of "means" in the utterance, although he does not stress these words to the extent that Jeff and I do when we quote this line. Jeff and I both stress different words in the quote to give an exaggerated stress pattern to the phrase, basing this somewhat on the actual stress that Inigo places on the words; this highlights the playful intertextual reference by marking it as "different" from the surrounding talk.

In the following example, Dave and I had been reminiscing to Paula about a recording that we remembered having to listen to for a course in graduate school on phonetics and phonology. In this class, our professor, Lisa Zsiga, had recorded audio files of herself saying the phrases, "Did Maddy win the medal?" and "Maddy won the medal" with different intonation contours, which we had to download and transcribe. Paula did not remember the recording even though she took the same class as us. So there is an epistemic imbalance present here and a somewhat awkward interactional dilemma where Dave and I are reminiscing about a shared experience that

Paula likely also had, yet cannot remember. Here, Dave mimics the recording in an increasingly ridiculous manner, which triggers both him and Paula to make a media reference to something else entirely. Paula uses word stress and exaggerated loudness to punctuate the reference. This briefly changes the epistemic territory of the talk.

(2)

1	Dave	We had to transcribe that!
2		And it was like,
3		<high-pitch> "Did ^Maddy have the medal?"
4		<high-pitch> "M-^Maddy had the ^medal!"
5	Sylvia	Haha!
6	Paula	Hahahaha!
7	Dave	Maddy had mad maddy mad mad mumuhuhmuhmuh,
8		[madmadmadmadaaaamamama!
9	⇨ Paula	["muhmuhmuhmuh" [hahaHA!
10	Sylvia	[and we just had to listen to [Lisa over and over again.
11	⇨ Paula	[(h) "PORK CHOP →
12		^SA:NDWICHES!"
13	Dave	Ha yeah.

I learned through a playback interview with the participants that Dave and Paula's verbal behavior in lines 8–9 and Paula's exclamation in lines 11–12 are a reference to a parody of a 1980s American *GI Joe* cartoon public service announcement about fire safety, uploaded to YouTube in 2006. In the parody video, all the voices are dubbed over with relatively nonsensical dialogue, to humorous effect. The video opens with two cartoon children in a kitchen which starts to catch on fire. The child who started the fire while cooking stands immobilized and is dubbed simply repeating a monosyllabic sound, until a GI Joe enters the kitchen and yells, "Pork chop sandwiches!" before he leads them to safety. So, in this excerpt of the conversation, Dave's mockery of the recording, "Maddy had mad maddy mad mad mumuhuhmuhmuh madmadmadmadaaaamamama" (lines 7–8) reminds both him and Paula of the GI Joe parody where the child repeats a similar monosyllabic sound. They both start making this sound together in lines 8–9. Paula then signals her reference more explicitly to the YouTube video by yelling loudly, "PORK CHOP SA:NDWICHES!" (line 11) and stressing the first syllable of "SA:NDWICHES." Dave further engages with the reference in line 13, when he laughs and says "yeah." Here, the fact that both Paula and Dave have seen this YouTube video briefly serves as a moment of fun shared identity affirmation among two people from the Millennial generation who share epistemic access to the same absurdist YouTube videos.

There are many similar examples in my data set where speakers attempt to mimic word stress as it occurs in the intonation contour of the referenced media (103/148; 70%). The reproduction of a particular intonation contour lifted from a media text is often distinguishable by virtue of the particular placement of word stress. Speakers replicate specific intonation contours to accurately depict and signal the original media text being appropriated, especially when the humorous intonation contour itself is a critical part of why the media text is worth referencing. To this point, Zsiga (2012) notes that intonation can be used to bring a referent into focus, and in many of the examples, there is something distinctive about the original intonation contour of the media text that makes it quotable. In other words, many of the media texts themselves make use of a specific intonation contour to bring a referent into focus, and then speakers attempt to reproduce this in their media references.

The following excerpt occurs some time after example 1, in the same conversation where Paula and I had been discussing the difficulty in defining *intertextuality*. As seen earlier, Jeff and I shifted the epistemic territory of this talk via a reference to *The Princess Bride*, (re)framing the interaction as playful. This playful frame eventually led to extensive wordplay around the word *intertextuality* itself. In this example, Jeff participates in that play frame by signaling a media reference through replicating the intonation contour of the original media text, stressing a particular part of the reference.

(3)

1	Paula	Hey, I have nothing against intertextuals.
2		OK?
3	Dave	[Ha.
4 ⇨	Jeff	["Not [that [there's anything ^WRO:NG with that."
5	Sylvia	[Hahahaha.
6	Paula	[They're just ^people. They're ^ju:st people.
7	Jeff	Mhm.

Paula makes a pun using the word *intertextual* as a stand-in for something like *intersexuals* (maybe even *transsexuals*) when she says, "Hey, I have nothing against intertextuals. OK?" (lines 1–2). Jeff responds to Paula's joke with a media reference: "Not that there's anything WRO:NG with that." Vowel lengthening, raised pitch, and loudness are all present in Jeff's media reference, and they actually function in this case to repeat the exact intonation contour of the media text being referenced—the popular American television situation comedy show *Seinfeld*, which ran from 1989 to 1998. In season 4, episode 17 of the show, a running joke begins where a newspaper journalist, and then others, are mistakenly led to believe that best friends Jerry Seinfeld and George Costanza are a gay couple. Seinfeld responds to the mistake initially by loudly exclaiming, "We're not GAY! Not that there's anything WRONG with that." Vowel lengthening, loudness, and a pitch accent on 'wrong' are all present in this media text and they function to create a distinctive intonation contour, resulting in a humorous, repeatable phrase. After this initial usage, the quotable phrase "Not that there's anything wrong with that" is used multiple times throughout the show as a call-back by different characters.

Becker (2006) observes that a variety of 90s media (*Seinfeld* included) presented homosexuality in ways that allowed "Socially Liberal, Urban-Minded Professionals" ("Slumpies") to pay lip service to gay rights and demonstrate trendiness by consuming vaguely gay-friendly media, while ultimately reinforcing existing heteronormative structures and anxieties. Thus, the catchphrase, "Not that there's anything wrong with that," which Jeff quotes from *Seinfeld* invokes the same heteronormative anxiety embedded in the show, especially in this context as it is used to engage with wordplay around dominant "Slumpie" discourse regarding tolerance for LGBTQ+ identities ("I have nothing against intertextuals"; "they're just people"). The playful repetition, punning, and referencing of this discourse simultaneously others LGBTQ+ sexualities while also (re)affirming the heteronormative identities within this group of friends.

Since the emphasis of "Not that there's anything wrong with that" is on the word "wrong" in *Seinfeld*, the phrase itself takes on an intonation contour consisting of a high pitch accent on "wrong" (also stressed via loudness and vowel lengthening) followed by a low falling tone. This is the intonation contour that Jeff uses when he quotes the TV show in this example. By mimicking the distinctive intonation contour of the source text, this imitation signals a media reference. I confirmed in playback that Jeff, Paula, and I had seen this particular *Seinfeld* episode. Thus, the reference temporarily serves to bring us together as Millennial friends who are familiar with the same TV show that was enormously popular when we grew up in the 1990s, while also reinforcing the heteronormative anxiety embedded in the show.

In sum, stress is the most common way that speakers phonetically signal media references in my data set. Stress highlights the media reference as significant for the listener. Stress is often present in the media text itself, co-occurring with a particular intonation contour, and then this intonation is reproduced when speakers reference that media. These Millennial friends use these contextualization cues to effectively signal media references to each other, and this enables group participation in recalling and savoring prior shared media experiences as American Millennials who have seen the same films, TV shows, and YouTube videos. The American media referenced in this section features primarily white (also Jewish, in *Seinfeld*) characters. One of these characters (Inigo Montoya) is actually presented as Spanish even though the actor who plays him is Jewish American, and his performance of a Spanish accent is referenced by Jeff. The heteronormative anxiety of *Seinfeld* is also referenced. The preponderance of referencing white American media produced in the late 1980s to the early 2000s in this data set is already noticeable within these first three examples. Referencing this media and the stereotypes embedded within (see also Wahl 2010 on *metastereotyping*) reinforces different aspects of the speakers' shared identities as heterosexual white American English-speaking Millennials.

"You shall not pass!": Pitch Shifts

Shifting to a noticeably higher or lower pitch than the speaker's usual pitch is also a common way that speakers in my data set signal media references (85/ 148; 57%). Following Couper-Kuhlen and Selting (2018), pitch refers to the location of a pitch configuration in a speaker's overall voice range; it can range from mid (the norm) to extra high or extra low.

Part of the reason that pitch shifts are used so often in my data is because speakers are frequently voicing others who have a noticeably higher or lower pitch than the speaker who is referencing the source text. The following excerpt precedes example 2; here Dave had been trying to bring up a particular scholarly journal article on the topic of semantics, which prompts me to recall the activity that our professor, Lisa, had us do in her Phonetics and Phonology course on intonation contours. Here I "display forgetfulness" (Goodwin, C. 1987) as I try to remember what the exact phrase was that Lisa had recorded herself saying for the activity. While I am showing that this is a temporary forgetting of the phrase, Paula seems to be lacking any epistemic access to this coursework experience. This epistemic mismatch among the three graduate students, along with my sudden shift in topic, creates an interactional dilemma. This dilemma shifts the activity of talk to something akin to a word search, and it shifts the participation framework as Dave tries to supply the intertextual reference that I am seeking. Initially, Dave provides the reference to the recording in his typical pitch, but I do not show evidence of having heard him or recognized his utterance as the reference for which I was searching. Then, however, Dave switches to a very high pitch to imitate our professor's higher-pitched voice while providing the correct reference. This time, I respond accordingly.

(4)

1	Sylvia	No, Lisa did those recordings that were like-
2		What were they, like-
3	Paula	Which one-
4	Dave	"^Ma:ddy bought [the medal."
5	Sylvia	["What is Mar- ^Mary gonna-"
6	Dave	No:=
7	Sylvia	=What the fu(h)ck wa(h)s-
8	Dave	It wasn't the- [She wasn't lookin at the se^mantics.
9	Paula	[Wha(h)t?
10	Sylvia	No:!
11	Dave	<high-pitched> "^MA:DDY GOT THE MEDAL."
12	Sylvia	YEAH, ^THA:T!
13		When we were in Phonol- [yeah-
14 ⇨	Dave	<high-pitched>["^MADDY HAS THE ^ME:DAL."

This example shows how important a shift in pitch can be in signaling a media reference. At first, Dave provides the phrase that I am searching for, with "Maddy bought the medal" (line 4) but in his typical pitch. I do not register that he is supplying the reference, however, possibly due to the combination of my overlapping with Dave (line 5), still searching my own memory for the right phrase, and Dave still using his typical pitch as he says the phrase. It is apparent that I do not recognize that he is supplying the correct reference at this point because I still attempt to come up with the phrase myself, saying, "What is Mar- Mary gonna-" (line 5), which prompts Dave to utter an exasperated, "No:" (line 6), which confirms the interactional dilemma at play here. I laughingly begin to ask, "What the fuck was-" still not having recalled nor recognized the phrase.

Finally, Dave says the phrase again, but this time he says it very loudly and with a noticeably higher pitch, in an approximation of Lisa's higher-pitched voice: "MADDY GOT THE MEDAL" (line 11). Dave's timing (with no overlap), loudness, and much higher pitch draw attention to the phrase and effectively signal it as the reference I had been searching for, and I respond accordingly, "YEAH, THAT! When we were in Phonol- yeah" (lines 12–13), with no further hesitation, repair, or indication of confusion. Dave's pitch shift and loudness here are crucial in effectively signaling a media reference, albeit a very in-group one, to a listener. This example shows how a noticeable gendered shift in pitch can be used to make an intertextual reference recognizable, allowing Dave and I to recall and reminisce about a shared coursework media experience as graduate students.

In the next excerpt, I shift my voice to a noticeably lower pitch to quote a male character in a more widely known media source. Here, Paula and her partner Todd's fierce Bengal cat, Hydra, has jumped to the top of the fridge in the kitchen just as Jeff tried to reach out and pet her, leaving his hand petting the air. While there does not seem to be an epistemic imbalance here, the funny (but also sad) moment could perhaps have created a bit of the kind of interactional awkwardness that media references are so useful in smoothing over.

(5)

1	Paula	She's like, "No. NO this is MY kingdom!"	
2	Sylvia	Haha.	
3	Dave	"I will repel the attackers."	
4 ⇨	Sylvia	*<low-pitched >*"/You /shall /not /[pa:ss!"	
5	Jeff		[No-[yeah hahahaha.
6	Paula		[Hahaha.
7	Dave		[Hahaha.

Here, perhaps triggered by words like "kingdom" (line 1) and "attackers" (line 3), I make a reference to the film *Lord of the Rings: The Fellowship of the Ring* (2001), voicing the wizened wizard character Gandalf when he dramatically yells, "You shall not pass!" (line 4) at a fictional menacing creature called the Balrog. My use of a lower-than-typical pitch here (along with a slower rhythmic pattern), mimicking the lower-pitched voice in which Gandalf yells, is part of what effectively signals this media reference to Jeff, Paula, and Dave. They all laugh in recognition, thus sharing with me this moment of recalling this fantasy film that was extremely popular during Millennial adolescence. In fact, this is the second example I have analyzed so far wherein speakers reference high fantasy films (recall the *Princess Bride* quote in example 1). Both of these fantasy films are notably directed by white individuals and feature primarily white actors. This affinity for popular high white fantasy appears frequently throughout the media references of this Millennial friend group, contributing to a white Millennial "nerd" identity, which will become even more clear throughout the rest of the book.

So far, examples 4 and 5 have demonstrated how speakers sometimes manipulate their pitch when they make a media reference. Speakers often shift their pitch when quoting someone who has a noticeably different pitch from the speaker, and, in examples 4 and 5, this has something to do with gendered performances of voice. In Dave's case, this means using a higher pitch to approximate his professor Lisa's voice, and, in my case, this means using a lower pitch to quote the fictional wizard Gandalf. Speakers might also alter their pitch to reference another speaker in a less noticeable way. For instance, in example 1, when Jeff voices Inigo Montoya from *The Princess Bride*, he lowers his pitch slightly when he says, "I don't think it means what you think it means" (line 9) in an attempt to perform what he likely perceives as a lower-pitched voice than his typical speaking pitch.

However, sometimes pitch shifts are not so straightforward. They do not always have to do with gendered performances (although they often do), and they do not always match up with the source text being referenced. The next example occurred in a conversation with Jeff at the house, after the eventful camping trip described at the outset of this book. Relevant to understanding the next excerpt is recalling the event of the participant and housemate Todd's best friend, Aaron, vomiting in the tent that Paula, Todd, Dave, and I were sharing with him, which forced us to sleep outside. Here, Paula and I reminisce about the day after that incident. That morning, some of Aaron's other friends canoed and kayaked to the island where we were camping to join us for breakfast, and they were confused as to why we slept outside. Note that while Paula and I recall a specific conversation that morning, it is not clear that Todd or Dave were present for this, and Jeff did not go camping with us. So there are different gradients of epistemic access to this event, and in addition to the topic itself being rather unpleasant, this imbalance might have created a slight interactional dilemma where some speakers were excluded from sharing in this experience. In any case, pitch is doing a lot of interactional work in this example. It is used to voice other speakers, to give voice to imaginary utterances, and, ultimately, it is used to voice a media reference (harsh voice is also an element of some of the talk here; this voice quality consists of constriction of the vocal chords, resulting in something like a rough or growling sound).

(6)

1	Todd	<whistling throughout>
2	Paula	I love how in the- that girl in the morning,
3		I think- I think it was Daniel's girlfriend.
4	Sylvia	Oh yeah, yeah.

5	Paula	When she was- when-
6		Like, *<high pitch>* "Why were you guys sleeping outsi::de?"
7	Sylvia	Yeah [she was so ^ba::ffled.
8	Paula	[(We're like) "Because...Aaron puked in the tent." And she's like,
9		*<high pitch>* "Ha::::::"
10	Sylvia	Yeah, and then, like-
11	Paula	*<high pitch>* "O::H! You're serious! [I thought that was a ^joke!"
12	Sylvia	[like, *<high pitch>* "I-"
13		*<high pitch>* "I thought you guys were ^joki:ing!"
14	Paula	No.
15	Sylvia	It's like, why: would we jo(h)ke abou(h)t tha(h)t?
16	Dave	*<low pitch, harsh voice>* "Do I ^look like I'm [joking?"
17	Paula	[Hahahaha(h).
18	Sylvia	[Ahahaha.
19	Jeff	"Oh that's ^FUnny to you."
20	Dave	Hahahaha.
21	Jeff	*<low pitch, harsh voice>* "WELL YOU GO in there."
22	Dave	Ha.
23	Paula	(h)And-
24	Jeff	And as one they rose chanting and pushed her into the tent [and sealed it.
25	Dave	[Haha.
26	Sylvia	Aha[haha!
27	Dave	[Haha.
28 ⇨	Todd	*<low pitch>* "One /of-
29	Dave	*<harsh voice>* "HA: HA HA:!"
30 ⇨	Todd	*<low pitch>* "One /of /us."
31	Dave	*<harsh voice>* "HA: [HA HA:!"
32 ⇨	Jeff	[*<low pitch>* "One /of [/us". Ha. "O:ne-"
33	Paula	[Hehe.
34	Dave	Haha.
35	Sylvia	Ha.

In lines 6–13, Paula and I voice the girlfriend of one of Aaron's friends (Daniel), using a very high-pitched voice to express what we perceived as her vapidity in questioning us about why we were sleeping outside, and in thinking that we were joking when we told her that Aaron had puked in the tent. Slobe (2018) coined a phrase for this kind of high-pitched mockery of a young, white woman: Mock white girl (MWG). A higher and more dramatic range of pitch is one of the linguistic features that characterizes MWG performances.

The MWG performance that Paula and I do here, which "other" this kind of speaker, who we perceive as young and vapid, in turn creates a shared stance and identity between Paula and me as older, more serious, and perhaps even smarter or more educated in contrast.

This high-pitched MWG performance that Paula and I do is possibly what triggers Dave in line 16 to use a very low and harsh voice in contrast to perform what he called in playback a "survivor voice," moving into a play frame by asking, "Do I look like I'm joking?" This gets laughs from Paula and me, and is followed by Jeff using some loudness and saying, "Oh that's FUnny to you" (line 19), in a hypothetical dialogue with Daniel's girlfriend, and then he uses a low-pitched harsh voice to say, "WELL YOU GO in there" (line 21). Jeff then shifts to a playful imaginary story-telling perspective, narrating, "And as one they rose chanting and pushed her into the tent and sealed it" (line 24).

This all leads to Todd, who had been whistling up to this point, making a media reference when he begins to chant rhythmically with a low pitch, "One of us" (lines 30 and 32). This reference originates in the controversial 1932 cult horror film *Freaks,* which features a cast of actual carnival sideshow performers. Specifically, the reference is to the infamous wedding reception scene for circus trapeze artist Cleopatra and sideshow performer Hans, in which Cleopatra is accepted by the other sideshow performers despite her being a "normal" outsider. They chant, "We accept her, we accept her. One of us, one of us. Gooba-gobble, gooba-gobble." This chant has been intertextually recirculated in over 30 films and TV shows.

Jeff picks up on the reference and rhythmically repeats it, also with a slightly lower pitch than his typical speaking pitch (line 32). In playback, Todd and Jeff were not able to identify a single source where they might have heard this chant. In *Freaks*, the mixed-gender chanting being referenced here is actually rather high pitched, but in intertextual references to the chant in other TV shows and films, the chanting is often low pitched. Additionally, Todd and Jeff might produce the reference with a lowered pitch since much of the talk that preceded it was uttered with lowered pitch, or they might be using a low pitch to add to the overall creepiness of the hypothetical dialogue and story that Dave and Jeff had created. In any case, here low pitch and a particular rhythmic intonation are used to signal a media reference, following prior performances involving pitch alterations. Todd's and Jeff's low-pitched chanting of this song brings them together as friends who both know this chant through previous media exposure.

These excerpts collectively illustrate how a shift in pitch can be used to cue a media reference, often in conjunction with other linguistic features, like intonation or loudness. In many cases, speakers are adjusting their pitch to try to approximate, or sometimes to mimic, the pitch of the speaker in the media they are referencing. Overall, the pitch adjustment often occurs when the person being quoted uses a noticeably higher or lower pitch than the speaker's baseline pitch. This often results in men raising their pitch to quote a woman, and women lowering their pitch to approximate the perceived lower pitch of a male speaker. These pitch shifts in turn highlight the speakers' typical speaking pitch relative to the others they are voicing. At other times, a pitch shift occurs that does not seem to match up with the referenced media text, but it still functions to cue a media reference. While there are different variations, people often shift their pitch in some way when they reference media in conversation. Not only do pitch shifts function to effectively signal media references, but they also construct unique individual and group identities.

The Role of Smiling and Laughter in Making Media References

Although it is impossible to know every time when someone might have been smiling in my audio-recorded data, smile voice is typically acoustically perceptible due to lip retraction and mouth widening that occurs with smiling (Tartter & Braun 1994). The shape that we make with our mouths when we smile changes the sound and loudness of our utterances, and we are generally able to hear this in each other's voices. People likely smile more often than they actually produce laughter, and thus laughter often (but not always) coincides with smile voice in my data. Media references in my data set are made with smile voice 39% of the time (57/148), and speaker laughter occurs with references 26% of the time (39/148). Laughter is considered to be a vocal marker of humor, which can influence listeners to perceive an utterance as humorous (Meyer 2015).

While examining smile voice and laughter, I noticed that the women in the conversations I recorded used smile voice and laughter to signal media references more often than the men. Goffman (1976:48) observes that "it appears that in cross-sexed encounters in American society, women smile more, and more expansively, than men." Tannen (1996:196), adopting a concept introduced by Goffman (1977), suggests that "ways of talking that pattern by gender" can be referred to as *sex-class linked*, meaning that they are "linked to the class of women or men rather than necessarily to individual members of these classes." Tannen (1996:216) further asserts that "in our culture, smiling is a sex-class linked behavior; in other words, women tend to smile more than men." Tannen's explanation for the reason that smiling is a sex-class linked behavior is that women are expected to smile more than men. Expanding on this explanation, she writes, "Women are seen as severe and lacking in humor if they rarely smile, whereas men who do not smile often are far less likely to meet with negative reactions" (1996:217). It is not clear if Goffman and Tannen would have hypothesized that the phenomenon of women smiling more than men could be extended to laughter, but several researchers have found that women respond to humor with laughter more than men (Dreher 1982; Bogaers 1993; Easton 1994; Makri-Tsilipakou 1994). In my data set, women both audibly smiled and laughed significantly more than men did in the conversations when making media references (gender and laughter reach significance at $p < 0.01$; gender and smile reach significance at $p < 0.01$). It would be interesting to see if men smile and laugh together at higher rates when no women are present; however, since I was a participant in the conversations I recorded, I did not have the occasion to record a conversation with only men present. Yet I want to underscore that men *do* smile and laugh together occasionally in my data set, just at a lower frequency.

In the example below, Dave and I are preparing to leave his house to drive to the grocery store to buy some chicken to cook for dinner. Our talk about our plans is somewhat epistemically isolating to the rest of the group of housemates present, and might have created a bit of an interactional dilemma for them. However, Paula and I again start to reference the recording that Dave and I had referenced two minutes earlier (in examples 2 and 4), of our professor, Lisa, saying, "Did Maddy win the medal?" and "Maddy won the medal" with different intonation contours, which we had to transcribe for homework. Here, the reference to the recording is simultaneously intertextual and intratextual, following Hamilton's (1996) distinction, since it refers to the recording itself which was heard many months ago, and to talk within the current conversation that occurred just a couple of minutes ago. I perform the reference drawing on the exaggerated intonation contours that Lisa had used in her recording, but I now use them for our current talk about buying chicken. Paula and Jeff join in, and as our intertextual and intratextual play grows increasingly absurd and metadiscursive, layering reference upon reference, the "shared hilarity" (Chafe 1994) of the situation builds. Eventually, both Jeff and Dave start to smile and laugh as they make additional references.

(7)

1	Dave	You ready?

2   Sylvia   Yeah. Should I bring my wallet or anything or are you gonna buy the →
3   chicken?
4   Dave   ^I'll buy the chick[en.
5   Paula   [Ha! Hahaha(h).
6   Sylvia   "Are ^you: gonna buy the chicken?" . . .
7   [Hahaha.
8   Jeff   ["Are you going to ^buy the chicken."
9   Paula   [<smile voice> "ARE <harsh voice> ^YOU GONNA BUY THE →
10   CHICKEN?"
11   <smile voice> "ARE YOU GOING TO BUY THE ^CHICKEN?"
12 Sylvia   Ha.
13 Jeff   "ARE YOU GOING TO ^BUY THE CHICKEN?"
14 Paula   <smile voice> "ARE ^NO:T YOU GOING TO BUY THE CHICKEN?"=
15 Dave   ="I wanna die [dot jpeg."
16 Paula   [Hahahaha.
17 Jeff   Hahaha.
18 Paula   (h)(h)
19 Sylvia   <high-pitch, smile voice> "I wanna di:e" ha.
20 Paula   Hahaha.
21 Dave   Hahahaha.
22 ⇨ Jeff   <smile voice> "DO YOU WANT TO ^DI:E?"
23 Sylvia   Hahaha.
24 Dave   ["I ^WA::NT TO DIE."
25 ⇨ Jeff   [<smile voice> "Do you ^WA:NT to die?"
26 Sylvia   Hahaha.
27 ⇨ Jeff   <smile voice> "Do ^yo:u want to [d-" haha.
28 Paula   [(h) [<laughing> (h)
29 ⇨ Dave   [Ha. <yells> "^I:::! wa(h)nt →
30   to(h) di(h)e."
31 Sylvia   Alright alright let's go:

Dave's response, "I'll buy the chicken," with contrastive stress on "I'll" (line 4) to my question, "Should I bring my wallet or anything or are you gonna buy the chicken?" (line 2) reminds both Paula and me of the preceding playful "Maddy won the medal" sequence that had occurred just a couple minutes earlier. This is evidenced by Paula's laughter (line 5) and by my altered intonation and otherwise unnecessary repetition of the question with, "Are you gonna buy the chicken?" (line 6) (mimicking "Did Maddy win the medal?").

Paula and Jeff both begin to playfully repeat this phrase with various intonation contours (lines 8–14).

Dave, exasperated, makes an entirely different media reference, saying "I wanna die dot jpeg" (line 15), quoting an internet meme. This meme originally derived from a JPG (a format for compressing image files) image of a dolphin leaping out of the sea; behind it is a starry night sky with a rainbow accompanied by the text "I wanna die" in comic sans, a casual font based on comic book lettering (see Figure 2.1). The humor of the meme derives from the incongruence of the rainbow and dolphin with the bleak message conveyed in comic sans. This meme used to actually be referenced in internet message boards simply via the text "iwannadie.jpg," as a humorous reaction, which explains why Dave says the title of the file name aloud here. Paula and Jeff respond to this reference with laughter (lines 16–17), while I repeat the reference with a high pitch and smile voice (line 19), causing Paula and Dave to laugh. Notice that once Dave laughs, Jeff begins to use smile voice to make references. Jeff repeats the intonation contour that we had been using for "Did Maddy win the medal?" asking loudly with smile voice, "DO YOU WANT TO DIE?" (line 22), and repeating this question with stress placed on different parts of the question two more times, smiling all the while (lines 25 and 27). While Paula and I laugh throughout this,

Figure 2.1 iwannadie.jpg

Dave finally laughs, before yelling, "I want to die" (lines 29–30), breaking up with laughter throughout.

Here we see two men, Jeff and Dave, using smile voice and laughter as they reference media, after Paula and myself also do so. In this mixed-gender setting, all of the participants, including Jeff and Dave, are smiling and laughing together, which ultimately functions in expressing the shared hilarity of this moment of word play. It might be the case that Dave and Jeff smile and laugh while making these references precisely because of the escalating intertextual metadiscursive play that occurs here, which induces situational shared hilarity in this group of friends. This example shows that smiling and laughing do not occur solely as cues for signaling media references, but to express shared enjoyment and humor derived from making such references. As we can see in this example, the references made are also signaled phonetically via stress and intonation contours, loudness, pitch, and the semantic content of the reference in the case of the "iwannadie.jpg" reference. While speakers smile and laugh when making media references according to gendered expectations, they also do so, regardless of gender, for functions related to rapport, group solidarity, alignment, and overall enjoyment of the conversation.

Performing Stylized Accents

The performance of marked accents (differing from the speakers' own typical accents) occurred in 31% (46/148) of the media references in my data. By accent, I mean a distinctive mode of pronunciation of a language, often associated with a particular nationality, locality, ethnicity, or social class. Speakers sometimes perform stylized accents when the source text they are referencing involves an accent noticeably different from the speaker's typical pronunciation. This happens only occasionally among the American Millennial friends I recorded, because they generally consume American media which typically is presented in (standardized) American English. However, there are still many notable examples in my data where speakers use "depictive delivery" (Clark & Gerrig 1990), using specific vocal attributes to voice characters from films, TV shows, memes, and video games who have distinctive accents (see Sierra 2019 and chapter 4 for additional examples).

There have been many relevant prior studies on linguistic stereotyping in U.S. media. Dragojevic et al. (2016) find that Standard American English and Foreign-Anglo accented speakers are over-represented on American primetime television, while Non-Standardized American and Foreign-Other accented speakers are largely under-represented. Dobrow and Gidney (1998) analyze children's cable and network television cartoons, finding that gender and ethnicity are marked by dialect stereotypes. Additionally, Lippi-Green (2012) examines accent portrayals in Disney movies, revealing that villains and characters with negative roles, traits, and physical appearances are more likely to be portrayed speaking with foreign accents than characters who speak Mainstream U.S. English.

Other studies on stereotypes and linguistic representation in American media focus on specific linguistic and cultural stereotypes. In her influential work on *Mock Spanish*, Hill (1995, 1998) posits that linguistic representations of underrepresented languages and language varieties in American media usually function as "mock language" (see also Ronkin and Karn 1999; Chun 2004) because only the most prominent stereotypical features of the varieties are invoked. Hill considers Mock Spanish to serve as covert (or "off the record") racism in public spaces. Bucholtz and Lopez (2011) similarly find that linguistic performances of Black English by European American actors in Hollywood films are "linguistic minstrelsy" (681): mock language that "reinscribes stereotypes about African Americans and their language." Like Mock Spanish, linguistic minstrelsy is used to caricaturize and parody Black speech and culture, and can also be considered covert racism (see also Lopez and Hinrichs 2017).

Mock language is also examined in stand-up comedy (Chun, 2004; Furukawa, 2015; Pérez, 2013), and in these contexts, researchers argue that comedians' mock language use can be interpreted as subversive, rather than racist. This interpretation relies on the comedians being perceived as authentic members of marginalized communities. However, Labrador (2004) examines how Hawaiian comedians use *Mock Filipino* to position immigrant Filipinos as outsiders, reinforcing their subordinate position in the social hierarchy of Hawaii. Thus in all of these contexts, even in humorous ones like stand-up comedy shows, mock language can be interpreted as a form of covert racism. This point is crucial to my own analysis of stylized accent performances in media references. I show how covert racism gets reproduced in conversational media references when speakers are not critical of the stereotypes in the media that they reference. My analysis builds on the research on mock language in scripted performances, to analyze how mock language is appropriated in unscripted everyday performances. While the studies reviewed in this section assume stereotypes in media have a direct effect on consumers, the stereotypical media or scripted performance itself is the focus, rather than the everyday uptake of media stereotypes. I take the next step in this book by analyzing how media stereotypes are appropriated in everyday interaction.

The vast majority of the examples of media references in my data that use mock language are made by one speaker: Jeff. Jeff outperformed me in example 1 by performing a stylized Spanish accent to quote Inigo Montoya in *The Princess Bride*, and in other instances he performs British, French, Indian, Polish, and Russian accents. Jeff makes 63% (29/46) of the total amount of media references performed with stylized accents across the data set. Paula, in comparison, makes 24% (7/46) of the total amount of media references performed with stylized accents. Todd performs stylized accents only in three media references and I perform them stylized two references. Dave never performed stylized accent. These numbers point to individual conversational differences, since this is clearly not a gendered phenomenon in my data, as is the case with smile voice and laughter. Rather, Jeff as an individual is, in the first place, a prolific media-referencer, contributing around one third of all the media references in my data set, and he makes half of his media references by performing accents.

Why does Jeff perform so many accents in his media references? Jeff told me in playback that as a child of an Egyptian and Lebanese father and an American mother of German, Irish, and Czech descent, he grew up in international circles in Washington, D.C. He expressed a belief that his upbringing and exposure to many foreign languages and their English accents might have led to him developing a familiarity with various foreign English accents. He also told me that he realized at an early age that performing accents made others laugh, and that this became an incentive for this kind of linguistic performance. In addition, Jeff once took an improv acting class, where he was encouraged to mimic various accents. Paula, who also performs accents frequently in her media references, also has experience in both improv and stand-up comedy. Indeed, stand-up comedy students are often taught explicitly how to engage in ethnic and racial stereotyping for laughs (Pérez 2013).

The excerpt I present below follows example 2, where Dave and I had been reminiscing about the recording that our professor Lisa had us listen to and transcribe in order to learn about intonation contours. Here, Jeff, who was not in our graduate program, becomes involved in this epistemically isolating talk by shifting both the epistemics and thus the frame of talk. He does this by making a reference to the 2003 American film *The Room*, which many of these friends have seen. Although this film's producer, director, writer, and mysterious lead actor Tommy Wiseau intended this film to be a serious and personal one (according to friend and co-star Greg Sestero and journalist Tom Bissell 2013), it was a commercial flop, and has come to be regarded as the "Citizen Kane of bad movies" (McCulloch 2011). It has become a popular cult film for the irony-loving Millennial generation, complete with participatory midnight screenings like those that have occurred for decades with the American musical comedy horror film *The Rocky Horror Picture Show* (1975). While Wiseau's home country is publicly unknown, people have speculated he is European and likely Polish; he has stated that he grew up in Louisiana and spent time in Paris, and Sestero and Bissell (2013:2) remark that Wiseau speaks with "an Eastern European accent that has been hit by a Parisian bus." In this excerpt, Jeff voices Wiseau's character, doing so with vowel lengthening, intonation mimicry, lowered pitch, and the performance of a stylized accent. This is actually the third time in the conversation that Jeff has attempted to quote this exact piece of dialogue from Wiseau, but I present the following excerpt because here his contribution is finally acknowledged by the group, likely due to his loudness and the good timing of the reference.

(8)

1	Dave	Maddy had mad maddy mad mad mumuhuhmuhmuh,
2		[madmudunudmadmunadaaamamama!
3	Paula	[Muhmuhmuhmuh[hahaHA!
4	Sylvia	[and we just had to listen to [Lisa over and over again.
5	Paula	[(h) "PORK CHOP →
6		^SA:NDWICHES!"
7	Dave	Ha yeah.
8	Paula	That's hilarious.
9	Sylvia	[And it was like "no:!"
10 ⇨	Jeff	[*<low-pitch, with Polish accent>* <u>You're breaking my hea:rt Lisa:!</u>"
11	Sylvia	Ha[haa!
12	Dave	[Haha[ha!
13	Paula	[Ha[haha!
14	Jeff	["You're tearing me apart, [Lisa."
15	Sylvia	*<low-pitch, with Polish accent>* ["You're tearing me →
16		aPA:RT!" ha.
17	Paula	Haha.
18	Jeff	*<low-pitch, with Polish accent>*"You're tearing me apa:rt, Lisa:!"
19	Paula	Hahahaha (h) hahaha (h)

My reminiscence that "we just had to listen to Lisa over and over again" (line 4), referring to the professor who taught Paula, Dave, and me, provides an opportunity for Jeff to make a reference to become involved in the conversation. He references a scene in *The Room* where Wiseau dramatically yells to his fiancée, also named Lisa, "You are tearing me apart, Lisa!" In fact, according to Sestero and Bissell (2013), Wiseau is himself referencing a line from James Dean in the iconic American film *Rebel Without a Cause* (1955). Jeff signals the reference to this line with vowel lengthening, lowered pitch, and the performance of an ostensibly European accent, saying "You're breaking my heart Lisa!" in line 10. Whereas after the previous two times Jeff had made this reference, none of us had responded or acknowledged his contribution to the conversation, this time, everyone laughs (lines 11–13). This reference brings us all together in this moment of shared hilarity, which occurs since most of us (excluding Paula) had epistemic access to *The Room*, having seen it previously.

Instead of ending his referencing there, however, next Jeff self-repairs the quote, in his typical voice, saying, "You're tearing me apart, Lisa" (line 14), replacing "breaking my heart" with "tearing me apart," which is what Tommy Wiseau actually says in the movie. I overlap Jeff, repeating his reference and showing appreciation, or savoring it (Tannen 1989/2007), by using vowel lengthening, lowered pitch, and accented speech with "You're tearing me aPART!" (lines 15–16). Not to be outdone, Jeff then repeats the reference, again with the performative accent, but this time with "tearing me apart" instead of "breaking my heart," so that the result is an accented: "You're tearing me apart, Lisa!" (line 18). The excerpt ends with Paula laughing and she then orients back to the Maddy recording. In this example, Jeff performs a marked accent to mimic a film actor with a different English accent from his own, and this accent is part of what signals his reference effectively to his interlocutors. While the speakers all laugh at this media reference, we are partially also laughing at Tommy Wiseau and the way he speaks, which is partially encoded in the accent performance. As Phillips and Milner (2017:105) observe, laughter at *The Room* is "fetishistic; it stems from identifying with an *us* who laughs, and laughs uproariously, at a man's sincere cinematic efforts." Thus, the fetishistic laughter at a performance of Wiseau's speech in this excerpt has the effect of othering Wiseau and those who might sound like him. This in turn reaffirms the sameness of this American friend group and how they speak English.

Earlier in this same conversation, there had been a lapse in talk. Paula is trying to get her reluctant kitten, Liam, to sit with her. Here, Paula performs the idiolect of Worf, a character from American science fiction television series *Star Trek*. This is followed by Jeff portraying a media stereotype of American Indian speech.

(9)

1	Paula	*<high pitch; talking to cat>* Come he:re.
2		Be snuggles.
3		…
4		*<Worf voice; low pitch>* "I have no desire to be snuggled."
5 ⇨	Jeff	*<HIE; low pitch>* "Again the humans drive us from our ancestral la:nds."
6	Paula	Hahahahahaha!
7		*<inhale>*
8		Hello sweetie.
9 ⇨	Jeff	[*<HIE; low pitch>* "There is no place in this ho:me for our people."
10	Paula	[*<high pitch>* Come he:re!

When Paula performs the voice of Worf as her cat, she uses a lowered pitch and a formal, ceremonious style. The actor who plays Worf, Michael Dorn, is African American, although this is not a racial category that explicitly plays a role in the fictional *Star Trek* universe. Yet Mirzoeff (1999:206–207) observes that in this show, "The culture of the Klingons began to resemble revised western stereotypes of civilizations such as the Zulu, the Vikings, and various Native American nations as a proud, warlike, and principled race." This connection between the fictional Klingon culture and western stereotypes of civilizations including Native American nations, along with Paula's use of lowered pitch and a formal style, are likely what trigger Jeff to make an entirely different kind of cultural media reference in his next utterances.

There was no indication in the conversation nor in playback that Jeff recognized the Worf reference. He said that Paula's utterance "gave [the cat] dignity or ferocity" and that her depiction was like an "honorable warrior." Indeed, Jeff seems to adopt the lowered pitch and ceremonious style Paula performs, when he says, "Again the humans drive us from our ancestral lands" (line 5). Meek has described the kind of speech Jeff performs here as "Hollywood Injun English" (HIE), which she defines as "a composite of grammatical 'abnormalities' that marks the way Indians speak and differentiates their speech from Standard American English" (2006:95). Meek finds there are specific linguistic features used in performing HIE in film, TV, and some literature. She shows that this speech style functions in tandem with stereotypical characteristics typically assigned to Indigenous Americans, and argues that both the speech forms and pejorative aspects of Hollywood Indigenous characters reproduce Native American otherness in contemporary popular American culture.

Here Jeff uses a similar lowered pitch to voice the cat, and a "formalized, ornate" and "slow, ponderous delivery," all of which characterize HIE (Meek 2006). In HIE, intonation and use of pauses are distinct, as pauses are longer and occur more frequently. Meek observes "the atypical use of pauses has a leveling effect on intonational contours, which creates a ponderous, monotonic pace suggestive of a lack of fluency (or a type of ungrammaticality)" and "this ponderous style may be used to represent an eloquent speaker performing oratory" (2006:98–99). Meek also notes that lack of tense marking is the most prevalent morphosyntactic feature of HIE available due to deletion of auxiliary or modal verbs. This can be seen in Jeff's construction, "Again the humans drive us" instead of something like "Again the humans have driven us." Paula laughs in line 6, and goes back to talking to her cat, Liam. In line 9, Jeff continues his HIE performance with "There is no place in this home for our people" (line 9), with lowered pitch and slow delivery. Meek states that HIE is phonologically identical to SAE; however, the scholarly commentary on the International Dialects of English archive makes note of "hard" and "lengthened" [r] in some samples of older Native American male English speakers; this is present here when Jeff says "our" in "our people" (line 9). The effects of this kind of media referencing are similar to those of mimicking Tommy Wiseau's accent in *The Room*. Jeff's use of HIE in this example others the accent and those whose speech it mimics, while simultaneously constructing his and his friends' national and ethnic identities as white European American speakers of SAE who are not Native Americans. Moreover, Jeff's use of HIE activates and reinforces western stereotypes about Native Americans. Thus, this insertion of HIE in conversation provides an example of a "covert racist" practice, similar to the use of Mock Spanish (Hill 1995).

In playback with the group, I asked Jeff what he was referencing in this example, anticipating it was some media reference to which I simply did not have epistemic access. Todd offered, "Indian trope?" before Jeff said, "That's me doing a Native American thing . . . whenever people are driven out of a place, I kind of do that? It's kind of terrible?" Jeff not only demonstrates that he has the metapragmatic awareness to identify what he was doing, but also that he is aware that this kind of accent performance is problematic. This playback response provides evidence of an ambiguous ("it's kind of") negative evaluative stance ("terrible") towards this instance of linguistic and ethnic stereotyping. By acknowledging that this performance is "kind of terrible," Jeff also resists the identity of being someone who unknowingly reproduces stereotypes. However, as the speaker in these conversations who makes the most media references and performs the most accents, it seems Jeff had put aside his metapragmatic awareness of the problem to be comedic and construct a humorous identity in this white space. Indeed, Mannell (1977) suggests "humor activates a 'playful judgment set' in which one's usual attitudes towards socially unacceptable actions or sentiments are temporarily suspended" (273);

similarly, Husband (1977) argues that humor "blunts" the audience's "critical sensitivity" to events one would normally find socially unacceptable (268).

The playback interview continued with Jeff further explaining, "I do the whole like sad Indian chief talking about being him and his people being driven off their ancestral lands . . . I was doing that because the cats were being inconvenienced by Paula's attempt to snuggle them and they would run away." When I played back Jeff's utterance—"Again the humans drive us from our ancestral lands" (line 9)—he explained, "I'm continuing the sad Indian chief thing." Jeff's repeated mention of the "sad Indian chief" is reminiscent of the televised 1971 environmental pollution Public Service Announcement (PSA) later dubbed "The Crying Indian," which features Italian-American actor Iron Eyes Cody portraying a Native American. As he stands aside a highway, car-flung trash lands at his feet, and the camera zooms in as he sheds a single tear. In further playback via email, when I asked Jeff if he was familiar with this PSA (without reminding him of the specific conversation I was analyzing), he wrote, "I was dimly aware that the material was sourced from some kind of nature advocacy video, but I couldn't have told you the date, title, or that it was a PSA." He continued, "In fact, I think (not sure) I may have got it from *The Simpsons*" and sent me a YouTube link to a scene from the TV show.

The Simpsons is, to date, the longest-running American sitcom, and it experienced its "Golden Age" of popularity during Millennials' youth and adolescence. The scene Jeff sent me is from season 9, episode 22 of *The Simpsons*. Titled "Trash of the Titans" (1998), it is clearly referencing the 1971 PSA. It features an empty potato chip bag fluttering from a truck on a road, landing at a pair of moccasined feet. These feet are revealed to belong to a stereotypical Native American character with long braids and a feather in his hair (also featured in the PSA), and the camera zooms in on him as one tear pours out of his eye (see Figure 2.2). Jeff's later identification of this media text provides one clue as to where part of his HIE stereotype performance of a "sad Indian chief" might have come from. This points to how the kinds of media we consume not only provide us with fun references, but also expose us to stereotypes—which we then reproduce in our everyday interactions (see also Wahl 2011). This recirculation of media stereotypes reinforces a limited worldview, and might even contribute to the sociopolitical divisions that exist in society.

In Jeff's reflections on this exchange, he wrote, "I think I intended a sort of transgressive/black humor." Kotthoff (2006) has discussed how stereotypes in jokes can bring forth sensitive issues in affirmative or subversive ways, and here Jeff cites "transgressive/black humor" as conditioning this kind of stereotyping as permissible. He concluded with, "In other people's usage, perhaps

Figure 2.2 Still image from *The Simpsons*, season 9, episode 22: "Trash of the Titans" (1998)

there could also be a subtle swipe against the PSA . . . a kind of gentle mockery of the intent of the PSA, rather than a more mean-spirited mockery of Native Americans themselves (although admittedly I could see either motivation being possible)." Overall, Jeff demonstrates he is aware of the complex double-sided nature of stereotyping humor, its motivations, and its effects. Still, his reproduction of ethnic and linguistic stereotypes in the form of conversational media references raises questions around why some white Americans feel comfortable engaging in this sort of linguistic behavior. This reproduction of ethnic, linguistic, and also gender stereotypes will be further examined in the following chapters.

To summarize, the performance of stylized accents is another contextualization cue for signaling media references, particularly when the character being voiced has an accent noticeably different from the speaker's voice. Certain individuals, like Jeff, perform accents much more than other speakers. Accents, in part, serve a function of signaling other voices, especially in the context of voicing specific characters or character stereotypes in cultural media. Additional evidence for this is provided by the fact that Paula, Todd, and I also perform accents on occasion, albeit to a lesser extent than Jeff. Overall, these performances of accents simultaneously other certain accents and their speakers, while also reinforcing the sameness of the Mainstream U.S. English that these Millennial friends speak.

"Spam spam spam spam!": Singing

Similar to the performance of a stylized accent as a contextualization cue to signal media references, singing only serves to signal media references in my data when the source text calls for it. Singing itself is somewhat marked in everyday conversation that is not otherwise about music (Azios & Archer 2018). When singing does occur, it can serve a variety of functions, such as to request, inform, share emotional stances, resolve interactional problems, shift topics and key, distance from actions/activities, construct humorous and clever identities, and manage (dis)alignment, knowledge distribution, and decision-making rights (Frick 2013; Stevanovic & Frick 2014; Warnock 2015; Azios & Archer 2018). Singing occurs in my data set when speakers invoke the melody and/or words of a song, either from a film or TV show, or from a stand-alone song (e.g., a song produced by a musician or group for radio play, etc., but not as part of a film or TV show). In my data set, 38 media references involve singing, which means that these speakers are singing in a little over one quarter of their media references (38/148; 26%). In some instances, the speakers-turned-singers invoke primarily the melody and only some words from the original song referenced, replacing the song's lyrics with new ones based on the local context. Warnock (2015) refers to this kind of singing as *formulaic improvisation*, writing that there is little research on the emergent structure of sung formulaic texts and mechanisms through which texts are modified and created anew. I contribute to our understanding of this process (see example 10 in this chapter and example 10 in chapter 3). In addition, there are a few cases where speakers quote a song without attempting to reproduce the original melody of the song being referenced. For instance, at one point in a conversation that took place among women in a graduate student lounge, my friend Holly states declaratively (but jokingly), "And then I got high" referencing the song "Because I got High" by musician Joseph Edgar Foreman, better known by his stage name, Afroman (see example 5 in chapter 3).

In the next example, Hydra, the cat, has just leapt to the top of the fridge in the kitchen again. As seen earlier in example 5, Hydra jumping to the top of the fridge had become rather expected and not unusual, although it was still relatively new at this time, which is demonstrated by how I comment on it below. There is an additional transcription symbol introduced here: a musical note symbol (♫) indicates singing a media reference (following the conventions of Frick 2013).

(10)

1	Sylvia	<*sing-song intonation*> There she ^go:es.
2	Paula	"Tha:r sh(h)e [blo:ws" haha.
3	Sylvia	[Hahaha.
4 ⇒	Jeff	[♫"There she go:es again." ♫
5 ⇒	Sylvia	♫"The:re [she: [go:es," ♫
6	Todd	[I want one of those (???)
7 ⇒	Paula	♫["go(h):es," ♫
8 ⇒	Sylvia	♫["Cli:mbing o:n the fridge" ♫ haha.
9 ⇒	Paula	♫["There she go(h)es" ♫ hahahahahaha!
10 ⇒		♫"On the [fridge agai:n" ♫
11	Sylvia	[Hahaha.
12 ⇒	Paula	<*fades out*> ♫"Da da da: da da:" ♫

I remark on Hydra's jump onto the fridge, saying, "There she ^go:es" (line 1) with sing-song prosody, with a high pitch accent followed by a low falling tone over the word "goes" (this is not a reference to any media). Paula builds on my contribution after a slight pause when she laughingly says, "Thar she blows" (line 2), which commonly refers to sighting a whale (in the 1851 book *Moby Dick* by Herman Melville about whaler captain's quest for a white whale, the dialogue is actually "There she blows!"). Jeff is then the first one to reference the pop song "There She Goes" (1990) by the British band The La's, saying, "There she goes again" with sing-song prosody. Then I reproduce the song, mimicking the melody by singing it with vowel lengthening in each word, and raising my pitch with each word: "There she goes" (line 5). Paula joins in laughingly with "goes" (line 7), and continues with "There she goes" (line 9), demonstrating both uptake of the reference and alignment by singing the same phrase with the same pattern of intonation (Stevanovic & Frick 2014; Azios & Archer 2018). I then participate in *formulaic improvisation* (Warnock 2015) by modifying the song's lyrics while maintaining the original melody, singing instead, "Climbing on the fridge" (line 8). After Paula breaks into laughter at this change (line 9), she collaborates in the joint activity of formulaic improvisation, creating new lyrics for the song with "On the fridge again" (replacing the original lyrics of "There she goes again"), and then repeats the melody and fades out with "da da da da da" (line 12). The fact that both Paula and I have epistemic access to this song and use it in this instance to mock a pet functions to bond us together as Millennial friends who grew up hearing this song on the radio and in popular films from our youth that featured it in their soundtracks, like *The Parent Trap* (1998).

Like speakers performing accents to mimic media that features marked accents, speakers often reference songs by singing them, as seen in example 10.

As Warnock (2015) observes, singing can contribute to an individual's clever, humorous, and playful persona. In the conversations I recorded, Paula sings the most references, followed closely by Jeff, and then Dave. I only sing once out of the 15 media references that I make (in a conversation that had more instances of singing than any other), and another friend, Tiffany, sings in one of her only two media references when she briefly pops into a graduate student lounge conversation (see example 8 in chapter 3). Paula, Jeff, and Dave might be more confident in their singing abilities than other speakers. Even though I was more self-conscious about singing at the time of recording, I felt comfortable singing "There She Goes" by The La's in example 10 because my younger brother and I used to sing this song quite frequently growing up. Additionally, since Paula and Jeff are the only friends with improv and stand-up comedy experience, it makes sense that they would incorporate singing in their interactions more than the other friends, along with accent performances, to construct their playful and humorous identities.

In the next excerpt, Paula had been complaining about receiving a large amount of spam emails from an adult website. This awkward discussion of spam email, which is also epistemically isolating since it focuses on Paula's specific inbox, leads to her housemates Jeff and Todd singing a song from a film together which smooths over the awkwardness.

(11)

1	**Todd**	Everyone-
2		^Every site probably does that though, right?
3	**Paula**	Nah- I- I swear I get more from them [than from like (??)
4	**Sylvia**	[You can just unsubscri:be?
5		I always just [control f unsubscribe on my- on like every email.
6	**Paula**	[I th- I feel like I have, maybe I haven't.
7	**Todd**	It's actually required by law that they- r- uh give you an →
8		option to do that on email.
9	**Paula**	Jeez I totally thought I had th- well?-
10	⇨ **Jeff**	♫ "SPAM spam spam spam" ♫
11	⇨	[♫ "SPAM spam spam spam" ♫
12	⇨ **Todd**	[♫ "SPAM spam spam spam" ♫
13	⇨	♫ "SPAM spam spam spam" ♫
14	⇨ **Jeff**	[♫ "SPAM spam spam spam" ♫
15	⇨ **Todd**	[♫ "Spammety SPA:M (wonderful) spa:m" ♫
16	⇨ **Jeff**	♫ "SPAM spam spam spam" ♫
17		. . . Yes.
18	**Todd**	Y'all are terrible backup singers.
19	**Sylvia**	Sorry.

Here Jeff begins loudly singing the "Spam Song" from a sketch in British comedy show *Monty Python* (1970) in line 10. The sketch being referenced is about a restaurant that serves Spam, a shortening of sp(iced ham), in every dish, and where patrons sing "Spam!" over and over again. According to the Merriam-Webster dictionary, this song is actually where the term *spam* in the sense of *spam email* originates. The singing stands out from the surrounding talk here, and Todd recognizes the song and joins in singing it with Jeff at the second bar (lines 12–13). The two continue singing momentarily (lines 14–16), and when they stop there is a brief silence, after which Jeff says "Yes" (line 17). Here, singing this song brings Todd and Jeff together as friends who have seen this sketch. However, it temporarily also excludes Dave, Paula, and me, since we had never seen this sketch. This is noticeable here in how Todd admonishes us for being "terrible backup singers" (line 18) along with my apology (line 19); I had no idea what this song was at the time. Todd and Jeff actually continue talking about the song for another minute or so, first debating whether or not they were referencing the same thing, then agreeing that they were, and eventually quoting other lines from the sketch.

In these examples, singing is used as a contextualization cue which stands out from surrounding talk in order to signal references to well-known songs. In some cases, speakers recognize the songs and join in, while others do not. Certain individuals sing media references more than others. Often speakers change the lyrics of the song to fit the melody to the current context, while other times they stick with the original words. Despite other studies that have found that singing is not a very common occurrence in adult conversation, singing is actually used relatively frequently in the conversations I recorded, although less than other contextualization cues used to signal media references. This is undoubtedly in part because only a few media references necessitate singing.

Contextualizing Media References in Everyday Talk

In this chapter, I examined how media references are signaled through specific contextualization cues in everyday talk across five conversations among Millennial friends. Building on Gumperz's (1977, 1982) and others' work on contextualization cues (e.g., Gordon 2002, 2008, 2009; Günthner 1999; Straehle 1993; Tannen 1989/2007; Tannen & Wallat 1993), this analysis has shown how media references are not only signaled by word choice itself, but they are also indicated in the speech stream through phonetic, prosodic, and paralinguistic cues that have meaningful intertextual ties to media texts. In the excerpts I analyzed in this chapter, friends introduce prior shared media texts into new contexts of everyday talk, creating intertextuality, which might be considered successful when other friends are able to "get" the references. In order for listeners to pick up on the references, speakers must signal them in some way. In other words, they must use contextualization cues to make media references stand out in the ongoing stream of talk, making such cues act as metaphorical oars in the stream of talk that interlocutors can use in order to participate in playful intertextual conversation. Media references cannot be interpreted by listeners if they do not know the prior text, but even then, listeners cannot necessarily interpret a media reference by its content alone if it is not skillfully signaled in the speech stream by the speaker.

The wealth of media references that my friends and I made in the five conversations in this study allowed me to uncover the specific contextualization cues that these speakers generally use when they are signaling media references. I showed how these speakers rely primarily on word stress, consisting of vowel lengthening and loudness, often reproducing specific intonation contours from media in order to mark a reference as something worth paying attention to in talk. I also demonstrated how noticeable pitch shifts are often used to signal media references, particularly when speakers are reproducing a media text that was originally uttered with a pitch significantly higher or lower than the speaker's typical pitch range. Additionally, I showed that audible smile voice (and presumably smiling), laughter, performance of stylized accents, and singing were used, albeit with less frequency, to signal media references. I showed how smile voice and laughter are associated with gender in this data, with women tending to use smile voice, smiling, and laughter more frequently than men to signal their playful appropriation of media references.

While the performance of stylized accents and singing are less common in my data set, I showed how certain individuals like Jeff and Paula might be more inclined to perform accents or sing songs to invoke media texts which themselves include marked accents and musicality. Thus, this chapter builds on previous work on contextualization cues by applying this concept to the yet relatively uncharted territory of how media references are signaled in talk beyond simple lexical repetition. At the same time, it illuminates our understanding of how intertextual processes unfold in talk. In addition to pointing out how intertextual media references are often signaled to remedy epistemic imbalances and interactional dilemmas, in this chapter I have also begun to explore the kinds of identities the speakers construct as they signal intertextual media references. In this chapter, the speakers construct their identities as

Millennials who have seen many of the same films, TV Shows, and YouTube videos. They also construct their identities as friends who are nerds, who are white, who speak Mainstream U.S. English, and who are overall rather hetero-normative in their behavior. Individual identities as graduate students and as humorous and clever people are also constructed in signaling specific media references.

While the data set exceeds 140 examples that were taken from five different conversations, it is important to point out that this data set is still only a small glimpse of human interaction, among particular friends from a certain generation, within a specific age range, and with particular media consumption practices. All of these factors are contextually relevant, and while they condition the prolific use of media references, they also constrain the generalizability of the findings to some extent. It is also possible that there are contextualization cues that I missed. As an independent researcher trained primarily in discourse analysis, I was able to account only for contextualization cues that were readily apparent through my own auditory perception. This means that I have not done close phonetic analysis of these cues, in part because they often occur in moments of overlapping turns of talk among different speakers which would make a systematic phonetic analysis difficult, if not impossible. I have also prioritized paying attention to the media references themselves, and it is possible that closely analyzing the phonetic qualities of all of the talk surrounding the references would provide additional insights. For example, word stress is a common feature of any talk in English, and it would be interesting to know how often it occurs generally in talk compared to how often it occurs with media references. Since I worked from audio-recorded data, it is possible that embodied contextualization cues also occurred that I was not able to account for here (for work on non-verbal embodied cues used to signal intertextuality, see Clark & Gerrig 1990; Streeck 2002; Sidnell 2006; Eearis & Cormier 2013; Thompson & Suzuki 2014; Blackwell et al. 2015; Stec et al. 2015).

Despite these limitations, it is likely that the more common contextualization cues that I found to signal media references—stress (vowel lengthening and loudness), intonation, and pitch shifts—are likely used to signal media references in other instances of everyday interaction due to their high frequency in this data set. While smile voice, laughter, performance of stylized accents, and singing occur less frequently as contextualization cues for signaling media references, they nonetheless provide interesting insights into gendered behavior (in the case of smile voice and laughter) and individual behavior (in the case of performed accents and singing) in everyday conversation. These less common contextualization cues also illuminate the constraints and affordances that media condition in the appropriation of media texts in everyday talk when such media portrays characters with various accents or singing. Despite the potential constraints on the analysis, in this chapter I have provided a starting point in a systematic analysis of the contextualization cues that are used to signal playful intertextual media references in everyday talk.

3

"I'm a sweet intertextual"

Demonstrating Engagement with Media References

While signaling intertextual media references is important for interaction, how such references are then taken up by listeners is also crucial for ongoing conversation. If someone makes a media reference, but no one demonstrates any uptake or engagement with the reference, it's the conversational equivalent of driving a car into a dead-end street. As is the case in the unexplored territory of the cues that signal media references, scholars have not yet focused specifically on how listeners demonstrate their engagement with media references. However, in many cases they have made the implicit assumption that speakers show understanding of intertextual jokes when they play along, laugh, or repeat (e.g., Gordon 2002 & Beers Fägersten 2012). In order to thoroughly understand the intertextual process of infusing talk with prior shared media texts, the precise mechanisms of engagement with such references must also be fully explored.

In this chapter, I provide analysis of 148 media references that were signaled by speakers across five conversations, focusing now on the ways in which listeners demonstrated their engagement with media references. I also analyze additional playback interview data I collected, in which I asked the participants for their insights regarding their responses to media references. Like chapter 2, here I also highlight moments where media references might be functioning to smooth over epistemic (knowledge) imbalances and awkward interactional dilemmas. However, many of the examples in this chapter simply show people having fun with media references, for no apparent purpose other than the enjoyment of playful talk in a group setting. Group and individual identities are often constructed in these moments of playful media referencing, and, like the previous chapter, I will also comment on this where it surfaces. This chapter contributes to the study of media intertextuality in talk by analyzing how groups of Millennial friends mutually engage in media references to demonstrate their group participation and group identity construction.

Millennials Talking Media. Sylvia Sierra, Oxford University Press. © Oxford University Press 2021.
DOI: 10.1093/oso/9780190931117.003.0003

The Joint Construction of Meaning

Gumperz (1982:167) acknowledges the importance of both speaking and listening in producing meaning, writing that "the signaling of speech activities is not a matter of unilateral action but rather of speaker-listener coordination involving rhythmic interchange of both verbal and nonverbal signs." Gumperz focuses on the signaling mechanisms of meaning in talk, and his concept of *conversational inference* relies on the idea that signaled language demands active interpretation based on prior linguistic experience. However, Gumperz does not examine the precise ways in which listeners indicate they have interpreted their interlocutor's meaning. This is my objective here—to analyze how listeners show engagement with speech activities that have been signaled by interlocutors, specifically examining the case of intertextual media references. In order to understand intertextuality as an interactional process, speaker-listener coordination is of paramount importance. As Hamilton (1996:64) writes, "Any investigation of intertextuality in face-to-face conversations ... where utterances are designed for particular interactional partners, must look at the degree of match between a [speaker's] use of intertextual ties and a listener's recognition of these ties as he or she works to understand the [speaker's] meaning."

Indeed, Bakhtin (1986) also recognizes that listening is a form of active participation, observing, "The fact is that when the listener perceives and understands the meaning . . . of speech, he simultaneously takes an active, responsive attitude toward it" (68). Scholars of interaction similarly suggest that listeners are not passive recipients but rather are active in constructing talk just as much as speakers. Erickson (1986, 2004, 2015) focuses on how listening influences speaking (and vice versa), and describes this interplay using the metaphor that "talking with another person . . . is like climbing a tree that climbs back" (1986:316). Supporting the idea that listeners can shape unfolding interactions, C. Goodwin (1986) shows that listeners also play a key role in providing frameworks for interpreting talk. Similarly, Duranti (1986) posits that speakers and listeners are equal conversational participants not because discursive roles are interchangeable, but because speaking action is oriented toward and ratified by listeners. Bringing these observations to the study of intertextuality in interaction, Tannen (2006) asserts that "conversation is not a passive endeavor of listening to others speak, nor a matter of serial passivity in which a person actively speaks then remains passive while another speaks" (600).

In this chapter, I present instances where listeners actively engage with media references that speakers have made, constructing shared identities by doing so. I show how they use minimal responses (like "yeah" or "yes") as a form of explicit recognition of media references, how they repeat references, laugh at references, and participate in playful frames of talk around references, often using some combination of these to engage with media references. Similar to how speakers deploy differing combinations of signaling mechanisms when they make media references, listeners also vary in whether they use none or all of these listening mechanisms, most typically using between one and three listening displays. In 18% (26/148) of instances, listeners did not use any listening mechanisms, which could be evidence that they did not hear the media reference (due to overlap in many cases), did not recognize it, chose not to acknowledge it, or possibly a listener responded simply with a smile, head nod, or some other embodied action that I did not capture with the audio recording. Much more commonly, however, listeners did audibly respond to media references, with responses to references occurring in 82% (122/148) of the examples.

Each of these listening behaviors, why they might be used, and what they mean for conversation are explored in this chapter. I begin with minimal responses as the rarest way that listeners show engagement with media references. Then I explore repetition as a way of demonstrating involvement with media references, which is relatively common in this data set. I then move on to laughter, which is the most common listening display overall. The final listening display that I focus on here is the construction of play frames. A series of researchers have treated "play" as a type of *interactional frame,* or talk activity, that may be metacommunicatively signaled in interaction (Bendix 1987; Bowman 1978; Glenn and Knapp 1987; Gordon 2008; Sherzer 2002). I show how play frames are a common way of responding to intertextual media references, incorporating all the other listening displays. Play frames are used for group identity construction based on shared experience with and knowledge of media references. I thus advance what previous studies have mentioned in terms of the importance of both speaker and hearer knowledge in intertextual processes, and contribute to the literature by showing that displaying listening via construction of a play frame is a complex process that goes beyond laughter, repetition, and statements of explicit recognition.

Four Ways Listeners Engage with Media References

"Yeah, yes, exactly": Explicit Recognition

Listener responses such as "yeah" and "yes" are commonly referred to as minimal responses. Minimal responses are used by a listener during a speech event to signal engagement with a speaker (Fellegy 1995:186; see also Choe 2018), and they are a primary means of displaying listening. Listeners occasionally use minimal responses to show what I call *explicit recognition* of a media reference. Explicit recognition, such as saying "yeah," "yes," or "exactly"—as opposed to implicit recognition, like laughter or repetition—might demonstrate recognition of the reference (or it may demonstrate "I get it" without knowing the exact reference). However, such explicit recognition was the least common way that listeners indicated recognition in my data. Only 11 out of the 148 examples (7%) exhibit explicit recognition on the part of the listener. For example, when one of the participants in my study, Paula, shouted, "PORK CHOP SANDWICHES!" in reference to a YouTube *GI Joe* parody video of the same name, her housemate Dave responded with a laughter token and "yeah" in response to the reference (in example 2 in chapter 2). Such a listening display might demonstrate some kind of recognition of the reference or, at the very least, demonstrate engagement with the reference (in this case, Dave did indeed know the source text, as confirmed in playback).

In the following conversation, the housemates Paula, Dave, Jeff, and I are talking in their dining room. Ironically, we had been engaging in word play around the word *intertextuality*, since Paula and I were studying the concept as graduate students in linguistics. Relevant to this excerpt is that I had just commented on how it looked like Paula was about to toast the vacuum cleaner with her alcoholic beverage, to which Jeff quipped, "You two have a very intertextual relationship." Here Dave uses the ensuing wordplay around the word *intertextual* to reference a film, and Paula responds with laughter followed by a minimal response showing explicit recognition.

(1)

1	Paula	*<laughingly>* Don't ju(h)dge our intertextual relationship!..
2		I'm just a woman who has intertextual desires, okay?
3	Jeff	*<slow, formulaic delivery>* Intertextual relations.
4	Paula	Ha[ha.
5	Sylvia	[Haha.
6	Paula	*<slow, formulaic delivery, low pitch>* In the biblical sense.
7	Jeff	Mhm.
8	Paula	*<slow, formulaic delivery, low pitch>* As in referencing the Bible.
9	Sylvia	M(h)m.
10	Dave	I was thinkin' more the *Rocky Horror* sense, but hey.
11	Paula	Mhm(h)m.
12	Sylvia	Haha.
13	Paula	Mhm..

14		That too
15	Dave	<low pitch> ♫ "I'm a- sweet inter^te:xtual." ♫
16	Paula	Hahaha!
17	Dave	Haha.
18	⇨ Paula	(h)(h)Yes.

Jeff's slow, formulaic delivery of "intertextual relations" (line 3) in this joking context about sexual relations makes Paula think of the stock phrase "in the biblical sense" (line 7), which she also delivers with a formulaic delivery and lowered pitch. This stock phrase also bears traces of sexual innuendo. In certain versions of the Bible, "to know someone" means to have sexual relations with them, as in Genesis 4:1: "And Adam knew Eve his wife, and she conceived and bore Cain." Therefore, saying something like, "I knew him . . . in the biblical sense" is sometimes used as a metaphor for "I had sexual relations with him." Paula then follows this up with, "As in referencing the Bible" (line 7). After both of Paula's contributions here, Jeff and I each give the minimal response "mhm," which might function as a sort of explicit recognition of her contributions, although they are not quite what I would call "media references" since they are not actually quotes from the Bible.

However, in playback, Dave told me he wouldn't have understood this joke about "the biblical sense." So instead, he contrasts Paula's biblical allusions with "I was thinkin' more the *Rocky Horror* sense, but hey" (line 10). Here Dave explicitly references the 1975 American musical comedy horror film *The Rocky Horror Picture Show* (RHPS). This film features a self-proclaimed "transvestite" lead character, Dr. Frank N. Furter. So Fred's "intertextual relations" (line 3) made Dave think of *intersexual* or *transsexual*, which in turn reminded him of RHPS's depiction of transvestism. Paula explicitly recognizes Dave's mention of RHPS with "Mhm" twice, in lines 11 and 13. Dave follows his mention of the film with a reference to it, signaling his reference with a low-pitched sung line: "I'm a sweet intertextual" (line 15). This is a reference to a line from the film's song "Sweet Transvestite," sung by Dr. Frank N. Furter in a low-pitched voice. The line is actually "I'm a sweet transvestite," but Dave revealed in playback that he had misremembered the line and thought it was "I'm a sweet transsexual," thus replacing "transsexual" with "intertextual" in a low-pitched sung reference.

Dr. Frank N. Furter's low-pitched vocal timbre has actually been analyzed as an aspect of the film that reinforces heteronormative masculinity (Reale 2012). Reale writes that "straight male fans can wear and mimic Frank's appropriations of femininity—they can even belt out "Time Warp" [another RHPS song] with any vocal timbre they choose—and they can do so without compromising their claims to masculinity" (2012:160). The RHPS reference is the only reference made to media portraying LGBTQ+ characters in my entire data set, and as such it warrants a brief discussion. Here we have a cisgender heterosexual man, Dave, referencing the lyrics of a tune sung by a bisexual self-identifying "transvestite" male character. If we follow prior analyses of the film, this is not at odds with Dave's sense of normative masculine identity, especially since he actually lowers his pitch to sing the lyrics. The film itself is an early attempt at some kind of representation of the LGBTQ+ community, and has many fans. Yet it portrays all of its queer characters as literal aliens, and Dr. Frank N. Furter as a flamboyantly manipulative and promiscuous person; promiscuity is commonly associated in a stereotypical manner with bisexuals (Zivony & Saguy 2018). Thus the film itself perpetuates stereotypes about LGBTQ+ individuals, and the film's insertion into talk here highlights the need for authentic LGBTQ+ representation in media.

Returning our focus to the ways in which media references are acknowledged by listeners, Paula responds to Dave's reference by laughing in line 16, and then catching her breath and saying "Yes" in line 18. She uses this minimal response for explicit recognition, and in playback confirmed that she had seen RHPS in college. Paula's engagement with Dave's media reference allows them to laugh and bond as friends who were both familiar with this outlandish cult film. At the same time, Dave's humorous quoting of Dr. Frank N. Furter, in addition to the playful talk leading up to his reference around an "intertextual relationship" (line 1), "intertextual desires" (line 2), and "intertextual relations" (line 3), might function in othering LGBTQ+ identifying individuals (which, arguably, RHPS itself does by portraying such people as aliens) while also reinforcing the heteronormativity of this friend group. On the other hand, however, the fact that Dave momentarily embodies a bisexual "transvestite" character by humorously quoting him in the first person to make a pun about intertextuality might be interpreted as alignment with that character or appreciation of the film. In this line of interpretation, Dave and Paula's shared identities as fans of RHPS are constructed here. Even if this latter interpretation is correct, the character and film referenced are nonetheless highly stereotypical, and the reference to the film in conversation might reinforce some of those ideologies. Minimal responses "mhm" and "yes" do interactional work to show recognition and appreciation of this reference.

What are some of the other contexts that might condition the use of minimal responses as recognition of media references? Minimal responses were sometimes used after a speaker first used recognitional demonstrative "that" (Enfield 2012) to point to a media reference, for example by saying "that song" prior to referencing a song by singing its tune. In these cases, speakers used "that" to draw attention to the fact that they were making a reference that should "activat[e] a common memory" (Ariel 1990/2014:53). This kind of explicit prefacing via using "that" and referring to the type of media—or in some cases even the source text itself—could explain why listeners then used minimal responses to indicate their uptake of the reference.

In the next example, three graduate students are chatting in a graduate student lounge at their university campus on a Friday afternoon: Holly, Miriam, and myself. Another graduate student, Tiffany, had left the room previously to go home but then returned. I had let her know when she first entered the room that I was recording. She had asked me for what, and I had replied that it was for a project on conversations among friends. Following a long silence in the room upon her return, Tiffany begins to narrate her thoughts on my recording conversations among friends. It is possible that she did this to remedy the awkward interactional dilemma of silence. Tiffany connects my recording of friends to our professor Deborah Tannen's recent book project on women friends. As she humorously relays her reflections, at one point she mentions "that conversation," referring to a conversation in a video that Deborah had recorded with which we were both familiar. I engage with her reference to this in-group media with a minimal response and some laughter.

(2)

1		Tiffany	When I was leaving? ...
2			I was thinking about the fact that you...
3			Well, you said,
4			that you were doing a conversation about ^friends,
5			And [then that-
6		Sylvia	[Mhmm.
7		Tiffany	Deborah's working on that book? About like-
8			women friends?=
9		Sylvia	=Mhmm.
10		Tiffany	And ^then, I was thinking...
11			about...
12			All the intertextual references that friends could make?
13			A^bout..Deborah Tannen?
14		Holly	Ha.
15		Tiffany	And her work on friends? Like-
16			repeating that conversation that those little girls had?
17	⇨		Like "my babysitter called Amber also [has contacts"?
18	⇨	Sylvia	[Oh yeah(h)

In lines 10–12, Tiffany tells me that she "was thinking about all the intertextual references that friends could make." Tiffany did not know at the time that I would be studying intertextual references among friends, yet she likely thinks of this topic because she was, like me, studying sociolinguistics and had been introduced to this topic through her coursework. Tiffany then describes how she had been thinking specifically of the intertextual references "friends could make about Deborah Tannen" (lines 12–13), our professor, "and her work on friends" (line 15). Then, she provides an example of an intertextual reference to a video of a conversation that Deborah had recorded and which she often featured in her talks on language and gender. Here, Tiffany introduces her reference to Deborah Tannen's video when she says, "like repeating that conversation that those little girls had?" (lines 15–16). The recognitional demonstrative "that" before "conversation" does some extra work to highlight the specific reference being made and to activate a common memory that she and I shared of having seen this video. The video features two little girls in a preschool sitting at a table coloring and talking together, when one of them suddenly looks up and says, "Did you know my babysitter called Amber has already contacts?" Deborah Tannen explains that by this, this girl means something like, "Did you know that my babysitter, named Amber, already has contact lenses?"

As Tiffany quotes the specific line from the video in line 17, saying "Like 'my babysitter called Amber also has contacts,'" I overlap her reference by saying "Oh yeah" (line 18) and laughing a bit, demonstrating with this minimal response that I recognize the reference. My minimal response here can actually be broken down into three parts. First, "oh" is a discourse marker that shows a shift in a speaker's orientation to information (Schiffrin 1987). Here, my use of "oh" shows that I am shifting to recognize the reference that Tiffany is making, and my use of the minimal response "yeah" which follows it works in tandem to demonstrate my recognition. My laughter token afterwards is another very common sign of recognition which I explore more later in this chapter. All in all, this example shows how using recognitional demonstrative "that" can do some extra work to point out a reference in talk. This can then cause listeners to respond with a minimal response demonstrating explicit recognition of "that" media the speaker is referencing. Here my response allows Tiffany and I to intersubjectively recall and reminisce about a shared graduate coursework media experience. Thus the media referencing here and Tiffany's and my mutual engagement function to construct shared identities as graduate students with shared memories of a very specific prior media experience.

Recognitional demonstrative "that" also occurred sometimes as a display of recognition itself, as shown in the following example. Three graduate students—Paula, Dave, and I—are talking in the dining room at Dave and

Paula's house. Dave had tried to bring up a research paper that only he had read on the topic of semantics, which afterwards reminded me of a specific phrase that our professor, Lisa Zsiga, had audio-recorded with different intonation contours as part of a homework assignment in her Phonetics & Phonology class. Here I try to remember the specific phrase (aloud), which creates a knowledge imbalance and awkward interactional dilemma, since Paula cannot recall the phrase at all, yet I stubbornly persist in trying to remember it even as Dave provides it while I talk over him. However, when I finally hear Dave provide the phrase, I use the minimal response "yeah" followed by recognitional demonstrative "that" to demonstrate recognition of the reference.

(3)

1	Sylvia	No, Lisa did those recordings that were like-
2		What were they, like-
3	Paula	Which one-
4	Dave	"^Ma:ddy bought [the medal."
5	Sylvia	["What is Mar- ^Mary gonna-"
6	Dave	No:=
7	Sylvia	=What the fu(h)ck wa(h)s-
8	Dave	It wasn't the- [She wasn't lookin at the se^mantics.
9	Paula	[Wha(h)t?
10	Sylvia	No:!
11	⇨ Dave	<high pitched> "^MA:DDY GOT THE MEDAL."
12	⇨ Sylvia	YEAH, ^THA:T!
13		When we were in Phonol- [yeah-
14	Dave	<high-pitched> ["^MADDY HAS THE ^ME:DAL."

In line 1, I try to recall "those recordings," asking, "What were they" (line 2). After a lot of confusion in lines 3–10, Dave repeats the phrase uttered in the recordings, very loudly and with a marked higher pitch: "MADDY GOT THE MEDAL" (line 11). I respond accordingly, shouting, "YEAH, THAT!" (line 12). "Yeah" functions here as explicit recognition, and "that" refers to the reference as the exact one that I had been trying to remember; both function together as a way to show confirmation that Dave has supplied the correct reference. I then expand on this ratification by saying, "When we were in Phonol- yeah" (the false start "Phonol-" indicates that I would have said "Phonology") (line 13).

This example shows how an explicit recognition device "yeah" and demonstrative recognitional "that" can be used to show appreciation of an in-group media reference, allowing Dave and me to intersubjectively recall and reminisce about a shared coursework media experience. Thus the media reference here and Dave's and my mutual engagement in the referencing both function to construct shared identities as graduate students with a shared prior media experience.

In sum, explicit recognition is the least common way that speakers respond to hearing intertextual media references in my data set. Media references are a subtle display of knowledge that indicate insider group membership (Norrick 1989), and explicit recognition of such conversational moves in some sense "undoes" the sense of enjoyment, or the rapport benefit of indirectness (Tannen 1984/2005) that speakers may get from signaling and understanding the references without any explicit language to indicate their doing so (see also the discussion on zero quotatives in chapter 2).

"A shared universe of discourse": Repetition

Repetition demonstrates and creates interpersonal involvement in conversation (Tannen 1989/2007). Tannen explains that "The pattern of repeated and varied sounds, words, phrases, sentences, and longer discourse sequences gives the impression, indeed the reality, of a shared universe of discourse" (1989/2007:62). A shared universe of discourse is created in my data set via the fairly frequent repetition of media references by different speakers.

Full or partial repetition of a media reference was used by listeners upon hearing a reference 39% (57/148) of the time. Thus, repetition is used by listeners fairly frequently, but less frequently than laughter or play frames in response to media references. While some repetition, especially with new twists, can be appreciated in a conversation, too much repetition could give off the sense that nothing new is being contributed to the talk. No one wants to sound like a parrot, simply repeating what someone else has already said. As Norrick (1994:15) writes, when speakers use repetition, "On the one hand, the repeat borrows recognizable elements from its original, but on the other hand, it differs from that original, if only through reference to it and contextual separation from it." In all of the examples from my data set that utilize repetition, the repeat is recognizable, but it is never exactly like the original.

In addition to repeating spoken words, speakers also frequently used repetition of melodies in response to media references to songs. Repeating the lyrics of a song in the tune of the original song quoted also demonstrates how repetition can function as a form of engagement upon hearing a media reference. The following example occurred on a Saturday evening as Dave and I were making dinner at his house. His housemate Paula tells their housemate Jeff that we are going to make pumpkin chocolate chip pancakes the following morning, prompting Jeff to break into song. It is possible that he starts singing a media reference here due to his relative lack of epistemic access to the baking activity and/or due to an interactional dilemma where this invitation to enjoy a meal that his women friends are going to make might feel a bit awkward, or even like an imposition. Paula engages with the song fully by repeating the same lyrics to the tune of the song.

(4)

1		Paula	Also tomorrow morning,
2			Jeff- you- (have) [(you [must be around)
3			[<sound of silverware clinking loudly>
4		Sylvia	[Oh my go:sh, ye:s.
5		Paula	We are making pumpkin chocolate chip..pancakes.
6		Paula	(It's gonna have-)
7	⇨	Jeff	♫ Making pumpkin pa:n[cakes ♫
8		Paula	[Haha(h)
9	⇨		♫[MA:KING- Making pumpkin [pa:ncakes ♫
10		Dave	[Haha.
11		Jeff	[♫(and?) a [pumpkin gonna put it on →
12			a pancake ♫
13		Sylvia	[Hahaha Is that gonna be →
14			our theme song?
15		Paula	[Haha ♫ Making →
16			pancakes makin' bacon [pancakes ♫
17		Jeff	[♫ That's what we're gonna make(h) ♫
18		Sylvia	[Um-
19		Paula	[♫ PUMPKIN PANCA::KES ♫

Here Jeff begins singing the "Bacon Pancakes Song," which is sung by the character Jake the Dog in the American animated television series *Adventure Time* that ran from 2010 to 2018. The show is notable for being created by a group consisting of a few young, creative Millennials. Indeed, despite being aimed at children, the show developed a fan base among adolescents and adults. In the episode "Burning Low," which aired in 2012, Jake the Dog sings the following lyrics as he is cooking a breakfast of bacon inside of pancakes: "Bacon pancakes, makin' bacon pancakes / Take some bacon and I'll put it in a pancake / Bacon pancakes, that's what it's gonna make / Bacon pancake!"

In Jeff's rendition of this song, he replaces "bacon" with "pumpkin," singing "Making pumpkin pancakes" (line 7). Paula immediately recognizes the song, as she halts her previous utterance (line 6), laughs (line 8), and joins Jeff in singing (line 9). In playback, Paula told me that Jeff and she sang this song together frequently, having even enjoyed watching various YouTube loop versions of it together. Jeff and Paula continue singing the song (lines 11–19) as Dave and I laugh in the background (neither of us knew this song although I try to participate by asking, "Is that gonna be our theme song?" in lines 13–14). This example shows how Paula's repetition of Jeff's initial media reference demonstrates her recognition of and engagement with the reference. By connecting this *Adventure Time* song with the topic at hand, the two friends bond as Millennials that have shared epistemic access to both this TV show made by other Millennials and loop versions of this specific song on YouTube.

Most examples show that repetition indicates appreciation and savoring (Tannen 1989/2007) of media references, especially in the way that listeners repeat, modify, and add on to references in new ways, further demonstrating their familiarity with the reference. This is not always the case. There was one example where a speaker repeated a media reference *because* she did not recognize it. This example took place in the graduate student lounge. Holly, Miriam, Tiffany, and I were sitting around the room talking. Relevant to this excerpt is that Holly, Tiffany, and I were around the same age, while Miriam was about 10 years older than us, making her the oldest participant in my data set, and the only member of Generation X. Holly and I had become close friends, while Miriam and Tiffany were friendly colleagues. In the excerpt I present below, I am complaining about having failed in my plan to go to the gym that afternoon after getting wrapped up in conversation with Holly, prompting her to make a media reference. Her reference is received with laughter by Miriam and me, but then Miriam repeats the reference with rising question intonation. Here, Miriam does not repeat the reference to demonstrate uptake but rather to indicate that she has *not* recognized the reference and to seek clarification.

(5)

1	Sylvia	I was gonna go to the gy:m and now I'm all demotivated.
2	Holly	I was gonna wo:rk on my di:ss,
3 ⇨		and..["♫ then I got :hi:gh:♫"
4	Sylvia	[and-
5		Got-
6		Ha[ha.
7	Holly	[Ha[haha.
8	Miriam	[Hahaha!
9 ⇨		Then I got high?=
10	Holly	=Yes I did! I [got ^really hi:gh!
11	Tiffany	[♫"Then I got high"♫
12	Holly	Haha.

After I complain that "I was gonna go to the gym and now I'm all demotivated" (line 1), Holly responds by partially repeating my words with "I was gonna work on my diss" (line 2) ("diss" refers to "dissertation"). Our repetition of "I was gonna" is reminiscent of the popular 2001 song "Because I Got High" by rapper Afroman. Holly references this song saying, "and . . . then I got high" (line 3), also echoing my "and now I'm all demotivated" (line 1). Afroman's song consists of him relating things he "was gonna" do, but failed to do when he smoked marijuana (e.g., "I was gonna go to class but then I got high"), with a chorus of "Cause I got high / Because I got high." Holly, Miriam, and I laugh (lines 6–8), demonstrating appreciation of Holly's humorous media reference, which might be humorous in part because Holly is not someone who would typically smoke marijuana. But then Miriam asks, with rising question intonation, "Then I got high?" (line 9). The rising intonation in Miriam's utterance seems to indicate that Miriam was repeating the reference in an attempt to seek clarification. As Tannen (2005) notes, in spoken discourse, listeners sometimes provide immediate feedback on what is currently being said and done in interaction through asking questions. However, Holly does not provide clarification, and instead, she responds affirmatively to Miriam's question in line 10 jokingly saying, "Yes I did! I got really high!" while Tiffany sings a line from the song in line 11, showing with her repetition of the tune that she also knows this song.

Rather than assume that Miriam did not know the reference and was indeed seeking clarification, I decided to email her and ask. In my email, I explained the piece of discourse I was examining, and asked her if she had heard the song at the time of the recording, or thought that she might have known the reference. Her response confirmed my initial intuition that she indeed did not recognize the reference:

"I don't know this reference and still don't. I don't watch TV or movies or the internet so I'm always THAT person who never gets anything. So I was being serious in my request for clarification—not knowing that it was a reference to a song—when I said, 'I got high?' I haven't heard that song (maybe I have but I wouldn't be able to tell you that I knew who sang it)."

This example and Miriam's insights about it demonstrate that repetition of a media reference is not always an indication of recognition. A speaker can, on the one hand, repeat a media reference to savor it, but on the other hand, repetition is likely a demonstration of lack of understanding when voiced with rising intonation. However, even though Miriam did not know this exact reference, her repetition of the reference crucially shows that she recognized that *something* was being signaled in the speech stream, and she attempted to participate in the group's playful talk by seeking clarification. If she thought Holly was being serious about getting high, she could have asked Holly something like, "You got high?" instead of repeating the first-person declarative clause, "Then I got high?"

Lastly, this example shows how listeners do not always "get" references, and sometimes, even among close friends, media references "fail" in much more noticeable ways than seen here (for example, receiving no uptake from any listeners, or causing confusion among speakers that leads to explanations and discussion). As I mentioned, Holly and I had developed a close friendship over a couple of years, while Tiffany and Miriam had more of a relationship as colleagues (and Miriam was significantly older than all three). Miriam attempts to participate in a conversation with younger graduate students about working on a "diss" by seeking clarification on a media reference, as she does not share the same experience of having heard the Afroman song on the radio with Holly, Tiffany, and me when we were all in our teens. She verified this in the email she wrote me when she said she didn't know it and didn't "watch TV or movies or the internet," not even mentioning radio. This example shows that while Holly, Tiffany, and I bond through shared knowledge of this in-group Millennial media reference, such references can also be used as a source of exclusion from the in-group (see also Duff 2002). However, overall this sort of repetition as seeking clarification is very rare in my data set. Even if a speaker does not fully "get" a reference, they are more likely to laugh or "go along" with it anyway, rather than ask for clarification. Most of the time, as I showed at the outset of this section, repetition serves for displaying group participation, appreciation, and savoring of media references as part of a shared universe of discourse.

"Pseudo-plausible worlds" and "shared hilarity": Laughter

Laughter is the most common way that listeners in my data respond after a speaker has made a media reference. Of the 148 instances of media references, 85, or 57% of the total examples, were coded for laughter on the part of the listener(s). It is safe to assume that when speakers laughed, they were also smiling. As Chafe (2001:39) observes, "Laughing typically is accompanied by the adjustment of facial muscles that we call smiling. It is unnatural to laugh without smiling at the same time." Why do people often smile and laugh when they hear a media reference? Firstly, laughter is a vocal marker of humor (Meyer 2015), and in my data most of the media references are meant to be humorous (although laughter can also simply signal "I hear you" even if something is not perceived as *really* funny; see Meyer 2015:22). Furthermore,

Chafe (2001) writes that laughter conveys "nonseriousness," which is triggered by "either imagining or actually encountering a world that is judged to be inappropriate to act on . . . a world that has some kind of pseudo-plausibility" (42). When speakers insert a line from a movie, or a melody from a popular song into their everyday talk, they are humorously proposing a pseudo-plausible world by melding a component of pop culture with everyday life. Tally (2014:146) writes that Millennials specifically enjoy humor that allows them to "inhabit the absurdist world."

Furthermore, Chafe posits that laughter and the feeling of nonseriousness that it expresses contain a property of contagiousness (see also Meyer 2015), which contributes to "shared hilarity," where people laugh together (Chafe 2001:40). Drawing from Tannen's (1986/2011) work on interpersonal relationships and the social need to demonstrate closeness and involvement with one another, and Norrick's (1989) research on the function of intertextual jokes, it is likely that shared hilarity has the benefit of constructing group accord and harmony in conversations. Indeed, Meyer (2015) observes that laughter shows affiliation and unity in a relationship (see also O'Donnell-Trujillo & Adams 1983).

In the next excerpt, the housemates Dave, Todd, Jeff, and Paula are in the dining room chatting with me. Jeff begins to tell us a brief anecdote about a recent interaction with Todd and Paula's kitten, Liam. Eventually Jeff sings a media reference to further involve us in this prior experience with Liam (shifting epistemics), and this causes Paula and I to laugh in recognition of the reference.

(6)

1	Todd	*<whistles throughout>*
2	Jeff	I w(h)as [si(h)tti(h)ng there on the sofa,
3	Sylvia	[(????)
4	Jeff	and like, Liam was just sitting there all like "bleh" like little cat loaf of →
5		cat bread just-
6	Sylvia	"Ca(h)t lo(h)af of [ca(h)t [brea(h)d" haha.
7	Jeff	[I just looked at him and he just looked like-
8	Paula	[Hahahaha.
9 ⇨	Jeff	♫ "No one knows [what it's li:ke..to be the ki:tty" ♫
10 ⇨	Sylvia	[Hahaha.
11 ⇨	Paula	[Haha.
12 ⇨		Hahaha (h) to be t- (h)
13	Jeff	I didn't know anything further than that, but its li(h)ke- he just had that →
14		look abou(h)t hi(h)m.
15	Paula	That's cute.

In this example, Jeff references the classic rock song "Behind Blue Eyes" (1971) by The Who. The original lyrics are: "No one knows what it's like, to be the bad man." Jeff humorously replaces these words with "No one knows what it's like, to be the kitty" in line 9. This causes both Paula and me to break into laughter at his humorous use of this song to describe the kitten's, Liam's, presumed melancholy in his cat loaf position. While both Paula and I recognized the tune of the song and its lyrics, we didn't know it well enough to contribute further lines, as we often do in other excerpts. This is evidenced here in line 12 when Paula makes a brief attempt to continue the song before giving up, and even Jeff then comments, "I didn't know anything further than that" (line 13), possibly meaning that he didn't know any of the rest of the lyrics (or maybe didn't know what was going on with Liam). Nonetheless, it is apparent in this example that by using a melody from a popular song, and infusing it with new lyrics about a pet cat, Jeff is proposing a pseudo-plausible world by merging a popular rock song with everyday life. Obviously Liam the cat cannot actually sing, but it's humorous to imagine him doing so, and to imagine him replacing the lyrics of a well-known song to voice his existential dilemma. As in other examples where the cats are a target of some mockery, this shared hilarity serves to bond Paula, Jeff, and me together as friends who know the same songs and who enjoy sometimes using them to poke fun at the pet cats.

This kind of mocking the cats via media references is present in another example rife with laughter. In this excerpt, Jeff, Dave, Paula, and I have been joking around about Liam and his love-hate relationship with the trash can in the kitchen, and its automatic opening and closing lid. Jeff had humorously commented that "Liam has created his own religion around that," leading me to joke that the trash can was Liam's "deity." Here, Jeff tells Paula a story about Liam's close encounter with the trash can earlier that same day (which I had also witnessed), and eventually the prior talk about the trash can as Liam's god re-emerges and leads to a media reference that is acknowledged with laughter.

(7)

1	Jeff	Todd got him to practically jump in the trash can today?=
2	Sylvia	=Oh yeah, that [was aweso:me.
3	Jeff	[Cuz like uh-
4		He- he was like playing with the fishing rod,
5	Sylvia	[Mhm.
6	Jeff	[He was like, "Meahh!"
7		A(h)nd it ope(h)ne(h)d and (he like)- [gnawed on the front ha(h)lf of i(h)t.
8	Sylvia	[Ahahahahaha!

9	Jeff	He was just sort of like ["aeh!"
10	Sylvia	[He was like ^half way [i:n [hahahaha.
11	Jeff	[Yep.
12	Paula	[O:::[:h!?
13	Dave	[Haha that's →
14		gre(h)a(h)t.
15	Jeff	He(h) [went "aeh!"
16	Paula	[O::::h!
17		He's like, "Wait, this is, this is against ^PLA:N!"=
18	Sylvia	=[Ahaha.
19	Jeff	=[He [came- he came face to face with his [go:d=
20	Paula	["Abort!"
21	Sylvia	[Ahaha=
22	Dave	=Hahaha.
23	Jeff	["Agh!"
24	Dave	[And it was darkn(h)e(h)ss.
25	⇨ Sylvia	He ["sta:(h)red [into the de:(h)phths"=
26	Dave	[Ha.
27	Paula	[(h)ha.
28		=(H)hahahaha[(h)
29	⇨ Dave	[And it "stared <*harsh voice*> [ba:ck into him."
30	⇨ Sylvia	[It "sta(h)red ba:(h)ck."
31		Hahaha.

In line 19, Jeff picks up our earlier thread of conversation about Liam's imaginary worship of the kitchen trash can, joking that when Liam jumped halfway into the receptacle he "came face to face with his god." In line 24, Dave says, "And it was darkness." Then I make a reference to a line from philosopher Friedrich Nietzsche's 1886 book, *Beyond Good and Evil*. This book was originally written in German, and the well-known line that I quote here can be translated as, "if you gaze long into an abyss, the abyss also gazes into you." I quote a variant of this translation in line 25, saying laughingly, "He stared into the depths" (replacing "gaze" with "stared" and "abyss" with "depths"). I believe I might have known the quote from reading and analyzing Alan Moore's graphic novel *Watchmen* (1986–1987) in college. Chapter 6 is called "The Abyss Gazes Also," a clear reference to the Nietzsche quote. While my reference is overlapped with some laughter from Dave and Paula (likely laughing about what was previously said), Paula laughs heartily at the reference in line 28, and in playback she confirmed that she was familiar with this well-known passage from Nietzsche. Dave completes the quote in line 29, also demonstrating his familiarity with it by saying, "And it stared back into him" as I overlap him and say, "It stared back" and laugh (line 30). Dave told me that he believes he knew the quote from a list of famous quotes on the internet. Paula's and my laughter around the use of this media reference conveys nonseriousness, triggered by imagining a pseudo-plausible world in which a cat's encounter with the depths of a trash can is akin to a profound observation from a famous 19th-century philosopher. The sense of nonseriousness is also amplified in the fact that we all perceived Liam as a bit clueless, especially in comparison to the other kitten, Hydra. This example also exhibits the contagiousness of laughter and resulting shared hilarity both before and after the media reference. This laughter and shared hilarity allow the speakers to experience and show their engagement with one another. More specifically, the laughter arising from the media reference demonstrates mutual engagement around knowledge of a 19th-century philosophical aphorism, which is likely shared by many college-educated American Millennials.

In another excerpt, three graduate students—Tiffany, Holly, and I—are continuing our conversation from example 2 in the graduate student lounge. Here, Tiffany continues to narrate her thoughts to Holly and me on the notion of our professor Deborah Tannen (referred to here as "she") analyzing intertextual references in our recorded conversations. As Tiffany humorously relays her thoughts, at one point she mentions "that song" to reference a well-known track among Millennials, before singing its tune and lyrics. I engage with her performance of this song with laughter.

(8)

1	Tiffany	Or like, how would she [^kno:w,
2	Holly	[Hahahaha!
3	Tiffany	What [the source text was?
4	Holly	[(h)
5	Tiffany	If, she had a recording, of the interaction you and ^I had two days ago?
6	Holly	Ha[haha
7	Sylvia	[Ha[ha (oh man)
8	Tiffany	[Where we both started singing that s[o:ng?
9	Sylvia	[Oh yeah yeah.
10	⇨ Tiffany	♫ "Backstreet's Back, alright!" ♫
11	⇨ Sylvia	Haha.
12	Tiffany	And ^then, it got stuck in my head=
13	Holly	=Ha[haha.
14	Sylvia	[Haha.
15	Tiffany	And it's stuck in my head right now.

In line 5, Tiffany refers to a prior "interaction" she and I had "two days ago," in which she recalls that "we both started singing that song?" (line 8). In line 9 I use the discourse marker "oh" with minimal response "yeah yeah" (line 9), demonstrating that I also recall this interaction. Then, in line 10, Tiffany performs a well-known part of the song we had been singing together, "Everybody (Backstreet's Back)" (1997) by American boy band Backstreet Boys. This bop was extremely popular when we were both children, and Howe and Strauss (2000:242) even include it in their description of "new made-for-Millennials music."

After Tiffany sings the line "Backstreet's Back, alright!," I react to her performance of the song with laughter (line 11). Some of the laughter response could be due to the feeling of nonseriousness provoked in picturing a pseudo-plausible world where our professor somehow obtained a recording of our previous conversation in which we sang this song together, and in the idea that she would be baffled by our singing. Tiffany's and my mutual engagement with this song thus comes about in part via our previous singing of it, and in part through our memory of the singing occasion. Tiffany expresses this engagement through her renewed performance of the song, and I express it via laughter. This mutual engagement allows us to bond as women of the Millennial generation who grew up as fans of the Backstreet Boys and similar boy bands. This similarity between us is reinforced in the context of this excerpt since our professor is not of our generation—according to Strauss and Howe (1991) she is among the youngest members of the Silent Generation—and would likely not recognize a Backstreet Boys song reference.

It became clear throughout listening to the conversations, reflecting on which media I intuited that certain speakers were familiar with, and then confirmed in playback, that sometimes speakers laughed not because they necessarily recognized the reference, but for other reasons. Reflecting on her laughter in response to a media reference to the film *The Room* for example (see example 8 in chapter 2), Paula admitted in a follow-up email that she had never seen *The Room* and clarified, "I think I might have been laughing at the general goofiness of the comment . . . even without knowing the reference." There are at least two other examples where speakers revealed in playback that while they were laughing at a media reference, they did not actually "get" the reference. Paula's statement highlights two interesting things about laughter as a form of engagement with media references. First, speakers might not always be laughing because they recognize a reference, but because they pick up on an attempt at humor, perhaps sensing that something is being referenced without knowing exactly what. Secondly, speakers laughing in response to a media reference might be due to the contagiousness of laughter, or due to previous, possibly unrelated humorous utterances. As Chafe (2001:40) observes, laughter and the feeling of nonseriousness is "slow fading"; that is, it "affects our experience over relatively long intervals." In addition, speakers might prefer to "fake" their recognition or understanding of a media reference by laughing, rather than not react at all, or rather than interrupt the flow of talk with a question like, "What is that from?"

In sum, smiling and laughter are the most common ways that listeners responded to media references in my data set. Chafe's observations on laughter are helpful in understanding why laughter was so common, and many of the examples lend credence to his notion that people laugh at the imagining of a pseudo-plausible world. The shared hilarity that media references often provoke contribute to involvement in the conversation, mutual engagement as members of a generation who share many of the same references, and a feeling of camaraderie among the speakers.

"Like that *Beauty and the Beast* song": Participation in a Play Frame

By now it should be clear that almost all of the media references made by Millennials in this book are made in a playful manner. Many of the examples that I have already analyzed occur in *play frames*, or stretches interaction where play is the primary activity. Actively participating in a play frame building on the original media reference is the second-most-common way that speakers respond to a media reference (after laughter), and, unlike laughter, this response can undoubtedly be considered a sign that listeners actually thoroughly recognized and understood the signaled media reference . Most of the references in my data set were coded as involving at least one listener participating in a play frame, whether brief or extended, involving the original media reference. Extended play frames around media references were my original site of focus in this line of research (Sierra 2016) and are the focus of this section as well as the next two chapters.

Here, I first examine a shorter instance of a play frame as an example of how listeners can demonstrate their recognition of a media reference. In this case, the first media reference made is to graduate student Dave's and my previous referencing of the recording of our professor Lisa saying, "Did Maddy win the medal?" and "Maddy won the medal" with different intonation contours (in example 3). The referencing of this earlier talk occurs about two minutes later, when Dave (my partner) and I were about to leave the house to drive to the store to buy chicken to cook for dinner. Here, the reference to the recording is simultaneously intertextual and intratextual, following Hamilton's (1996) distinction, since it refers to the recording itself which was heard many months ago, and to the current conversation, just a couple of minutes ago, where Dave and I had been initially referencing the recording. In the example below, I perform the reference through intonation mimicry and it is purely phonetic, drawing on the exaggerated intonation contours that Lisa had used in her recording but not repeating any of her specific words; housemates Paula and Jeff demonstrate recognition of the reference through their repetition and participation in a play frame around the reference.

(9)

1	Sylvia	Should I bring my wallet or anything or are you gonna buy the chicken?
2	Dave	^I'll buy the chick[en.
3	Paula	[Ha! Hahaha(h)
4 ⇨	Sylvia	"Are ^you: gonna buy the chicken?"
5 ⇨	Paula	["ARE ^YOU: GONNA BUY THE CHICKEN?"
6 ⇨	Jeff	["Are you going to ^bu:y the chicken."
7 ⇨	Paula	"ARE YOU GOING TO BUY THE ^CHI:CKEN?"
8	Sylvia	Ha.
9 ⇨	Jeff	"ARE YOU GOING TO ^BU:Y THE CHICKEN?"
10 ⇨	Paula	"ARE ^NO:T YOU GOING TO BUY THE CHICKEN?"=
11	Dave	="I wanna die [dot JPEG."
12	Paula	[Hahahaha!
13	Jeff	Hahaha!

Dave's response, "I'll buy the chicken" (line 2) to my question, "Should I bring my wallet or anything or are you gonna buy the chicken?" (line 1) reminds both Paula and me of the preceding "Maddy won the medal" sequence that had occurred just a couple of minutes earlier. This is evidenced by Paula's laughter (line 3) and by my own intonation mimicry and otherwise unnecessary repetition of the question, with "Are you gonna buy the chicken?" (line 4) (mimicking "Did Maddy win the medal?"). Thus line 4 is the first instance of the media reference appearing again, and the following utterances by Paula and Jeff are the listeners' responses to it. First, Paula participates in the new play frame by repeating my question, but more loudly (line 5), and then Jeff says, "Are you going to buy the chicken" (line 6), also showing his recognition of the reference and contributing to the play frame. Paula again speaks loudly, saying, "ARE YOU GOING TO BUY THE CHICKEN?" (line 7) and Jeff increases his volume as well, repeating his previous question, "ARE

YOU GOING TO BUY THE CHICKEN?" (line 9). The sequence ends after Paula contributes the ungrammatical, "ARE NOT YOU GOING TO BUY THE CHICKEN?" (line 10). She is latched by Dave, who makes yet another media reference with, "I wanna die dot JPEG" (line 11). This is a reference to an on-line JPEG, or photographic image, of a dolphin leaping out of the sea with a rainbow behind it with the text "I wanna die" in comic sans font (see example 7 and Figure 2.1 in chapter 2). Paula and Jeff respond with laughter (lines 12–13).

Whereas example 9 demonstrates a relatively fleeting play frame, example 10 below is an instance of an extended play frame. This example shows how listeners demonstrate their mutual engagement with an inter-textual media reference through participation in a play frame that hinges on referencing a specific media text. The example occurred in the dining room, after a lull in the conversation when housemates Paula and Dave had been playing with one of Paula's kittens. Here, the housemates reference a scene and song from the 1991 Disney film *Beauty and the Beast*. I present the example in smaller excerpts due to its length.

(10a)

1	Paula	You know what time it is?
2		Gin and toni:c ti:me
3	Dave	[Gin and tonic time?
4	Sylvia	[<*high pitch*> Gin and toni::c!
5	Paula	[???-
6	Dave	[You gonna be dru:nk [by the time we get back.
7	Jeff	[Oh I ^love gin and tonic time!
8	Paula	[Hahaha.
9	Sylvia	<*high pitch*> Gin and toni::c!
10	Paula	Haha[hahaha can som-
11	Dave	♫ ["Gin and tonic party time gin and tonic party time yea:h" ♫
12	Sylvia	<*high pitch*> Gin and toni::c!
13	Paula	Can someone make sure the floor is clean [for me haha (?)

After Paula announces it is "gin and tonic time" (lines 1, 2), meaning that she is going to mix gin and tonic for herself to drink, Dave, Jeff, and I all react in various ways to her declaration, which eventually "triggers" Jeff to make a media reference. Dave repeats her, asking "Gin and tonic time?" (line 3) and says, "You gonna be drunk by the time we get back" (line 6), while I cry out with a high pitch, "Gin and tonic!" three times (lines 4, 9, 12). Dave loudly references a popular internet flash animation and song from the early 2000s,

"Peanut Butter Jelly Time" in line 11, participating in *formulaic improvisation* (Warnock 2015) by replacing the original lyrics with "Gin and tonic party time." In playback, Paula explained that when she said, "Can someone make sure the floor is clean for me" (line 13), she was referring to previous times when she had drunk gin and tonic and laid down on the floor. In the same playback session, Jeff explained that he had said, "Oh I love gin and tonic time!" (line 7) because he enjoyed when Paula drank and behaved humorously. This moment in the conversation was perhaps a bit awkward since no one was drinking alcohol, yet Paula announces that she will drink (line 2). The speakers' various reactions to her announcement could be interpreted as seeking a way to deal with this subtle interactional dilemma. These reactions trigger Jeff in the next segment to reference *Beauty and the Beast*, specifically the song "Belle" which is sung early in the film. Paula and Dave demonstrate recognition of the reference through their repetition and ultimately via their active participation in a play frame around the reference. This play frame ameliorates the awkward interactional dilemma.

(10b)

14	⇨ Jeff	[This is where everyone PO:PS ou(h)t,
15		Gi(h)n and-
16	⇨	Like- like- like that [*Beauty and the Beast song,*
17	Paula	*<high pitch>*[<u>"Gin and tonic"</u>!
18	Jeff	they're like *<French accent>* "<u>BON^jo(h)ur</u>!"
19	Paula	Ha *<high pitch, British accent>* "<u>Gin and ^tonic? Gin and ^tonic</u>"!
20	Jeff	*<high pitch, British accent>* "<u>Gin and ^tonic</u>"!

The shouting and singing (lines 4–12; example 10a) after Paula's initial announcement (line 1; example 10a) triggers Jeff's semi-active conscious (Chafe 1994), and he is reminded of a scene and song in the 1991 animated film *Beauty and the Beast*, where townsfolk pop out of windows, a chimney, and a pillory, enthusiastically calling out "Bonjour!" in rapid succession to the protagonist, Belle. His semi-active conscious could also be triggered by the fact that in the song, Belle describes how people in the town do the same thing every day, and "gin and tonic time" implies a daily activity. Jeff compares the current real-life situation to the film scene, constructing a play frame of "we're in this movie" by saying, "This is where everyone POPS ou(h) t, 'Gi(h)n and-' Like- like- like that *Beauty and the Beast* song" (lines 14–16). Paula picks up on Jeff's reference almost immediately, as she overlaps him, laughing and repeating his earlier "Gi(h)n and-" (line 15) with "Gin and tonic!" (line 17). Jeff continues elaborating on which scene he is referring to with "they're like 'BONjo(h)ur!'" ["Good morning," in French] (line 18), another example of this speaker performing other accents and languages for humor. As in other examples, this brief linguistic performance temporarily highlights that these speakers do not typically speak French together. This in turn others French speakers while reinforcing the group's typical use of English. Paula laughs again as she and Jeff repeat, "Gin and tonic!" (lines 19, 20) imitating the cry of "Bonjour!" in the song "Belle" in a moment of formulaic improvisation. Paula's laughter and repetition of Jeff's words demonstrate her appreciation of the *Beauty and the Beast* reference.

In the next excerpt she and Jeff appropriate further lines and melody from "Belle" to engage in a play frame based on shared discursive knowledge about this film and song, which enables their shared imagination of a pseudo-plausible world where Paula is a drunken Belle. The creation of this play frame hinging on knowledge of *Beauty and the Beast* allows the friend group to bond as Millennials who have all seen this film as children, and can now use their knowledge of it to playfully tease one of its members. Indeed, Strauss and Howe (1991) observe that as children, Millennials were the first generation taken to see G-rated films made specifically for them as viewers. They also note that such films stressed civic virtues such as optimism, cooperation, and community, all of which are evidenced by the cooperative townspeople enthusiastically singing "Belle" together in *Beauty and the Beast*. This portrayal of an optimistic cooperative community effort might be part of what lends the song to be appropriated by a group of Millennial friends here to do some complex interactional work. In the next excerpt, the friends continue the play frame by referencing the melody from the film's song while also doing more formulaic improvisation in modifying the song's lyrics to humorously fit the current context.

(10c)

21	Paula	♫ There goes she-
22		Ha[ha "Oh there she go(h)es she's drinking lo:ts [o:f liquo:r" ♫
23	Sylvia	[Ha.
24	Jeff	♫ ["getting shit-faced" ha
25	Paula	Ha! haha (h) Ju::st getting shit-faced …
26	Dave	♫ (??) "ONCE AGAI:N!" ♫ [from his room]
27	Paula	Hahahaha (h)(h) o:h.
28	Jeff	Haha.

Paula and Jeff launch entirely into the play frame consisting of formulaic improvisation, as Paula laughs and replaces the original words from "Belle,"

"There goes the baker with his tray, like always" with "There she go(h)es she's drinking lots of liquor" (lines 21, 22). Jeff overlaps Paula with "getting shit-faced" (i.e., drunk, line 24). Paula laughs and savors Jeff's contribution, "Just getting shit-faced" (line 25), and this repetition contributes to the construction of the collaborative play frame. After a brief silence, Dave chimes in from his bedroom (he had left the dining room earlier) with "ONCE AGAIN!" (line 26), joining in the play frame and causing Paula and Jeff to laugh in a moment of shared hilarity.

In the next lines, Jeff contributes to the play frame by continuing to invent new lyrics to humorously fit the current activity to the tune of the song.

(10d)

29	Jeff	♫ "GIN AND TONIC ARE HER TWO: MAIN FOO:D GROU:PS" ♫ heh
30	Paula	Hahahaha!
31	Jeff	Heh heh.
32	Dave	Haha.
33	Jeff	♫ "SHE'S HAD NOTHING ELSE TO EA:T" ♫
34	Paula	(h)
35	Jeff	♫ "EVERY MORNING JUST THE SA:ME" ♫
36	Paula	Hahahahaha (h)
37	Jeff	♫ "WITH EYES [A-" ♫
38	Dave	♫ ["THE HANGOVER'S GONE AW[A:Y" ♫
39	Paula	[Hahahahaha!
40	Jeff	♫ "WITH EYES AS RED AS FLAME" ♫
41	Dave	Haha.
42	Jeff	♫ "SHE'S OFF TO FIND ANOTHER (??)" ♫ heh, I dunno.
43	Paula	Haha[hahaha!

Jeff sings loudly and with a lowered pitch, mimicking the male character Gaston in the film, "GIN AND TONIC ARE HER TWO MAIN FOOD GROUPS" (line 29), laughing afterwards and inviting laughter from Paula and Dave (lines 30, 32). He continues singing, "SHE'S HAD NOTHING ELSE TO EAT" (line 33). While these lines are sung to the tune of the song but do not lift any actual words from the song, his next line is an exact repetition of one of the lyrics from the film's song: "EVERY MORNING JUST THE SAME" (line 35). Jeff attempts to continue the play frame, "WITH EYES A-" (line 37) but Dave cuts him off with his own play frame contribution of new lyrics to the tune of the song, "THE HANGOVER'S GONE AWAY" (line 38). Jeff then persists in his original attempt, "WITH EYES AS RED AS FLAME" and tries to add one final line before giving up in lines 40–42: "SHE'S OFF TO

FIND ANOTHER (??) heh, I dunno." The next lines show the speakers stepping out of the play frame and then stepping back in.

(10e)

44	Dave	[Haha.
45	Jeff	Haha.
46	Dave	DRANK DRA::NK!
47	Jeff	Heh Belle's like the town drunk.
48	Dave	AHHHHH!
49	Jeff	(LOOK WHAT I GOT) BLAGHHHH.

Dave yells, "DRANK DRA::NK!" (line 46), which seems like it could be a reference to something, but playback did not clarify whether or not this was the case. Jeff then laughs and briefly steps out of the play frame, providing some metacommentary: "Belle's like the town drunk" (line 47). This prompts both Dave and Jeff to return to the play frame, as they voice this hypothetical character of "Belle the town drunk" with specific character role-playing, yelling, "AHHHH" (line 48) and "(LOOK WHAT I GOT) BLAGHHHH" (line 49). Whereas before the play frame seemed to involve positioning Paula as the character Belle, now Dave and Jeff shift to both taking up Belle's role as "the town drunk." However, Paula returns to the song that they had been singing and reincorporates the topic of gin and tonic in the play frame, as she voices her own "character" within the frame.

(10f)

50	Paula	♫ "CUZ I'LL NEVER GET MALARIA:: CUZ OF ALL THE →
51		QUI:NINE IN THE: DRI::NK" ♫
52	Dave	Ha.
53		♫ "SO WHEN MOSQUITOS COME AROUND" ♫
54	Paula	Hahahaha.
55	Dave	♫ "EVERYONE ELSE (HAS) HIT THE GROUND" ♫
56	Paula	Haha.
57	Dave	♫ "EXCEPT FOR QUININE I HAVE INSIDE [ME:" ♫
58	Paula	[Hahahaha(h)(h)hahaha!
59	Jeff	Ha.

Paula continues the song and thus the play frame by connecting tonic water with quinine and malaria, singing, "CUZ I'LL NEVER GET MALARIA CUZ OF ALL THE QUININE IN THE DRINK" (lines 50-51) to the tune of the part of the song where Belle sings, "Oh, isn't this amazing? It's my favorite part because, you'll see." Here Paula is voicing a specific character, thus briefly taking on the role of a drunken Belle that her friends have assigned her. Dave laughs (line 52) and then picks up the topic of malaria by also singing in Belle's role to the tune of the song, "SO WHEN MOSQUITOS COME AROUND, EVERYONE ELSE (HAS) HIT THE GROUND, EXCEPT FOR QUININE I HAVE INSIDE ME" (lines 53, 55, 57). Paula laughs after each of Dave's lines of the song (lines 54, 56, 58), and Jeff laughs at the end (59). This is the end of this extensive play frame that functioned here to resolve interactional awkwardness by having fun with media references. In the next lines Paula orients back to the "real world."

(10g)

60	**Paula**	(h)O:h.
61		But really alcohol is a problem people. Haha.
62	**Dave**	Depends on your definition of pro[blem.
63	**Paula**	[I concur...
64		*<clears throat>*
65		*<silence, followed by a toilet flushing in the background>*

Paula inhales and sighs, "Oh" (line 60) and then orients away from the play frame and back towards real life, saying, "But really alcohol is a problem people" and laughing (line 61). This statement acts as a buffer between the play frame the speakers had just been involved in, where drinking alcohol was taken lightly and seen as a humorous topic, and real life, where Paula sarcastically pokes fun at their previous play frame. Here Paula is also perhaps saving face, since this play frame could be interpreted as threatening her positive face, or desire to be liked (Brown & Levinson 1987), as it pokes fun at her drinking habits. Dave also orients back to a real-life frame, and shows alignment with Paula in also bolstering her positive face, saying, "Depends on your definition of problem" (line 62). Paula overlaps and aligns with him, with "I concur" (line 63). She clears her throat, and the room is silent until the sound of a toilet flushing in the background is heard. This awkwardness is then remedied by turning the topic to one of the kittens' reactions to the sound.

In sum, this example shows how speakers can construct an extended play frame in response to an initial media reference. Here, they create a play frame of "we're in this movie" over the real-life frame of "Paula is preparing a drink," in response to Jeff's initial film reference. This play frame demonstrates group orientation around remembering shared knowledge of a film and its accompanying song. Such play frames also feature laughter and repetition, and as Bowman (1978) asserts that smiling and laughter maintain play frames,

I argue that repetition also serves that function here. A developed play frame like the one analyzed here which makes use of story line, character behavior, voices, melody, and lines from a film song allow Millennial friends to smooth over an interactional dilemma by bonding through shared childhood memories of a popular Disney film. This referencing constructs shared group identity based on that shared epistemic access and experience, while also constructing individual identities as humorous and playful. Needless to say, Paula's identity construction as someone who enjoys getting tipsy on gin and tonic is also active here.

While play frames around media references are extremely common in my data set, not all media references lend themselves to extended play frames, such as the *Beauty and the Beast* example. For instance, if the media reference is simply a single catchphrase, such as an isolated line from a TV show or film to which no one responds in the original source text, it is difficult to build a play frame around that. Listeners are more likely to use a minimal response, repetition, or smiling and laughter in such cases.

Engaging with Media References

This chapter has explored joint construction of meaning and its importance in intersubjective intertextual processes. I have analyzed how different Millennial friends demonstrate engagement, enjoyment, and shared orientation to intertextual media references through four different displays of listenership: minimal responses, repetition, laughter, and participation in play frames. I showed that minimal responses are occasionally, albeit rarely, used to express uptake of a media reference. I explained the rarity of minimal responses by virtue of them having a dampening effect on the rapport function of indirectness in "getting" a reference without having to explicitly register it. I also analyzed how listeners sometimes repeat the original media reference to savor it, often making it their own by modifying it in the process. I additionally demonstrated how laughter, and presumably smiling, is by far the most common way that listeners respond in my data when hearing media references. Applying Chafe's (2001) theorizing on laughter, I posited that when speakers smile and laugh in response to hearing media references, it is because they are faced with a pseudo-plausible world that triggers a feeling of nonseriousness. I showed that while these friends might explicitly affirm, repeat, or laugh at a reference, this does not always indicate understanding the reference, as seen with Miriam's repetition with rising intonation (in example 3, line 9) and Paula's laughter (in example 4, line 4). However,

displaying explicit recognition, repeating, laughing, and smiling are all generally used as ways to participate in the group and to display identities as those
who "get it."

Participation in a play frame around a media reference, which often
incorporates many other listening behaviors, was the second-most-common
way that interlocutors responded when hearing media references, and also
functions as a way for speakers to participate in an in-group based on shared
knowledge of media. Through referencing a popular 1990s Disney film seen
in childhood, for instance, these adult friends are able to play, sing, and laugh
together as Millennial friends with shared media experiences and knowledge.
The various listening mechanisms allow these friends to bond through shared
engagement with media references to films, TV shows, YouTube videos, songs,
memes, and books that they have previously been exposed to as Millennials
who grew up in the U.S. The listening responses also do work for the friends
who were graduate students together, so that they can reminisce about shared
graduate coursework media experiences. In engaging in play frames based on
an initial media reference, the listeners also construct their individual identities as playful, clever, and humorous.

The same caveats about speakers signaling media references in chapter 2
also hold for this analysis of listener uptake in response to media references—
the five conversations analyzed here are a just a sample of human interaction
among particular individuals. Furthermore, it is possible that I missed some
indicators of listening devices, especially considering that I worked from
audio recordings, and any embodied indications of listening (such as nodding) are unfortunately unknowable. I also have not done close phonetic analysis of the turns at talk that I analyze here, in part because they often occur in
moments of overlapping turns of talk among different speakers which would
make a systematic phonetic analysis difficult, if not impossible. Despite these
limitations, smiling, laughter, repetition, and participation in play frames can
likely be observed in many other conversations as a way of demonstrating enjoyment of media references, due to their high prevalence in this data set.

As I mentioned at the outset of this chapter, sometimes the participants did
not respond at all to intertextual media references. Of the total 148 examples
of media references, 26, or about 18%, did not include any of the four categories of listener uptake that I observed. There are a few possible explanations
for why people did not react or demonstrate any uptake of certain intertextual
media references. One explanation, which I observed in some of the examples,
is that at least one other speaker overlapped with a speaker who made a media
reference. This might have resulted in the speaker making the reference
going unheard. Another possibility is that while a speaker signaled a media

reference, their audience did not know the source and simply remained silent rather than pretend they did, laugh along, or ask what the reference was. Yet another possibility is that the media reference was recognized, but the listener did not demonstrate uptake because they were tired, bored, or for whatever other reason did not feel like showing their recognition. Finally, participants in the conversations could have been smiling or nodding in recognition of a media reference, but since I only audio-recorded the conversations, I have no way of knowing. While the instances where speakers do not demonstrate uptake of the media references are interesting in their own right, in some sense they are also "dead ends" in terms of examining conversational involvement. Instead, I chose in this analysis to focus on how conversational participants did show uptake because it is crucial for appreciating the equally important roles of speakers and listeners in intertextual talk as they construct shared group identities based around shared media experiences and knowledge.

4

"Friends don't let friends skip rat day"

Referencing Memes, Shifting Epistemic Frames, and Constructing Intertextual Identities

The analyses presented in chapters 2 and 3 demonstrated how speakers use contextualization cues to signal media references in conversation and how listeners display that they have understood references. This chapter and the next one shift focus from the *how* of media references, that is, the mechanics of signaling and recognizing references, to the *why* of media references— why people make them in the first place. Specifically, in this chapter I explore how media references are used for two interrelated interactional processes: epistemic frame management and intertextual identity construction. By *epistemic frame management*, I mean the way in which speakers not only manage the *frames*, or talk activities, that they are participating in, but also simultaneously manage *epistemics*, or the knowledge required to engage in the conversation. In my data, speakers use humorous media references to enact these epistemic frame shifts, shifting their talk to a play frame while also shifting the conversation to one in which most of those present can participate due to their shared *epistemic access*. These epistemic frame shifts are, in turn, ultimately conducive to different kinds of intertextual identity construction that rely on shared knowledge of media. Additionally, in these two chapters, I move from focusing on references to "old" media, like books, songs, films, and TV shows, to exploring references to "new" media with which the Millennials in this study engage: internet memes and video games. I continue to analyze additional playback interview data I collected, in which I asked the participants for their insights regarding their media references. Although studies of intertextuality in interaction have acknowledged the importance of shared knowledge in creating meaning, how this unfolds moment to moment in conversation and impacts identity construction has only been minimally explored. I demonstrate how bringing the conversation analytic study of epistemics into dialogue with intertextuality and framing provides new insights into how shared knowledge of media can be mobilized for resolving awkward interactional moments and, ultimately, for identity construction.

Millennials Talking Media. Sylvia Sierra, Oxford University Press. © Oxford University Press 2021.
DOI: 10.1093/oso/9780190931117.003.0004

My analysis continues to build on Goffman's (1974, 1981) observation that speakers laminate frames in discourse. I explore how speakers use media references to laminate play frames in their conversations. I also further expand on Gordon's (2002, 2008, 2009) work, in which she argues that intertextuality and frames are fundamentally linked. Additionally, in this chapter I build on work that focuses on some of the interactional functions that shifting frames serves in conversation. I draw on Tannen's (2006) study of intertextuality and framing in a couple's arguments, in which she analyzes how arguments are referenced and reframed over the course of a single day. Tannen (2006) finds that "restoring harmony was accomplished in part by reframing in a humorous key, and in ways that reinforced the speakers' shared family identities" (2006:597). Similarly, M. Goodwin (1996) finds that shifting frames in various contexts (in arguments, during stories, and in service encounters at airports) works to solve *interactional dilemmas*, or awkward and unpleasant moments in interaction. Importantly, Goodwin writes that "shifting frame[s] is not done capriciously, rupturing ongoing discourse; it occurs in orderly ways as practical solutions to interactional dilemmas, reshaping the speech event, or constructing distance from the tone of the activity in progress" (1996:71). In the examples I analyze in this chapter, I argue that speakers often use internet meme references to create humorous play frames to lighten the mood.

However, creating humorous play frames is not the only interactional work that speakers are doing in many instances when they reference media. They are often also managing epistemics, or the distribution of knowledge, in their conversations. Heritage (2012) proposes that an epistemic engine is actually a driving factor in talk, so that any epistemic imbalance results in speakers attempting to equalize the imbalance. In other words, when speakers do not share the same knowledge in conversation, they tend to work to correct this inequity through their talk. Additionally, Raymond and Heritage (2006) show how speakers manage epistemics to construct social identities. Specifically, they analyze how two friends, Vera and Jenny, balance epistemic stances in assessments of Vera's grandchildren in a phone conversation. For example, at one point Jenny makes an epistemic assessment: "They're a lovely family now aren't they." This assessment is marked as "downgraded" with the tag question "aren't they," which invites Vera to give a response and evaluate her own family and grandchildren independently from Jenny. Vera responds, "Mm: They are: yes," acknowledging her primary epistemic right to assess her family. Through negotiating epistemic stances, these women manage interactional identities regarding their rights to assess the epistemic territory of the grandchildren. More generally, speakers tend to draw on what they know about in order to express themselves as individuals with particular relations to knowledge and to each other. In this chapter, I argue that speakers are simultaneously shifting frames as they readjust epistemics in their talk, and ultimately these interactional processes lead to different kinds of individual and group identity construction based on shared Millennial experience and knowledge of media, specifically focusing on the case of internet meme references.

In chapter 3, I showed how speakers participating in play frames around an intertextual media reference is the surest sign that they have thoroughly recognized and understood the reference. In this chapter, I analyze examples where Millennial speakers use intertextual references to memes to engage in play frames as a way to deal with awkward epistemic imbalances and interactional dilemmas. These shifts to play frames also coincide with epistemic shifts; in other words, speakers shift the knowledge territory, or epistemic territory (Heritage 2012; see also "epistemic domain" in Stivers & Rossano 2010) of the talk, which may also be considered part of the interactional dilemma itself. A main objective of this chapter is to show that these shifts, which occur both in the activity of the talk (the frame) and in the epistemic territory of the talk, can be considered as interrelated shifts that depend fundamentally on the shared media reference being signaled and recognized by the speakers involved. I argue that media references are discursive units of knowledge that can be signaled, recognized, and incorporated into epistemic frame shifts, accomplishing complex interactional work.

At the same time, this chapter highlights how the references to internet memes in particular invoke various cultural stereotypes. Stereotypes are reproduced in everyday talk for various interactive functions, such as complaining (Stokoe 2003, 2009), resisting participation in stereotypical activities (Robles and Kurylo 2017), justifying stereotypical behavior, solving interactional problems, scapegoating (Kurylo 2013), bullying, shocking, claiming the floor, keying the informal tone of social encounters, creating intimacy and solidarity, amusing, and managing a variety of personal and social identities (Condor 2006). Since accusing someone of stereotyping is a face-threatening move (Van Dijk 1992) with moral consequences (Stokoe 2003; Stokoe and Edwards 2014), stereotyping in everyday talk usually goes unchallenged. This chapter explores how humorous intertextual meme references that reproduce stereotypes embedded in the memes serve different interactional and ideological functions, ultimately constructing different kinds of American Millennial identities.

Internet Memes

Evolutionary biologist Richard Dawkins (1976) introduced the original concept of memes, analogous to biological genes, to describe cultural ideas that are spread by copying or imitation. The concept has been extended to activities, catchphrases, and media such as images and videos (often with accompanying text) spread virally via the internet, often as mimicry or for humorous purposes. Shifman (2013:362) describes internet memes as the "propagation of content such as jokes, rumors, videos, or websites from one person to others via the Internet." Segev et al. (2015:2) describe memes as being bound together by two forces: a shared quality that is specific to each meme family, constituting its singular essence, and more general qualities of form, content, and stance that draw on the conventions of the broader memetic sphere.

In recent years there has been a proliferation of internet-based studies on memes, which inform my study of how they are appropriated offline in face-to-face interaction. Scholars have analyzed internet memes as a participatory new online media (e.g., Zappavigna 2012; Shifman 2013; Milner 2013a; Wiggins & Bowers 2015; Milner 2016), even claiming that they are speech acts in their own right (Grundlingh 2018), with humor, amusement, ambiguity, and in-group expressive experimentation being understood as key functions of memes (Lankshear & Knobel 2007; Shifman 2013; Dynel 2016). As Milner and Phillips (2017) summarize, online behaviors (including memeing) are inherently ambivalent. Such behaviors are "simultaneously antagonistic and social, creative and disruptive, humorous and barbed" (Milner and Phillips 2017:9).

Some researchers have focused on how and why memes spread online. In an earlier overview of memes as a new online language, Davison (2012) argues that the key to the success of memes and their generative nature is the explicit removal of authorship. Yang (2017) provides a more nuanced explanation for the spread of memes, finding that the common properties of spreadable memes are simplicity, coherence, utility, expressivity, and publicity. In a similar vein, Laineste & Voolaid (2017) find that memes are more likely to spread when there are multiple interpretations accessible to different audiences, and when the original meme is open to further modification by those audiences.

Memes have also been analyzed as a collectivization tool online (Milner 2013b; Gal, Shifman & Kampf 2015; Aguilar et al. 2017), which, in addition to simply bringing people together in online communities, can also be used for meaningful social change and online activism (Fuica González 2013; Milner 2013b, Bayerl & Stoynov 2014; Huntington 2015; Kligler-Vilenchik & Thorson 2015; Davis, Glantz & Novak 2016) as well as general online political participation and dissent (Rintel 2013; Adegoju & Oyebode 2015; González Espinosa et al. 2015; Martínez-Rolán & Piñeiro-Otero 2016; Al Zidjaly 2017; Ross & Rivers 2017; Smith 2019).

Memes have become such a ubiquitous part of culture and everyday life that Segev et al (2015) propose that they are forms of contested cultural capital, while Harvey and Palese (2018) propose a framework for building critical meme literacy in the classroom and for engaging students in creating their own memes. While most of the studies on memes situate their focus on the creation, spread, and use of memes online, few studies have yet analyzed how texts from internet memes can be appropriated by speakers in everyday face-to-face conversations offline (cf. Sierra 2019), which is the phenomenon I present here. The first three examples in this chapter involve speakers making references to memes that draw on stereotypes about women: The Strong Independent Black Woman meme and The Overly Attached Girlfriend meme. The last two examples involve speakers making references to memes that draw on stereotypes about men: memes about "skipping leg day" and the Long Hair Don't Care meme. Together, these memes in turn create and perpetuate digital stereotypes—or "cybertypes" (Nakamura 2002).

As observed by Milner (2016:91), "many memes are characters based on stereotypical conventions." This has been confirmed in other studies on memes. In Shifman's (2014) early study of YouTube meme videos, she finds that the majority of these videos feature men (rather than women), and that most of the men fail to meet prevalent expectations of masculinity either in appearance or behavior. She refers to this as "flawed masculinity" (Shifman 2014:76–77). Shifman writes that "a future exploration of the positions users take up when mimicking these videos—whether they mock or venerate their less-than-perfect masculine protagonists—is ... crucial for our understanding of the implications of this mode of representation" (Shifman 2014:78). Women appear as protagonists in only 10–16% of memetic videos (Shifman 2014; Gal, Shifman & Kampf 2015), and when they do appear, gender-related stereotypes surface of needy women who are too talkative and too emotional (Shifman 2014:157). Importantly, Shifman (2014) observes that new meanings may be added to such memes through the discursive practices of the users who imitate them.

Through analysis of meme video appropriations and reenactments online, Gratch (2017) shows how the circulation of memes can both perpetuate and subvert racial, class, and gender stereotypes. Eschler and Menking (2018) also find that "starter pack" memes specifically express prototypes of social identities that contain potent imagery and messaging around race, ethnicity, and gender. Additionally, Yoon (2016) notes that most memes about racism perpetuate colorblindness by mocking people of color and denying structural racism. At the same time, Dobson and Knezevic (2017) find that memes stigmatize poverty and social welfare. Lastly, Kanai (2016) observes that interpreting memes also requires readers to operationalize gendered, classed, and raced classificatory knowledges. Shifman writes that future research should attempt to understand how memes are used by different groups, encouraging researchers to explore to what extent internet memes constitute a "global" language, and to what extent specific local cultures create their own "discrete memetic vernaculars" (2014:173–174). In this chapter, I attempt to answer the second part of this question, addressing local identities and how this specific group of Millennial friends creates their own memetic vernacular in their everyday conversations.

For each case in this chapter, I present the interactional context and the conversation first, followed by an explanation of the meme referenced and the analysis of its appearance in offline conversation. The analysis demonstrates that intertextual meme references are used in these instances to construct play frames, often functioning to resolve epistemic and interactional dilemmas. In each case I also analyze how the insertion of stereotyping memes in conversation affirms certain individual and group identities, not only vis-à-vis shared knowledge of the memes but also in the ways that these meme references other the groups of people represented within them. This othering of swaths of US society in turn highlights shared identities of the speakers.

Referencing Memes in Everyday Talk

"She's a strong independent woman"

It is a Saturday night at my partner Dave's house, and his housemate Paula and I are chatting in the dining room. Paula had just tried to pick up her kitten, Liam, who had stuck his leg out against her chest in defiance as she did so. Here, we comment on and voice Liam's behavior. Then we comment on the behavior of her other kitten, Hydra, which leads to Paula making a meme reference.

(1a)

1	Paula	Liam's like "NO::! See, leg is ^ou:t!"
2	Sylvia	*<high-pitch, to cat>* What is that?
3	Paula	(?????)
4	Sylvia	"No(h) se(h)e le(h)g is out."
5	Paula	*<high pitch>* Le(h)g is [out!
6	Sylvia	[Haha does that mean-
7		that's [how you know he doesn't wanna be he(h)ld?
8	Paula	[He's just like-
9		He's like "NO:"! Yeah, [it's like- like-
10	Sylvia	[Stick the leg o(h)u(h)t?
11	Paula	Stick the leg out,
12	Sylvia	Dis-legs himse(h)lf [from you(h)?
13	Paula	[Exactly.
14		And I'm like, *<high pitch>* "But I wanna cuddle!"
15		and they're like, ["NO::!"
16	Dave	["I wanted to be free:::!"
17	Sylvia	["No:::"
18		Liam's the- Hydra like- almost never lets me pick her up.=
19	Paula	=Definitely . . .
20		*<quietly>* Definitely. She's more..
21 ⇒		"She's /an /in/de/p[en/dent /wo/man."=
22	Dave	[(You want?)
23	Sylvia	=Yep.
24		*<1.5 second silence>*
25 ⇒	Paula	"who /don't /need /no /ma:n" . . .
26	Sylvia	She only did the other day,
27		when I was bringing her from- downstairs up here and then →
28		she kinda like was just like *<high pitch>* "ok[ay:!"
29	Paula	[She's like →
30		*<high pitch>* "Ok! This is fine."

In line 18, I shift from talking about Liam to commenting on Hydra's behavior, observing that she "almost never lets me pick her up." This is a first position epistemic stance (Raymond & Heritage 2006), which expresses my knowledge about Paula's cat, Hydra. Paula latches onto my observation, affirming it by repeating "Definitely" twice (lines 19–20), which is an upgraded epistemic stance, as Paula is the one who has primary epistemic rights to assess her pet cat. Whereas Raymond and Heritage (2006) examine two friends "owning grandchildren" via their epistemic negotiations, here two friends appear to be managing the epistemics of "owning cats." Paula continues her epistemic assessment of Hydra, first saying "She's more.." (line 20). After a brief pause, she says instead, "She's an independent woman" (line 21), with a marked rhythmic intonation. What does this new rhythmic intonation indicate?

The rhythmic intonation (and Paula's utterance that follows it) provides evidence that she is referencing an internet meme; specifically, The Strong Independent Black Woman meme. While on the surface, the idea of a Black woman being strong and independent might seem positive, this meme refers to the limiting stereotype of the sassy Black woman stock character frequently portrayed in films and television shows (much of the following discussion also appears in Sierra 2019). According to the memetic reference website, Know Your Meme, a Facebook page called "Being an independent black woman who don't need no man" was launched on June 11, 2011, gaining over 47,000 "likes" in the following three years. On August 6th, a Body Building Forums member created a thread with *ASCII art* (a graphic design technique that consists of pictures pieced together from printable computer characters) "strong black woman" *copypasta* (characters that can be copy and pasted on a computer). YouTuber Liz Charles uploaded a video on October 4th of a young white man saying, "I'm a strong black woman I don't need no man." Despite the person recording the video (presumably Liz Charles) saying, "I probably shouldn't put this on YouTube, it sounds racist," at the time of writing the video has over 87,000 views. The meme is often repeated in an ironic manner by white (often male) people (see Ilbury 2019). On February 8th, 2012, Redditor karmanaut posted the ASCII copypasta to the circlejerk subreddit, receiving more than 3,200 upvotes and 145 comments before being archived. On May 25, 2012, a Quickmeme page titled "Strong Independent Black Woman" was created with an image of a Black woman with pouted lips, one hand on her hip and the other used to wag her finger with the accompanying text: "I AM A STRONG INDEPENDENT BLACK WOMAN WHO DON'T NEED NO MAN," as shown in Figure 4.1. It is likely that this is the image Paula has in mind when she references the meme in example 1a, as she confirmed in a playback interview.

Along with the restrictive cultural stereotypes presented in this meme, where Black women are independent and sassy, drawing on the stereotype of the "angry Black woman"—a well-established racial trope which renders Black women as aggressive, obnoxious, and lacking vulnerability and empathy (Harris-Perry 2011), the meme also makes use of a linguistic stereotype. As Bucholtz and Lopez (2011:699) observe in Hollywood films featuring stereotypical usage of African American English (AAE), "The full grammatical range of the variety is restricted to the emblematic use of a few features." In this meme, AAE is emblematized with the grammatical feature of negative

Figure 4.1 "Strong Independent Black Woman" meme

concord (Labov 1972:699) in the construction "don't need no man" as well as the absence of third-person singular -s in the use of *don't* for *doesn't*, a well-documented feature of the variety (Green 2002). Despite slight variations on this meme, negative concord persists throughout all versions. This linguistic stereotype reinforces a raciolinguistic ideology (Flores & Rosa 2015) that all Black women, and thereby possibly all Black people, speak AAE.

After Paula references this meme, I respond with a minimal response "Yep" in line 23. Here I affirm receipt of the reference, but my lack of laughter or any other uptake is somewhat marked, as is the relatively long pause that follows. Paula then completes the meme's template by saying, "who don't need no man" (line 25). This reference relies on epistemic access to a meme, yet even though Dave and I both knew the meme, we do not engage with the reference here. Instead, Paula's reference is again followed by a pause, before I continue expanding on the observations about Hydra that I had been making prior to Paula's meme reference. Paula orients to this talk, overlapping me and continuing to talk about Hydra's behavior. Referencing the Strong Independent Black Woman meme here briefly constructs a play frame which imagines the cat Hydra as a "strong independent woman." It also subtly reinforces the stereotype within the meme about Black women's personalities, along with the linguistic stereotype embedded in the meme. By referencing this meme, stereotypes about Black women are reinforced, and Black women are othered. At the same time, the speaker's contrastive identity as a white woman using this meme to joke about her kitten is foregrounded in contrast to the invocation of a stereotype of Black femininity.

The next excerpt occurred a couple of weeks later on a Friday night at Dave's house. Two of Dave's housemates, Jeff and Paula, are hanging out in the dining room with Dave and I. Jeff had been joking about hypothetical scenarios where the pet kittens Hydra and Liam might try to kill the housemates. Dave has just commented on how the aggressive kittens needed the housemates alive in order to let them into the basement (a space from which they were typically banned but occasionally slipped into). Here Paula references the Strong Independent Black Woman meme again (this excerpt is also analyzed in Sierra 2019).

(1b)

1	Dave	They still don't have a strategy for getting in the basement,
2		though=
3	Jeff	=Mhm.
4	Dave	without us.
5		So they need us arou:nd so they can get in there.
6	Sylvia	Yeah.
7	Jeff	As long as we're useful to them, they let us live.
8	Sylvia	Yeah.
9	Dave	Yep. Well, Liam needs lovin'.
10	Paula	(high pitch) He[does.
11	Dave	[Hydra on the other hand don't give a shit.
12	Jeff	[Hydra knows only-
12 ⇨	Paula	["Sh- hey, she's a ^stro:ng independent..African woman."
13	Sylvia	mh!
14	Dave	[Damn right she is.
15 ⇨	Paula	[("She don't need no man.")
16 ⇨	Jeff	[("Who don't need no man.")
17	Paula	(h)[(??)
18	Jeff	[(She u:h..
19		She knows only sarcasm and loathing.

Like I did in example 1a, here Dave and Jeff take epistemic stances about Paula's cats in lines 1–7. In line 9, Dave observes, "Well, Liam needs lovin'," dropping the "g" in "loving," which is a classic non-standard indexical marker of tough masculinity (e.g., Fischer 1958). Dave follows this up with a non-standard syntactic construction in "Hydra on the other hand don't give a shit" (11), using "don't" in place of "doesn't." This non-standard construction might also carry connotations of toughness. Dave's swear "shit" is also associated with masculinity (de Klerk 1997; Kiesling 2005:724) and aggressiveness (Coates 1993; de Klerk 1992, 1997). These subtle phonetic and syntactic choices are likely what trigger Paula to reference the Strong Independent Black Woman meme once again in connection to describing Hydra. Indeed, there is a widespread raciolinguistic ideology that equates AAE with being cool, tough, and masculine (Bucholtz 2011; Morgan 1999).

In line 12, Paula references the Strong Independent Black Woman meme again, saying "Sh- hey, she's a strong independent African woman." Paula replaces the meme's typical use of "Black" with "African." Initially, I thought the use of "African" might be due to some discomfort in saying the word "Black," or in an attempt to be "politically correct" and reach instead for "African American." When I presented Paula with this interpretation, she said that at the time, she thought the cats were an African breed. In any case, the meme is recognized by the group, and along with the shift in epistemics required to get the joke, it also creates a fleeting play frame of "Hydra the cat is a strong independent African woman." I emit a single laughter token in response to this meme reference (13), which is reminiscent of my initial minimal response upon hearing it before in example 1a, "Yep." Dave contributes, "Damn right she is" (14); the expression "damn right" is also associated with male language (Edelsky 1976) and for the speakers, it might also be associated with stereotypes of African American toughness. Both Paula and Jeff say something like, "She don't need no man," which is difficult to hear due to overlap of the three speakers and laughter particles within their talk (lines 15-16).

The reference simultaneously serves for both Paula's humorous identity construction as well as group identity construction based on shared knowledge of the meme. This brief epistemic play frame shift serves a social bonding function, where the speakers joke around with an internet meme due to their shared internet savvy, playfully drawing on the meme to bond through mocking a pet. In appropriating this meme and its AAE features, however, these friends also activate and reinforce a meme's linguistic and social stereotypes, which also others Black women. The joke's intertextual irony could perhaps also be interpreted as a dismissal of the linguistic stereotype and possibly also stereotypes about Black women's toughness, but the very repetition of these stereotypes reinforces them (see also Robles 2015, 2019). Furthermore, the stereotype itself is not questioned or discussed at all here.

In both of these examples, Paula briefly shifts to a play frame in conversation by referencing an internet meme which simultaneously shifts the epistemic territory of the talk from being only about her cat Hydra to also being about a meme featuring a stereotypical representation of a Black woman. In the first example, Paula's reference was not taken up by other speakers, but it still served to briefly alter the frame and epistemic territory of the talk. The second example showed the meme being used in a similar manner, but here there was more uptake from Paula's interlocutors, and so the meme reference not only served for a brief epistemic frame shift but it also served for her own humorous identity construction as well as the group identity construction of the speakers who participated in the meme reference. At the same time, referencing this meme gives off the speakers' identities as white friends who do not speak AAE, in contrast to the Black woman in the meme they reference here. Bucholtz and Lopez (2011) describe how through linguistic minstrelsy, white European American male protagonists in Hollywood films:

> exercise white privilege by utilizing linguistic features indexical of Blackness without being affected by the stigma that usually accompanies the use of such language. Once they have no further need for their Black-influenced personas, the white protagonists return to their standard language variety with a newfound racial and gender authentication conferred by their experience, while leaving hegemonic racial arrangements intact.
>
> Bucholtz and Lopez (2011:701–702)

While the example presented here is from unscripted everyday conversation rather than a film script, this observation can be considered in relation to my data. The speakers who use linguistic features lifted from a meme associated with being Black do so without any risk of stigma or negative consequences in this private white space. Once the meme reference has been made and recognized, the friends return to speaking their typical White Mainstream English (Alim and Smitherman 2012). This reference does nothing to challenge racial stereotypes in the moment, and in fact it reinforces linguistic, ethnic, and gender stereotypes.

However, discussing this example with the participants in playback interviews has led to some reflection among them, revealing their metapragmatic awareness. In discussing this meme reference and other examples from the data set, Dave stated, "Your data is white people being racist. I've come to terms with that. I've come to terms with the fact that that meme is racist . . . when I first participated in it, I didn't think it was, but now that I look at it in retrospect, it's unequivocally the case." This observation critiques the prior linguistic behavior, serving to distance Dave from the behavior and association with "white people being racist" by using past-tense constructions like "I've come to terms," "I didn't think it was," and "now that I look at it in retrospect." Paula also acknowledged in informal discussion around this example that stylized accent performances for humor's sake can be interpreted as offensive or racist.

Thus, the appropriation of the Strong Black Woman meme in conversation can be considered another example of "casual" linguistic and cultural stereotyping, or a "covert racist" practice, reminiscent of mock Spanish (Hill 1995). In this case, a covert racist practice consists of white speakers referencing a racist internet meme in everyday conversation. The fact that they are friends is important here. As Paula mentioned in playback, the closeness of the relationship between the speakers is what conditions using potentially offensive humor, and this has also been studied in other contexts (e.g., Wolfers et al. 2017). Furthermore, the fact that this meme reference takes place in a white space without any Black people present is likely relevant to its occurrence. Despite the apparent prioritization of humor and the construction of shared in-group identity over critical sensitivity, the analysis of this talk and bringing it to the speakers' attention shows the potential for metapragmatic reflection and reconsideration of linguistic and cultural stereotyping in everyday talk. Still, this example of a conversational meme reference containing AAE and a stereotype about Black femininity ultimately demonstrates how white speakers activate and reinforce the linguistic and social stereotypes represented in the meme, which has the effect of othering Black women and Black English speakers.

Interestingly, a spontaneous conversational reference to this data excerpt and metacommentary about it occurred about a year and a half after the initial recording, with different friends. I do not have an audio recording of this conversation, but I took notes after it happened, which I reproduce here. This example shows how a different group of speakers repeat the prior reference to the Strong Independent Black Woman meme, again activating and reinforcing the stereotypes of the meme. However, here the speakers' heightened metapragmatic awareness about the stereotypical nature of this meme results in immediate criticism of the reference.

This third example occurred after I had presented the above example 1b containing the reference to the Strong Independent Black Woman meme at an international academic conference (this example is also analyzed in Sierra 2019). Throughout the conference, I had spoken with two friends and colleagues from graduate school, Erin and Hana, about my ethical concerns regarding portraying my participants as engaging in racist linguistic practices. After the conference, Erin, Hana, and I had just arrived in a different country for some post-conference leisure travel, and were walking through a park when I said, "I love traveling because I feel like I can do stuff." Erin responded, "Because you feel independent?" The word "independent" triggered Hana to jokingly reference my data, saying, "You're a strong Black woman!" Erin then said, "Oh no, don't say that or we'll be in her data as racist." I echoed Erin, sarcastically saying, "Yeah, you'll be my racist friends." Then we might have smiled or laughed at the idea that this would end up in my work.

This interaction contains an intertextual reference to the Strong Independent Black Woman meme, as experienced through my analysis at a conference of the prior conversational reference to the meme. Hana's fleeting reference, "You're a strong Black woman!" again activates and reinforces the cultural stereotype present in the meme that Black women are "strong." It also reinforces the non-Black identities of the speaker (Hana is Korean) and of myself, the addressee. But, unlike the original example analyzed, this one contains spontaneous criticism about the meme reference itself, when Erin says, "Oh no, don't say that or we'll be in her data as racist." This instance, along with the playback data I have already described, shows that, in general, some metapragmatic awareness about cultural and linguistic stereotypes can result in reflective commentary after having made media references containing stereotypes. However, this specific instance shows something new—that elevated metapragmatic awareness (due to our former discussion and my presentation of the original example at a conference) can result in metacommentary immediately following a stereotyping media reference. In this case, Erin immediately and explicitly labeled this stereotyping media reference and people who reference it as being perceived as "racist," admonishing "Oh no, don't say that" with the implication that this kind of linguistic behavior is to be avoided. This example provides one other instance of how a reference like this might spread, while more importantly demonstrating that with elevated metapragmatic awareness of the stereotyping nature of such a reference, speakers are capable of immediately reflecting on this kind of linguistic behavior as problematic and unacceptable.

Taken together as a set, the first two instances of referencing the Strong Independent Black Woman meme construct intertextual identities as American Millennials who know the same internet meme. At the same time, these references also reinforce whiteness, heteronormativity, and humorous identities in a white space by ironically citing a meme featuring a stereotypical trope of Black femininity in relation to heteronormative expectations. In those instances, speakers shift the epistemic territory from pet cats to a popular meme, constructing a play frame where a female cat is recast as a "strong (African) woman." The third instance of quoting this meme in conversation refers both to its internet existence as well as to its appearance in the prior examples as featured in my own linguistic analysis at a conference presentation. This instance features metapragmatic commentary immediately following its reappearance in conversation. This last example reaffirms group identities as Millennial academics, and again highlights non-Black identities while also explicitly drawing attention to the meme and its use in conversation as a racist practice. This demonstrates that while media stereotypes are often unthinkingly inserted into conversation, it is possible to raise our awareness about this practice through explicit discussion of the problem.

"Who's texting us?"

The next example of a meme reference in conversation occurred almost immediately after example 1b. It begins with Jeff referring back to an earlier story he had told about the kitten Hydra leaping onto him and knocking him over. As the speakers try to deduce whether the cat who lovingly attacked Jeff was Liam or Hydra, they produce a series of utterances that eventually prompt Paula to once again reference a meme in relation to Hydra.

(2)

1	Jeff	I actually don't remember if it was Hydra or Liam.
2	Paula	Pro[bably Hydra, honestly.
3	Jeff	[(who pounced on me-) probably Hydra.
4	Sylvia	(Might have been) Hydra.
5	Dave	That's a much more Hydra [thing to do.
6	Jeff	[Like I've never known Liam to want →
7		snuggles that badly.
8	Sylvia	Hahaha.
9	Paula	(h)LOVE ME::[::
10	Jeff	[Hahaha.
11	Dave	(I'LL SINK MY CL[A::WS? I:::N?)
12	Jeff	[Like a litti::l needy..sharp..
13	Paula	girlfr[i(h)end?
14	Jeff	[ballistic miss[le.
15	Paula	[(h)
16	Jeff	co[vered in fur.
17	Paula	[WHERE HAVE YOU BEE:N?

18	Jeff	AGHHHH shu:mp.
19	Paula	You said you were coming back earlie:::r.
20	Jeff	<*high-pitch*> Who were you texting?
21	Dave	Ha.
22 ⇨	Paula	"<u>Who's texting u(h)s?</u>" Hahaha.
23 ⇨		"<u>Who(h)'s te(h)xting u(h)s.</u>" Haha.
24	Dave	Hahahaha.
25	Paula	(h)a::h.
26	Hydra	Meow.
27	Paula	[Meow!
28	Dave	[Meow!
29	Paula	Were you sad that we were making fun of you: I'm sorry.
30	Jeff	She's [like, "Hey guys, ^not COOL"
31	Paula	[I'm sorry sweetie.

In lines 6–7 Jeff takes the unmitigated epistemic stance that he has "never known Liam to want snuggles that badly." Then Paula cries, "LOVE ME!" as a form of *constructed dialogue* (Tannen 1989/2007), or dialogue created by a speaker to quote another party, for Hydra in line 9. In line 12, Jeff describes Hydra as "a little needy sharp" and Paula offers "girlfriend?" in line 13. Then, Paula produces more constructed dialogue for her cat, which furthers a new play frame that imagines Hydra as a needy girlfriend, calling out, "WHERE HAVE YOU BEEN" and "You said you were coming back earlier" (17,19). This prompts Jeff to also construct dialogue for Hydra in line 20, saying, "Who were you texting?" with a very high pitch. In line 21 Paula almost directly quotes the Overly Attached Girlfriend meme (Figure 4.2) repeating "Who's texting us?" twice, savoring (Tannen 1989/2007) the reference.

The Overly Attached Girlfriend meme is based around webcam images of YouTuber Laina Morris. Morris participated in a contest held by singer Justin Bieber that challenged fans to create a "Girlfriend" counterpart to his 2012 hit song "Boyfriend." Morris uploaded a YouTube video on June 6th, 2012, called "JB Fanvideo," which featured her singing a parody of Bieber's song. The video satirized elements of the Bieber lyrics that were perceived by some as clingy, featuring Morris staring at a webcamera with a fixed smile while singing about Facebook-stalking her boyfriend and related themes. The video quickly went viral, and the next day a post titled "Overly Attached Girlfriend" appeared on the online discussion board Reddit, linking to the Quick Meme website page also called "Overly Attached Girlfriend." The memes on Quick Meme feature webcam pictures of Morris and captions portraying her in the stereotype of an overprotective and clingy girlfriend. Initially, actual lyrics from

Figure 4.2 "Overly Attached Girlfriend" meme

her song were used for the captions, but then internet users started creating their own related captions. Figure 4.2 shows one example of the meme that is being referenced in example 1c, as it reads "Cell phone vibrates. Who's texting us?" While Paula makes the meme reference here, Jeff does not laugh, but Dave does. Thus, Dave ratifies Paula's meme reference and her humorous identity construction. Paula and Dave also briefly bond over referencing this meme, which also temporarily shifts the epistemic territory of the talk, but other friends do not participate in the brief play frame that imagines Hydra the cat as an overly attached girlfriend.

This meme features another stereotype about women in relation to men, but instead of portraying a Black woman who "don't need no man," this stereotype depicts a white woman who is too attached to a man. Paula and Dave playfully bond over mocking a pet cat while also referencing the Overly Attached Girlfriend meme's stereotype of a needy, clingy girlfriend. In line 29, Paula characterizes this referencing as "making fun" of Hydra when she addresses her meowing cat, and Jeff ventriloquizes Hydra, saying, "Hey guys, NOT cool" in line 30. Paula then apologizes to Hydra in line 31, saying, "I'm sorry, sweetie." This evaluation reinforces the interpretation that this meme stereotype is a negative one, and represents a type of behavior to be avoided. Like the Strong Independent Black Woman meme, this one also reinforces ideas around heteronormativity—in both memes, a woman is depicted as either being or not being in a relationship with a man. In referencing these memes, the speakers are reinforcing heteronormative behavioral norms, while also othering feminine heterosexual behavior that falls into two extremes of a heterosexual spectrum as either too independent or too clingy.

In all three of these examples, when other speakers take epistemic stances towards Paula's cat, Hydra, Paula humorously reorients the conversation slightly by referencing internet memes. These meme references briefly construct play frames about her cat which simultaneously shifts the epistemic territory of the talk. The references also serve for Paula's identity construction as a humorous individual, and for certain group members as Millennial friends who know the same memes and appreciate their insertion into everyday talk. At the same time, the memes referenced feature stereotypical depictions of women as either "too independent" or "too needy" in their relationships with men, reinforcing ideologies on what counts as appropriate behavior for heterosexual women. Thus all at once, these meme references reinforcing multiple stereotypes are managing epistemics, frames, and individual and group identity construction.

"Bro do you even paint"

While the first three excerpts analyzed in this chapter demonstrate how internet meme references can be used very briefly to reorient conversation in terms of framing and epistemics, the next example presents a cluster of related meme references being used for an extended epistemic play frame shift. The next two examples also differ in that rather than featuring meme references containing stereotypes about women being used to comment on a female cat's behavior, the memes referenced in these examples contain stereotypes about men's behavior and are referenced to comment on men's activities in the friend group. The first meme reference I present here emerges due to an epistemic imbalance underlying an awkward interactional dilemma. I show that an epistemic shift and a simultaneous shift to a play frame can be effective in resolving such dilemmas.

It is a Saturday afternoon at the house of Dave, Jeff, Paula, and their fourth housemate, Todd. Todd and his good friend John are sitting at the dining room table painting miniature model rats for the board game "Myth." As they paint the rats, they are simultaneously commenting on a YouTube video they are watching on Todd's laptop. In the video, Youtuber Robbaz is playing the video game "Kerbal Space Program" and flying an unusual cube-shaped spaceship that he made in the game. Paula, Dave, and I are also present at the table, when Jeff and his relatively new girlfriend Dee walk into the house. Dee was still relatively unknown to the group at this time, and it is possible she had never met John. This makes for some awkward conversation.

(3a)

1	Jeff	Oh hello.
2	John	Sup.
3		Video (??) camera again (??)
4	Paula	Meow,
5		Meow,
6		Hello=
7	Dee	=Hello ag(h)ain!
8	Paula	Hey!
9		How's it goin? <*kitten's paw gets caught in Paula's hair*>
10		Oh oh oh [eee.
11	Video	[(I just??)
12	Todd	[<*low pitch*>You have returned.
13		Wait, how is it alIVE!
14	John	I dunno.
15	Video	Rubik's- Rubik's Cube.
16	Todd	It ju(h)st fe(h)ll out of orbit!

This excerpt is rather unusual and may be considered awkward in many ways. As Jeff and Dee walk into the house, Todd and John are engaged in the peculiar activity of painting miniature model rats at the dining room table, a behavior that is epistemically limiting to Jeff and Dee, and results in some interactional awkwardness. When Jeff enters the dining room and says, "Oh hello" (line 1) his "Oh" indicates recognition that there are a group of people in the dining room but also perhaps surprise (Schiffrin 1987). The only person who greets Jeff immediately is John, with the minimal and rhetorical "sup?" (line 2) while Paula meows (lines 4–5), mimicking her cat, Liam, who had been meowing while hearing Jeff and Dee at the door a few moments earlier. Then Paula switches her attention and greets the couple with "Hello" (line 6) and is latched by Dee with "Hello again!" (line 7), indicating that the two had met and had perhaps just seen each other earlier. Paula asks Dee, "How's it going?" (line 9) but Dee never responds, and meanwhile Liam's paw gets caught in Paula's hair and she makes sounds of pain (line 10). Eventually Todd comments on the pair's arrival by announcing in a playful formal tone with a lowered pitch, "You have returned" (line 12), again suggesting that Jeff and Dee had been at the house earlier, probably before I arrived. However, then Todd and John both orient back to the YouTube video they are watching on the laptop (lines 13–16), which, along with the rat-painting activity, is epistemically isolating to the rest of the group, especially considering that the laptop was oriented towards Todd and John but away from most of the others present. This results in Jeff and Dee awkwardly standing in front of the group already seated at the dining room table. Next, Jeff tries to break the ice, and meme references come to the rescue.

(3b)

| 17 | Todd | How [is it- |
| 18 | Jeff | '[Painting all the ^miniatures?' |

Jeff indicates that there is an epistemic imbalance as he attempts to enter into the epistemic ecology by asking Todd and John what they are doing. He asks, "Painting all the miniatures?" (line 18). This phrase is a subtle intertextual media reference. There was a popular image from the webcomic and blog Hyperbole and a Half, where the artist Allie Brosh depicts herself excitedly shouting, "CLEAN ALL THE THINGS!" at the peak of her enthusiasm for doing chores. At the time of the recording, the phrase "(verb) all the (noun)" had become a rather popular meme in everyday talk. With this meme reference, Jeff begins to key the interaction as playful.

Todd begins commenting on the video again as Jeff questions him, but cuts himself short (line 17) to answer Jeff's question.

(3c)

19	Todd	We're painting ^ra:[ts today.
20	Sylvia	[Rats!
21	Jeff	Ah(h)!
22	Todd	We're painting ^ra:ts today.
23	Jeff	Today is ^ra:t day.
24	Dave	Hehheh[hehheh.
25	Jeff	[I forGO:T today [was ^ra:t day.
26	Paula	[It-

Todd addresses the epistemic imbalance with, "We're painting rats today" (line 19), and I also chime in with "Rats!" (line 20). Jeff responds with "Ah!" (line 21) showing a change of mental state with *ah*-receipt that acknowledges his relative lack of information (see Heritage 1984 & Schiffrin 1987 on "oh") and amusement with his laughter token. Jeff has already begun to construct a play frame with his meme reference (line 17) and laughter particle (line 21). Now he continues in that direction, appropriating Todd's answer and joking, "Today is rat day" (line 23) and "I forgot today was rat day" (line 25). Jeff explained in playback that he was eliciting a trope of "today is x day," as in "today is laundry day," implying humorously that "rat day" is a normal part of the household's weekly activities. Jeff is slowly shifting the epistemic territory of the talk as he attempts to become more engaged in the epistemically isolating rat-painting activity. While in regards to this activity he has relatively little knowledge, he is able to appropriate talk about it and combine it with another epistemic territory by invoking a trope, which also begins to develop a play frame in the interaction.

Now that a play frame trajectory has been established by Jeff, Paula joins in, using a specific media reference which assumes shared epistemic access to internet memes regarding the importance of "leg day."

(3d)

27 ⇨		It's LIKE [^"LE:G DAY."
28	Dave	[YOU SHOULDA KNOWN, FRE:D!

Building on Jeff's jokes about "rat day," Paula now participates in the play frame by making a connection to an internet meme with, "It's LIKE 'LEG DAY'" (line 27), producing the utterance loudly and lengthening the vowel in "leg" to draw attention to this meme reference. In playback, Paula said that she had recently run into Jeff as he was preparing to go to the gym, and he had told her about "leg day" and its associated memes. This might explain her exuberance at the chance to introduce the media reference into talk here.

The memes speakers reference in this conversation relate to a particular media stereotype of American heterosexual masculinity: the bro. The stereotypical behavior of a bro or bro culture more broadly can be indexed through activities and topics of talk (Kiesling 2019). The memes referenced in this conversation relate more specifically to the meme of the *curlbro*. According to the website Know Your Meme,

Curlbro is a pejorative slang term referring to gym-going men that focus on training their arms when weight lifting. It was used often on 4chan's /fit/ online message board and the BodyBuilding Forums to stress the importance of compound exercises and leg training or to mock those who perform curl exercises in the squat rack. Curlbros are often associated with the Jersey Shore 'guido' stereotype along with steroid use and excessive tanning.

Leg Day, then, is a day dedicated to lower body exercises in strength-building workout routines. According to Know Your Meme, discussions about leg day began in the early 2000s in online exercise discussion forums. A BodyBuilding Forums member uploaded a photo on July 22, 2012, of a man at a gym who appeared to have a bulky upper body but underdeveloped legs with the caption, "Friends don't let friends skip leg day" (see Figure 4.3). The caption used the phrasal template "Friends Don't Let Friends," which itself is an intertextual reference to the 1983 anti–drunk driving public service announcement slogan

Figure 4.3 "Friends Don't Let Friends Skip Leg Day" meme

"Friends don't let friends drive drunk." Sets of photographs, a Facebook page, and YouTube videos followed, exposing millions of internet users to these memes about the perils of skipping leg day. Recall that, Shifman (2012) finds that this kind of "flawed masculinity" is a common feature of memes more broadly, and calls for future exploration of the positions that internet users take towards such representations of masculinity.

Returning to the conversation, the shift to this meme-based play frame includes what has been observed as characteristic of frame shifts, that is, "radically different topic structures and participant orientations" (Schiffrin 1993:251). Whereas before, Todd and John's talk had been oriented towards the video they were watching, Jeff's frame shift introduces a new topic structure regarding the miniature model rats, and now everyone present orients towards this new topic. The fact that more speakers become involved also shows that the epistemic territory is shifting along with the frame.

After Dave overlaps Paula with "YOU SHOULDA KNOWN, JEFF" (line 28), Jeff responds apologetically.

(3e)

29	Jeff	I'm ^SO:rry!
30		[I forgot rat day.
31	⇨ John	[You ^NE:VER 'skip ^RA:T da:y',
32		what are you doi:ng.
33	⇨ Jeff	(Ne(H)ver 'skip r-')
34	Dee	Ha.
35	⇨ Jeff	'FRIENDS don't LE(h)T [FRIE:NDS [skip rat day'.
36	Dee	[Ha!
37	⇨ Paula	'[skip rat[day'.
38	Dave	[heh[hehhaha.
39	Sylvia	[hehheh.
40	Paula	Exactly.

Jeff mock-apologizes by saying, "I'm sorry! I forgot rat day" (lines 29–30), repeating part of his earlier joke. Here he acknowledges Paula's and Dave's contributions to the epistemic play frame shift and continues to engage in it, as a sort of role play where he is guilty of skipping "rat day," similar to how the internet meme places guilt on those who skip "leg day." Next, John becomes involved in the newly created play frame. He demonstrates understanding of the media reference that Paula made and, drawing from his knowledge about leg day memes, shows competence in this epistemic territory by admonishing Jeff, "You NE:VER skip RA:T day, what are you doing" (lines

31–32), lengthening the vowels in "never" and "rat day" to signal another leg day meme. Jeff begins to repeat John laughingly, "Never skip r-" (line 33), but cuts himself off before speaking again, loudly, drawing from his knowledge about this specific meme with "FRIENDS don't LET FRIENDS skip rat day" (line 35). Paula also fills in the formula with "skip rat day" (line 37). This reference elicits laughter as a sign of appreciation of the reference from Dave and I (lines 38, 40), and Paula affirms the reference with "Exactly" (line 40). In this excerpt, Jeff, Paula, and John construct a humorous play frame of "today is 'rat day'" that resolves an epistemic imbalance and interactional dilemma. This allows Jeff, Paula, and John to construct humorous individual identities. At the same time, this meme referencing works to draw them together as friends who know the same memes and can use them to self-deprecatingly make light of nerdy board game-related behavior within the group, while simultaneously othering and distancing themselves from stereotypical gym rat behavior.

Next, however, Todd orients away from the play frame and back towards the real-life situation of sitting at the table with the miniature model rats.

(3f)

41	Todd	Sylvia was over here being like,
42		"To:dd, (why don't you let me) [paint some ra:ts".
43	⇨ Jeff ·	'[BRO:, do you even p[ai:nt.'
44	Dee	[Haha[haha.
45	Dave	[HA!
46	Paula	*<low pitch, quietly>* 'Bro: do you [even pai:nt.'
47	Video	[(??)
48		You can control gravity!
49	Jeff	What is making that noise.

         <Conversation turns to the video playing on the laptop>

Todd makes fun of my previously expressed disgust at the rats by teasing, "Sylvia was over here being like, 'Todd, (why don't you let me) paint some rats'" (lines 41, 42). But then Jeff makes another meme reference: "BRO, do you even paint" (line 43). According to Know Your Meme, the rhetorical question, "Do You Even Lift?" is a "condescending expression used on body building and fitness forums to question the legitimacy of someone's fitness expertise or weight lifting routine." Jeff begins this expression with "Bro," which is also common online (a Google Image Search of the phrase provides a plethora of examples) and he replaces "lift" with "paint." Dee shows appreciation of the play, laughing more than she has previously (line 44), and Dave bursts into a single loud "HA!" (line 45). Paula repeats Jeff's reference quietly with a lowered pitch (line 47), performing enregistered "bro voice" (Kiesling 2019). The play frame abruptly ends when Jeff hears the video that Todd and John have been watching (lines 47, 48) and asks, "What is making that noise" (line 49). The conversation then turns to Todd explaining the video to Jeff.

While Jeff seems to have been successful in resolving the interactional dilemma for himself, Paula, and John, as they were the speakers who most actively contributed to the epistemic frame shift, there is less evidence that Dee recognized or understood the meme references, which means she may have lacked epistemic access to fully appreciate the play frame. When I asked Jeff in playback if Dee knew about the "skipping leg day meme," he told me he was not sure, and that he had never talked with her about it previous to this interaction. Therefore, while my analysis has focused on how Jeff, John, and Paula use meme references to reaffirm their own group identity as people who know the same memes and mock (but also, thereby, subtly reinforce and other) certain ideologies of masculinity as reflected in the memes, this interaction could also be interpreted as one that unintentionally excluded Dee. In the same way that referencing media can serve a bonding function, it can also serve as an exclusionary device, whether intentional or not (see also example 5 in chapter 3).

An exciting moment for me as an analyst came when, during a playback interview, Jeff provided evidence that he was actually somewhat aware of using his conversational moves to do interactional and epistemic work to alleviate awkwardness. After listening to the recording of the conversation, Jeff reflected, "I guess what I was going for was a way to make it a humorous situation in which everyone could participate and be put at ease." Jeff's reference to a "humorous situation" can be interpreted as the play frame, and his desire that "everyone could participate" speaks to the shared epistemic territory drawn upon for the intertextual meme references. His claim that he wanted everyone to "be put at ease" corroborates my interpretation that there was indeed an interactional dilemma here that Jeff was attempting to resolve by referencing memes and laminating a play frame on the conversation. This play frame lamination relies on simultaneously shifting the talk from a restricted epistemic territory with which only Todd and John can relate to a shared epistemic territory of memes. This allows Jeff and Paula to become actively involved in the conversation, and as they construct their own individual identities as clever and funny individuals, Dave, Dee, and I laugh at the humorous playful talk around meme references. Ultimately the meme referencing here serves to construct shared Millennial nerd group identity around knowledge of the same internet memes, which are used to playfully mock the group's nerdy behavior, while also distancing the men in the group from and othering bro culture by mocking its representations of flawed masculinity. This Millennial nerd group identity construction will become extremely prevalent in chapter 5.

"Long hair don't care"

Like example 3, the next example also contains commentary about men's behavior. Here we will see Jeff again use a meme reference to break into some epistemically isolating talk. However, this example differs a bit from the previous ones in that the epistemically isolating talk is about a prior real-life problem, rather than local epistemic rights in talking about pet cats or the immediate dilemma of walking into an awkward rat-painting scenario with a new girlfriend. In the example below, Paula, Todd, Dave and I are discussing the apparent nonchalance of Todd's friend, Aaron, during the camping incident recounted in chapter 1 where he had vomited in the tent we were all sharing.

(4)

1	Sylvia	I love though how like the whole next day we were just-
2		making fun of hi:m,
3		and like, l- and he like didn't ca(h)[r(h)e(h)
4	Paula	[He's v-
5		[I was thinking the same thing he's very stoic.
6	Todd	[He- he does NOT-
7		He does ^not care.
8	Paula	He's just like-
9		[He was just-
10 ⇨	Jeff	'[Long hair don't care.'
11	Paula	He[just like ^o:wns it he's like,
12	Sylvia	[He's just like "Yep, this happened."
13	Paula	"Yeah, psh."=
14	Dave	=Yeah?
15	Paula	"You know it."=
16	Dave	=Haha[haha.
17	Paula	["Yup.
18	Todd	[(???)
19	Paula	"That's [about what happened."
20	Todd	[(doesn't give a shit.)
21	Paula	Yeah.
22		No that was very..very impressive.

23	⇨ Jeff	'Lo:ng hair ^don't care.'
24	⇨ Paula	'[Lo(h)ng [h(h)air do(h)n't ca(h)re.'
25	Sylvia	[Hahaha.
26	Todd	[Aaron ^I:S 'long hair don't care.'
27	Jeff	Exactly.
28	Paula	(h)haha[haha.
29	Todd	[He's like "I threw up in the tent,
30		now I'm sleepin' outside, muh."

In line 3 I laughingly observe how Aaron "didn't care" that we were making fun of him the next day, and Paula aligns with me in line 5 by agreeing that "he's very stoic." Then Todd aligns with us in lines 6–7 by affirmatively stating "he does not care." This triggers Jeff to make a meme reference in line 10, saying, "Long hair don't care." This phrase has become text for a variety of internet memes featuring images of people, fictional characters, and animals flaunting long hair. While there is an isolated example of the phrase being used in a 1970 classified ad, none of the major periodical databases (e.g., LexisNexis, Factiva, Proquest) turn the phrase up before 2007. In 2007, American R&B singer/songwriter Lloyd produced a #1 hit single called "You," featuring Lil Wayne singing the lyric, "Me & lil' Lloyd baby, long hair don't care" (both men had long hair at the time). After this, the phrase spread to long-hair forums, Instagram, Pinterest, and other websites in the form of images of people and characters with long hair accompanied with the phrase "Long hair don't care."

Jeff, the only friend present who did not go on the camping trip, tries to become involved in the talk by referencing the internet meme "Long hair don't care" to comment on Aaron's hair style and behavior. When Jeff first references this meme in line 10, no one seems to hear him or pick up on it. Instead, there is overlapping constructed dialogue for Aaron in lines 12–19, furthering our description of his laid-back attitude in the face of embarrassment. But when the talk slows down a bit, Jeff persists in making the meme reference again in line 23. This time, Paula and I demonstrate appreciation of the reference through Paula's repetition (line 24) and my laughter (line 25). Todd states emphatically that "Aaron IS 'long hair don't care,'" (line 26) implying that Aaron embodies this expression. Jeff confirms this with "Exactly" (line 27).

Here Jeff uses this meme reference as a way to briefly shift the epistemic territory of the talk from the exact events of the camping incident to an internet meme. Jeff uses this meme reference as a way to become involved in the talk, similar to how in example 3, he references the leg day memes to become involved in the talk about the rat-painting activity. Also recall in chapter 3, he becomes involved in graduate students' talk about their professor Lisa by referencing the film *The Room* with "You're tearing me apart, Lisa!" Inserting media references like this into conversations constructs Jeff's identity as a humorous, clever, and fun person. It also allows him to participate in conversations where he lacks the same epistemic access as his interlocutors.

All in all, referencing this meme allows Jeff and the rest of the speakers present to briefly bond over their shared enjoyment of this meme. By referencing the Long Hair Don't Care meme in this context, the friends also subtly reinforce a gendered ideology that unconventionally long-haired men are "laid back," and, as they describe Aaron as embracing this flawed masculinity, they evaluate the combination of having long hair and not caring as humorous with their laughter. Jeff and Todd, the two men in the group with more conventional short haircuts, participate the most around this meme (as well as Paula, who was dating Todd). But Dave, the one man present with long hair, does not engage with this meme (he also said in playback that he did not know this meme). Both of these humorous meme reference examples ("leg day" and "long hair don't care") featuring stereotypes of different kinds of masculinities also function to manage the boundaries of what kinds of masculinities are valued, privileged, and expected within the group (see also Robles 2019).

Meme References in Everyday Talk

In this chapter, I have begun to bring framing, as well as work on intertextuality in interaction, into dialogue with the conversation analytic work on epistemics. Drawing from research on the epistemics of social relations and heeding both the call for work on epistemic ecologies (Heritage 2013) and the call for an epistemic discourse analysis (van Dijk 2013), I have shown how a close analysis of talk that engages in the most current theories of knowledge in interaction illuminates how intertextual references can be used as resources for knowledge management, frame shifting, and constructing identities. More specifically, I have shown how these Millennial friends use references to internet memes to create epistemic play frame shifts to resolve interactional dilemmas, while also constructing unique individual and shared group identities.

I have shown how interactions involving epistemic imbalances opened up spaces for epistemic frame shifts, and these shifts relied on internet meme references. In some examples, there were epistemic imbalances around owning cats which were remedied with meme references. In other cases, speakers used memes as a way to break into epistemically isolating conversations. The references were simultaneously used to construct lighthearted play frames, which also diffused awkwardness and allowed speakers to have fun and bond with one another through play. These frame transformations were dependent on the references to memes themselves which allowed the epistemic territory to shift to a topic to which at least most of the speakers had epistemic access. In turn, these references contributed to their shared group identity construction as Millennials who know the same memes and use them to poke fun at their own and each other's behavior (including that of their pet cats). By using their knowledge of memes to create epistemic frame shifts when faced with interactional dilemmas, these speakers simultaneously construct individual identities as humorous and clever people, while also constructing shared group identity around their knowledge of memes and how they use them.

Through my research on the internet memes speakers invoked in the conversations analyzed here, I learned that these memes reached their peak popularity in 2012–2013. Yet the conversations I analyze here occurred in 2015. This indicates that these Millennials, who were in their mid to late twenties, were a bit behind when it comes to popular internet memes. They were using slightly outdated memes in these conversations probably because they are not people who spend a lot of time in online discussion forums, where these memes were originally generated and circulated. Therefore, these participants are people who became aware of these memes second hand, through Facebook, Twitter, Buzzfeed, or other websites and, in Paula's case, via Jeff in a previous face-to-face conversation. Still, their shared knowledge of these specific memes does contribute to their unique epistemic ecology as people who can infuse their talk with such intertextual meme references to create epistemic play frame shifts when faced with interactional dilemmas. Furthermore, I have shown, that while these meme references are primarily used for group bonding, they might also exclude others who do not share epistemic access to the memes.

Here I have also focused on the stereotypes embedded within many internet memes. I showed how an internet meme seen on a computer screen referencing a limiting stereotype of African American women's perceived toughness is used in face-to-face conversation to playfully mock a pet cat. Internet memes mocking stereotypes of men who have unbalanced workout routines are deployed to tease friends about painting rat figurines for a board game. The connections made between these particular memes and real-life situations may be possible because these memes represent stereotypes of social behavior that then lend themselves to be mapped onto behavioral dilemmas for members of this group. Overall the meme references in conversation demonstrate that the boundaries of online versus offline social processes are porous (Blommaert 2017:44). In these examples, women quoted memes featuring stereotypes of women, while men did most of the meme referencing of memes featuring stereotypes of men. It is almost as if these speakers are looking to memes (and other media) for cues as to how to perform their gender identities. Or maybe they quote memes that confirm their preconceived ideologies around gender. It could also be the case that these speakers do not feel they have the epistemic rights to quote memes that do not reflect their own corresponding gender identities. In any case, referencing memes that contain stereotypes about racial, linguistic, and gendered behavior reinforces those stereotypes. Referencing memes more broadly also serves interactional functions. In particular, these references shift frames and epistemics to construct shared group identity around both knowledge of the memes and group behavior that is comparatively more normative than what is presented in the memes themselves.

5

"This is like an RPG where you pick up friends along the way"

Overlapping and Embedding Video Game Frames, Negotiating Epistemics, and Constructing Intertextual Identities

In chapter 2 I focused on the contextualization cues that the speakers in my data use to signal intertextual references to media, and in chapter 3 I showed how such references are responded to or shown to be understood by listeners. In chapter 4 I argued for conceptualizing intertextual media references as resources that can be used to make *epistemic frame shifts*, in which speakers not only manage the *frames*, or talk activities, that they are participating in, but also simultaneously manage *epistemics*, or the knowledge required to engage in the conversation. I have begun to show how these epistemic frame shifts are especially useful when speakers are faced with knowledge imbalances and related interactional dilemmas. In this chapter, I examine how the American Millennial friends in my study share prior texts from video games to "play out loud" in their everyday conversations (cf. Tovares 2012 on "watching out loud"), balancing their differing epistemic territories, while simultaneously navigating different frames. As Howe and Strauss (2000) observe, Millennials grew up with video games in the same way that Baby Boomers grew up with board games. The way that Millennials reference video games in their talk ultimately reinforces Millennial group identity construction in interaction. Heeding Hamilton's (1996) call for an intertextual analysis of identity construction and van Dijk's (2013) call for an epistemic discourse analysis, I draw on Tannen's (2006) analysis of reframing and rekeying, Gordon's (2009) analysis of overlapping and embedded frames, and Raymond and Heritage's (2006) analysis of epistemics in identity construction. I demonstrate how video game references in talk can be used as resources for epistemic frame shifts that are conducive to Millennial group identity construction.

I analyze in this chapter how the Millennial speakers in my study use shared video game references for epistemic management while simultaneously rekeying serious talk about real-life issues (such as work and money) to

Millennials Talking Media. Sylvia Sierra, Oxford University Press. © Oxford University Press 2021.
DOI: 10.1093/oso/9780190931117.003.0005

lighter, humorous talk that reframes such issues as being part of a lived video game experience. Specifically investigating how the reframing occurs, I elaborate on Gordon's (2009) descriptions of overlapping and embedded frames in family discourse. *Overlapping frames* occur when "an utterance is situated in (at least) two frames at once," with the utterance referring simultaneously to the present context and to a past context (Gordon 2009:116). *Embedded frames* refer to a situation in which a more specific frame is completely embedded in a more general frame (Gordon 2009:141). Gordon mentions the possibility of embedded frames within overlapping frames, but her emphasis is on how intertextuality is used to accomplish framing in family discourse, while also constructing the family as a social group with a shared set of prior texts. However, Hoyle (1993) examines how two boys playing ping-pong embed a more specific "player interview" frame within a broader "sportscaster play" frame. Her work shows how other frames can be embedded within play frames, and, while Hoyle does not use the term *intertextuality*, her analysis reveals how knowledge gleaned from previous experiences is mobilized in creating play frames.

Trester (2012) also examines the relationship between intertextuality and framing. She analyzes how intertextual play functions in the creation of new performance frames in an improv comedy group's backstage talk to construct community. Trester finds that *entextualization*, "the process of rendering discourse extractable, of making a stretch of linguistic production into a unit— a text—that can be lifted out of its interactional setting" (Bauman & Briggs 1990:73), serves as a framing device in her data; entextualization enacts a shift into a performance frame, where speakers engage in various intertextual, linguistic "games" (2012:256). She applies Goffman's (1961) work on *game moves* which create the emergence of a particular kind of play frame—a *game world*. Game worlds must exist in the real world since they are constructed in conversation, but they are surrounded by a barrier that allows for some properties of the real world to be included, if they are relevant to the game (Trester 2012:241).

Like Gordon, Tannen (2006) examines intertextuality in family discourse, analyzing how a couple's arguments are reframed and rekeyed over the course of one day. She defines *reframing* as "a change in what the discussion is about" and builds on Goffman's (1974) work on *key* to define *rekeying* as "a change in the tone or tenor of an interaction" (Tannen 2006:601). This focus on how intertextuality contributes to rekeying and reframing further illustrates how intertextuality and framing are intertwined. Additionally, Tannen finds that "restoring harmony was accomplished in part by reframing in a humorous key, and in ways that reinforced the speakers' shared family identities" (2006:597).

Shared interactional knowledge is required to carry out these framing and keying processes which ultimately lead to group harmony and identity construction. Beers Fägersten (2012) also finds that intertextual quotation of film texts is a way to rekey and reframe interaction, serving for conflict resolution in a family. Though they do not explicitly consider intertextuality, Norrick and Spitz (2010) similarly explore the use of humorous reframing and rekeying to restore harmony in conversation, and they analyze humor as a resource used to mitigate conflict in talk. Similar to the process of reframing and rekeying to restore harmony, M. Goodwin (1996) finds that shifting frames in conversation can solve interactional dilemmas, or awkward and unpleasant moments in interaction. Importantly, Goodwin writes that "shifting frame[s] is not done capriciously, rupturing ongoing discourse; it occurs in orderly ways as practical solutions to interactional dilemmas, reshaping the speech event, or constructing distance from the tone of the activity in progress" (1996:71). Thus, many of the studies on framing have shown that reframing, or shifting frames, can be used to resolve interactional issues.

I build on this prior work by arguing that when Millennial speakers shift talk from restricted epistemic territories about individual life experiences to shared epistemic territories relating to video games, they simultaneously use these game moves to create overlapping play frames (or game worlds), which are then strengthened by embedded frames containing *constructed dialogue* (Tannen 1989/2007), or dialogue created by a speaker to quote another party. When speakers take on character roles embedded within overlapping play frames, they become more fully engrossed in the play frame, and more distanced from the prior real-life talk. This allows speakers to overcome interactional hurdles they face in interaction. It also allows different speakers to become involved in conversation as well as active in constructing their identities as individuals, friends, Millennials, and members of a specific epistemic ecology.

Video Games

Video games, like other media, reflect patterns of domination and power that exist in offline society. Taking an early critical approach to video games, Thornborrow (1997) focuses on the male-centered discourses of the computer game–playing world. Relatedly, Iaia (2016) examines the dominance of English as a lingua franca in video games. Additionally, Wagener (2018) analyzes discourses of ethnic discrimination in online gaming. Despite the existence of domination and discrimination in both video game design and video game play, video games have also been researched as a tool for psycho-social good for children, adolescents, and young adults.

Linguistic research on video games has primarily focused on children playing video games in classroom settings. This research has examined issues such as how children talk about video games in the classroom, whether or not game play contributes to literacy (e.g., Lacasa et al. 2008; Apperley 2010; Berger & McDougall 2013), and especially how video games might be helpful to students in second-language-learning environments (e.g., Lim & Holt 2011; Hitosugi et al. 2014; Shiraz et al. 2016; Duran 2017; Ebrahimzadeh & Alavi 2017; Scholz 2017; Pitarch 2018; Sykes 2018; Blume 2019; Enayat & Haghighatpasand 2019).

Video gaming and its benefits for slightly older adolescents and young adults has been less studied. Folkins et al. (2016) examine applying principles of video game design to clinical therapy settings, while Finke et al. (2018) examine motivations of young adults with autism spectrum disorder (ASD) for playing video games, suggesting that video games can be a beneficial leisure activity for adolescents and young adults with and without ASD for developing communication and social skills. Additionally, a few studies examine how players interact with video games and each other while actively playing the games (e.g., Mondada 2012; Piirainen-Marsh 2012; Varenne et al. 2013). Notable gaps exist in the literature pertaining to adults who play video games, as well as in examining everyday conversations where speakers are not actively playing video games, but where the talk is nonetheless infused with video game references from prior game play experiences (cf. Sierra 2016).

Tovares' (2012) work on how a TV show serves as an intertextual resource in family conversations inspired my noticing of how my partner Dave and his friend group frequently used video games as intertextual resources in their conversations. As we glimpsed in chapter 4 when Dave's housemate Todd and his friend John were painting miniature figurine rats for the board game "Myth," Todd had a distinct passion for games. In fact, all of the housemates played board games occasionally, but in addition they were all avid video game players. Dave's other housemates, Jeff, Todd, and Paula frequently played games with each other on their mobile phones, while Todd and Paula (also romantic partners) also played games on the PlayStation and Wii in the basement. In addition, Jeff, Todd and Dave played video games at their personal computers in their individual bedrooms. Video games were such a shared experience in the house that in the front sitting room, Paula had painted a mural on the wall facing the entrance to the house depicting all the housemates, as well as Paula and Todd's two kittens, as video game characters (see Figure 1.1 in chapter 1). Arguably then, these Millennial housemates can be characterized, in part, by their love for playing video games, which contributes to a shared "nerd" Millennial identity also constructed via their discourse with one another as members of a unique epistemic ecology.

One recorded conversation among the housemates and me stood out for its rich use of video game references; that conversation is the first one analyzed in this chapter. I then began to notice when the housemates used video game references when I was not recording, so I started to supplement my recorded data with notes about conversations where video game texts seemed to function in the same way as the initial instance I had recorded. I often consulted with Dave afterwards when he had been present during the conversations to try to maintain accuracy in recalling the interactional details. Eventually, I recorded another conversation between Dave, his close friend from high school, Alan (not a housemate), and me featuring video game references, which is the second recorded excerpt I analyze in this chapter. I round out my analysis of these two recorded instances of video game references with some observations from my notes on the unrecorded conversational references to other video games.

Referencing Video Games in Everyday Talk

The first video game references that I analyze in this chapter refer to the independent video game *Papers, Please* (Pope 2013). *Papers, Please* is an unusual video game. It is an anomaly in that it is not necessarily a fun game (although it might still be entertaining). Instead, *Papers, Please* is a rather serious game: it focuses on the psychological toll of working as a male immigration officer in a fictional Eastern Bloc–like country called Arstotzka. Contemporary scholars view *Papers, Please* as an important new kind of game that interfaces with real-world politics, ethics, and morality (e.g., Formosa et al. 2016; Lohmeyer 2017; Kelly 2018). The game begins when the player "wins" the job of a male immigration officer through a state-run job lottery, requiring him to relocate with his wife, son, mother-in-law, and uncle from their home village to a state apartment. The player's main task is to inspect potential immigrants' documents at a checkpoint booth, similar to the checkpoints separating East and West Berlin during the Cold War. In fact, as Lohmeyer (2017:13) comments, "Every element about the appearance of the game communicates a type of Cold War aesthetic through minimal graphics and an intentionally drab color palate."

Some details about *Papers, Please* are particularly relevant to my analysis. If the player discovers discrepancies in immigration documents, the applicant must be interrogated and may be arrested when the player hits the "detain" button, which triggers a shutter at the checkpoint booth to slam shut. If this happens, "*Prostet*" is heard and a speech bubble on the screen from the guards' mouths translates this to "Out." A second speech bubble coming from the player's mouth says, "You should not have come." At times, applicants, like the character Jorji, notorious for forging false documents (see Figure 5.1), may attempt to bribe the player. If the player makes few mistakes, they may receive a plaque for "sufficience," which they can hang on their wall. Mistakes made and number of people processed in a given amount of real time representing a single day in the game affect the player's pay in "credits." The player then has to make decisions about how to cover basic expenses like rent, heat, and food for the family, as well as medical bills and birthday presents. As Kelly (2018) observes, the player does not interact with their family directly; instead, a balance sheet is provided at the end of each working day that lists which bills are unpaid, which relatives are dying, and how much harder the player will need to work the next day in order to keep family members alive. Thus the player is often faced with moral dilemmas about how to spend their credits, whom to let in the country, and whether or not to accept bribes. The workdays become more stressful as relations between Arstotzka and nearby countries deteriorate, and increasingly complicated guidelines are given for document inspections. Eventually, the player may become involved in a rebel group's plot to overthrow Arstotzka's government and the player's decisions have a direct effect on the outcome of the rebellion.

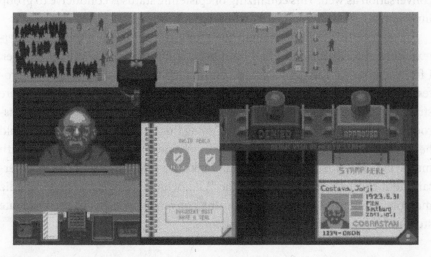

Figure 5.1 *Papers, Please*: Jorji Costava's fake passport

Papers, Please has become popular since its release and has won many awards, being praised for its sense of immersion and the intense emotional reaction it creates. Formosa et al. (2006) find that *Papers, Please* incorporates four key moral themes with which players must contend, providing a unique experience: dehumanization, privacy, fairness, and loyalty. The game's immersive emotional experience seems to lend itself to being used as a resource drawn upon for managing social relations in the conversations I analyzed in this chapter, especially considering the shared experience that Dave, Todd, Jeff, Todd's brother (another Millennial friend), and I had playing the game together in the basement of the shared house a few weeks before I began recording.

"We have been paid by 'Arstotzka'": *Papers, Please* References in Conversation

The first excerpt I analyze is from a Saturday night at the shared group house, where housemates Dave, Paula, Jeff, and I are having a lively conversation in the dining room. The speakers make references to *Papers, Please* here to rekey serious talk about money to a humorous key by adding an overlapping frame of a real-life video game experience. This rekeying and reframing rely on shifting the talk from a restricted epistemic territory with which only the graduate students can relate (all present except Jeff) to the shared epistemic territory of the video game experience, allowing Jeff to become involved in the conversation as well. This equalizing of epistemic status is conducive to group involvement and shared identity construction.

Previous to this excerpt, we had been joking around about the word *intertextuality*, since Paula and I had both been reading up on it (she for a paper, I for a seminar in the topic). I had commented that in my seminar, my professor had proposed an activity called "Intertextuality in the wild" where students could discuss events related to intertextuality outside of the classroom, but that I didn't think she saw it "going this far" (meaning that we would be joking about the word itself to such an extent). The excerpt starts with me saying "Intertextuality gone wild," making a reference to the adult entertainment commercials for *Girls Gone Wild*, which are likely a shared media memory for many Millennials. Soon the conversation turns to the graduate students' receipt of their payment stipends.

(1a)

1 **Sylvia** Intertextuality: "^gone wi:ld":..

2	Dave	WO[OO! REFERENCES! Woo!
3	Paula	[Hahaha speaking of gone wild, we got ^PAI:D!
4	Sylvia	[Oh yeah, ^finally:!
5	Dave	[Yeah, I know, right?

After my reference to the *Girls Gone Wild* commercials (line 1), Dave imitates them and calls attention to the topic of intertextual references, yelling loudly, "WOOO! REFERENCES! Woo!" (line 2) (the commercials often featured girls yelling "Woo!"). Then, Paula, after laughing and perhaps relating "going wild" with having money, says, "speaking of gone wild, we got PAID!" (line 3), referring to the fact that our first stipend checks of the academic year had just been deposited. Here, Paula changes the frame from joking about the word *intertextuality* to the frame of talking about being recently paid. Her loudness on "PAI:D" along with the elongation of the vowel effectively elicit the other two students' responses to this topic. I respond, "Oh yeah, finally!" (line 4), showing a change of mental state with "oh" (Schiffrin 1987). I orient myself to this new topic, aligning with Paula's excitement, and implying that this payment was overdue with "finally." Dave overlaps with me, saying, "Yeah, I know, right?" (line 5). Both Dave's and my "yeahs" signal alignment with Paula and show evidence of our equal epistemic statuses as graduate students.

Having received these responses from Dave and me, Paula takes another turn, continuing the frame change and also rekeying the conversation to be more serious.

(1b)

6	Paula	God, I can pay my fucking rent.
7	Sylvia	That [first check always seems so delayed.
8	Paula	[The- our (stipends came late?)

Paula's "God, I can pay my fucking rent" (line 6) stood out to me at the time of recording, as it does now, as relatively marked; its serious and tense tone, as well as notable lack of overlap, stand out in what had been a lighthearted conversation filled with laughter and simultaneous talk. In playback, Paula told me that at the time, she was running out of her summer job money and was hoping to avoid asking her parents for money. Paula's utterance here abruptly rekeys the previously playful frame (making fun of the term *intertextuality*) and furthers the serious frame of talking about money. She accomplishes this through various contextualization cues: the tone of voice, the exasperated oath "God," the expletive "fucking," and the semantic content of the statement itself, which relays that the reason Paula was so enthusiastic about being paid was because she needed to pay rent. I take up this serious key, aligning with Paula by commenting that the first check "always seems so delayed" (line 7). Then Paula explains to Jeff that our stipends came late (line 8). The fact that only the three graduate students (Paula, Dave, and I) could participate in the more serious talk regarding the epistemic territory of graduate stipend checks demonstrates that there is a knowledge imbalance between the three of us and Jeff, and the resulting interactional dilemma in this sequence of talk opens up a space for an epistemic frame shift which allows Jeff to participate in the conversation.

Next, Jeff responds to Paula's explanation that the stipends arrived late (line 8) with "Borat" voicing, perhaps attempting to rekey the serious conversation back to its original playful tone (Jeff confirmed in playback that he was referencing Sacha Baron Cohen's character Borat Sagdiyev, a fictitious Kazakh journalist who speaks with a stereotypical Eastern European accent, in the popular 2006 British-American mockumentary comedy film *Borat*):

(1c)

9	Jeff	*<Borat voice>*Ye:s. Ye:s.
10	Paula	*<Borat voice>*Yes. Yes. Hahaha.
11	Jeff	*<Borat voice>*Ye:s. It's nice.

The playful rekeying arguably begins with the Borat voice used by Jeff: "Yes. Yes" (line 9). This is followed by Paula's repetition: "Yes. Yes. Hahaha." (line 10). Jeff then continues, "Yes. It's nice" (line 11), which might be referencing Borat's catchphrase, "very nice." This stereotypical Eastern European Borat voice (which others Eastern European speakers while reinforcing American nationalities and Mainstream U.S. English within the group) leads into references to the video game *Papers, Please*. These video game references simultaneously initiate an epistemic shift and an overlapping play frame with the metamessage of "we are living a video game that we have played."

(1d)

12	⇨ Sylvia	We have been paid by "<u>Arsto:tzka</u>"..
13	⇨ Jeff	[hahaha <u>You [received some "cre:dits" for processing [the [language</u>.
14	Paula	[haha [haha [hahahahaha.
15	Sylvia	[hahaha [hahaha.
16	⇨ Jeff	You're lucky you drew this jo:b in the "<u>la:bor lottery</u>."

Triggered by the stereotypical Eastern European accent that Paula and Jeff had just been using, I was reminded of the video game *Papers, Please*, which draws heavily from life in the Soviet Union and East Germany. Perhaps responding to the interactional dilemma of the key and frame becoming so serious around money, I say, "We have been paid by 'Arstotzka'" (line 12), referring to the fictional country in *Papers, Please* and making an implicit comparison between our university and Arstotzka's bureaucratic government. This game move introduces a game world (Goffman 1961), and the hypothetical narrative develops an overlapping frame of "we are living a video game that we have all played" over the frame of "we are talking about real life." Following Gordon (2009), I suggest that the intertextual references to the video game create overlapping frames—two simultaneous definitions of the situation: the participants are engaged in talking about getting paid in real life, but in using intertextual references to discuss this, they are also simultaneously playing that they are living a video game that they have played in the past.

After a short but perceptible silence, perhaps trying to understand the connection, both Jeff and Paula laugh (lines 13, 14). Whereas Jeff had been silent while the three students discussed stipend checks (only participating with his Borat voice after Paula's explanation of the topic), now Jeff becomes much more involved in the conversation, presumably since the epistemic territory has been shifted to discourse about *Papers, Please*, of which Jeff has knowledge. Jeff draws from his knowledge of the video game and makes a game move to begin a "role play" (Gordon 2002, 2009), saying, "You received some 'credits' for processing the language" (line 13). In this way, he elaborates on the overlapping play frame by referring to our payment as "credits," the monetary unit used in *Papers, Please*. He jokingly describes our work as linguists as "processing the language," an overly formal, "newspeak" way of describing our work, reminiscent of how jobs are described in the video game (for example, the border control agent's job is "processing people"). This causes both Paula and me to laugh (lines 14, 15).

The laughter in these lines signals that the conversation has been rekeyed, "indicat[ing] a change of emotional stance" (Tannen 2006:601). As Chafe (2001:42) writes, laughter conveys non-seriousness. Here, reference to this game world contributes to "shared hilarity" (Chafe 2001), where all participants find the game world humorous. With the overlapping play frame, the conversation has been rekeyed from serious, even frustrated, to light-hearted and funny. Jeff continues this overlapping and rekeyed play frame with, "You're lucky you drew this job in the labor lottery" (line 16), referring to how, in *Papers, Please*, the player is assigned their job as a border control agent via a labor lottery. Notice how words like "credits" (line 13), "job" (line 16), and "labor" (line 16) still contain remnants of the real-life frame about being paid, and these contribute to the overlapping play frame while still anchoring the talk in the real-life frame about money and work.

Paula participates in the overlapping play frame by introducing an embedded frame, which strengthens the overlapping play frame as it moves the speakers further into the game world and further away from the original real-life frame. She constructs an embedded frame with a more specific meta-message by moving into an even more specific epistemic territory of the video game. She does this by referencing a particular character, Jorji, in *Papers, Please*, joking that the credits came from him, and then voicing him.

(1e)

17 ⇨	Paula	[THEY ALL CAME FROM JORJI. <u>JORJI'S LIKE "HE:Y!"</u>
18	Sylvia	[Yeah.
19	Dave	"He:y."
20	Jeff	[So-
21 ⇨	Paula	[<u>"I MAKE-A PASSPO:RT[A:!"</u>
22	Sylvia	[Hahahaha.

Paula contributes a game move, saying, "THEY [the credits] ALL CAME FROM JORJI" (line 17). Jorji is the middle-aged male character shown in Figure 5.1 who is known for appearing throughout the game at the checkpoint with false documents, like a passport, for example (line 21). With this specification of the epistemic orientation towards the game world, the "remnants" of the real-life frame about being paid, which were present up to this point in the overlapping frame, start to fall away—the only anchor to the real-life frame is in "they all came from Jorji" (line 17), where "they" refers to the "credits," but after this no other ties link back to the real-life frame about being paid.

Further epistemic orientation towards the game world is facilitated when Paula introduces an embedded frame by constructing a voice for Jorji, with "HEY!" (line 17) and "I MAKE-A PASSPORTA!" (line 21). This constructed dialogue (Tannen 1989/2007) evokes Jorji specifically because of the choice of phonetic detail, which contributes to "depictive delivery" (Clark & Gerrig 1990) of the character. The loudness of "HEY!" (line 17) contributes to portraying the overly friendly attitude of Jorji. The non-standard syntactic construction of "I MAKE-A PASSPORTA!" reflects the text of the syntactic structures that come from Jorji in the game. This syntactic construction, along with the inserted and elongated vowels in "MAKE-A" and "PASSPORTA" (line 21), construct a sense of "foreignness" to his voice. All of this requires very specific epistemic access to a single character in the game, and, via that character, non-Anglo American accents are othered while the group's American identities and Mainstream U.S. English are reinforced. This character voicing also constructs an embedded frame with a metamessage of "I am playing Jorji." Embedded within the overlapping play frame, Paula (and, briefly, Dave) enact Jorji's character—so they are living the role of Jorji for that fleeting moment, and are temporarily engrossed in that role. Also note that making a passport is completely unrelated to the original frame about being paid. This embedded frame of "Jorji is present in our life as a video game," with its very specific epistemic orientation, brings the conversation even further into the overlapping play frame of "we are living a video game," with very little remnants of the original real-life frame.

Note that while Dave repeats "Hey" (line 19), he is relatively uninvolved throughout the construction of the play frame. In playback he said, "I don't shift into those other frames a lot" and "I'm focused on getting real shit done" (i.e., focused on important practical issues in the real world). This suggests that willingness to participate in play frames may be linked to an individual's conversational style (as described by Tannen 1984/2005), and there is evidence of this again in Dave's behavior in *The Oregon Trail* excerpt I analyze later in this chapter.

Next, Jeff assigns specific game character roles to all of us, using his epistemic access to the video game to metacomment on the overlapping play frame.

(1f)

23	⇨	Jeff	So- Todd is 'your wi:fe' and-
24		Paula	Haha.
25		Sylvia	Hahaha.
26	⇨	Jeff	Dave is 'your mo:ther-in-la:w',
27		Dave	Ha.
28		Sylvia	Hahaha.
29	⇨	Jeff	And Sylvia is 'your so:n',
30	⇨		and [I'm 'your..u:ncle' or something.
31	⇨	Paula	[Haha and you 'drew me a pictu:re' hahaha.

In assigning familial game roles to his friends, Jeff is not actually in the play frame, but he is commenting from outside of it (see Gordon 2002). Jeff assigns Paula's real-life cisgender male partner, Todd, the role of Paula's "wife," (line 23); both recasting Todd as a woman and implying that in this imagined game world, Paula, a cisgender woman, is the male player. Dave, another cisgender man, is assigned the role of Paula's "mother-in-law" (line 26), casting him as woman along with Todd. Jeff assigns me (a cisgender woman) the role of Paula's "son" (line 29), thus casting me along with Paula as being male. Interestingly, Jeff assigns himself the only gendered game role that corresponds to his real-life cisgender identity expression as a man, saying, "and I'm your uncle or something" (line 30).

These character roles are not chosen at random; in the game the player is always assumed to be male, and has a wife, a mother-in-law, and an uncle. The video game thus reproduces salient ideologies regarding male gender (as being a default, and as playing a "worker" role) as well as reinforcing heteronormative sexual relations. In this portion of the conversation, Jeff assigns us all salient familial roles from the game in relation to Paula, who is cast as the male player in this play frame. Dave, Paula and I laugh throughout this stretch of the conversation, maintaining the non-serious key and participating in the shared hilarity of the play frame. Paula then accepts her positioning as the male character, and builds on the family roles from within the play frame. She again draws on very specific knowledge about the game, contributing to the overlapping play frame with "and you drew me a picture" (lines 31, 33). This refers to a game dynamic where if the player makes enough money, they can buy a crayon set for their son, who then draws a picture. The player can choose to hang up this picture on the wall at the immigration office.

While Paula's turns regarding the picture are voiced from within the play frame, I break the frame when I make a metacomment about our role-playing, drawing on epistemic access to the real world.

(1g)

32	**Sylvia**		I [love how-
33	**Paula**		[You drew me a :picture(h):
34	⇨ **Sylvia**		We- we all have like opposite gender ro(h)les in thi(h)s haha.
35	**Jeff**		Yeah! Ha.
36	**Sylvia**		Ha[haha.
37	**Paula**		[It is-
38	**Jeff**		I didn't really=
39	**Paula**		=It's very ^i:nterte(h)xtual [hahaha.
40	**Jeff**		[I didn't really think to-..
41			^Now we're just using that word for ^everything!

My metacomment that "I love how" (line 32) "we all have like opposite gender roles in this" (line 34) redirects our epistemic orientation towards our real-life situation of expressing cisgender identities that do not match the game gender roles Jeff has assigned. My positive affective stance towards this role-playing, in effect, names the play frame and ruptures it (see Tannen 1984/2005). But it also expresses my approval and enjoyment of the kind of gender-bending that Jeff is doing in the play frame. In turn, Jeff responds, "I didn't really-" (line 38), being cut off by Paula, and then persisting for a moment in line 40: "I didn't really think to-" before orienting to Paula's interjection of "It's very i:nterte(h)xtual" (line 39). It seems that in lines 38 and 40, Jeff was rejecting some agency in expressing that he "didn't really think to" assign us the gendered roles that matched our gender expressions. By doing so he rejects the notion that he would intentionally subvert dominant gender norms in this way, which again is interesting since he assigned himself the only gender role that matched any of the participants' gender identities. The group then returns to the previous frame that was active at the beginning of this excerpt, making fun of the word *intertextual* (lines 39, 41) for two solid minutes.

In this example, all the speakers had originally participated in a play frame as they joked about the word *intertextuality*, but then abruptly shifted to a serious real-life frame, where the three graduate students complained about their paychecks and rent. This unpleasant topic left Jeff out. But then the frame was quickly transformed with speakers drawing on their shared knowledge of the same video game to create a humorous overlapping play frame, which defined the situation as, "We are living a video game we have all played." This epistemic frame shift allowed Jeff to become actively involved in the conversation, and it helped the group overcome an epistemic imbalance and interactional dilemma.

When Paula acted out the video game character Jorji's role, the embedded frame that conveyed, "Jorji is present in this world" further strengthened the overlapping play frame and kept the conversation moving in a playful and non-serious direction. In sum, the serious (and epistemically isolating) real-life talk of checks and rent was completely dropped, and speakers instead drew on their equal epistemic access to participate in a play frame. This play frame also allowed Jeff, Paula, and me to discursively construct our individual identities as clever, humorous, and playful. In particular, it shifted Paula's identity construction from that of an annoyed graduate student trying to make rent to someone who can laugh and joke about her financial situation. Since this interaction also shows that the male-centric and heteronormative game structure of *Papers, Please* is subtly subverted when Jeff assigns us gendered game roles that do not match our real-life gender identities, I also had the chance to express an identity as a someone in favor of subverting traditional gender roles. More broadly, this play frame showcased our shared group identity as nerdy Millennial friends bound by a shared previous video game–playing experience and knowledge of shared prior texts from the video game.

Papers, Please References in Other Conversations

The same interactional processes around references to *Papers, Please* can be seen in other similar examples of everyday talk, which I did not have the opportunity to audio record, but which I observed and then wrote down in my notes. These examples provide evidence that this phenomenon of reframing interactional dilemmas and shifting epistemic territory with video game texts and thereby reinforcing group identity is prevalent among these Millennial friends.

The first example occurred at a restaurant one Sunday afternoon and involved housemates Dave, Jeff, Todd, and me. We had been remarking on how nice the restaurant was when Todd and Jeff began to talk about a dicey situation at work. Todd was Jeff's supervisor, and Jeff and Todd recalled that they had conducted Jeff's performance review at this very restaurant; this led to a rekeying and reframing of the conversation. After the potentially uncomfortable topic of the hierarchical work relationship between Jeff and Todd, and the specific recent performance review of Jeff, Jeff made a game move. He constructed an overlapping play frame, still anchored in the real-life frame, saying, "I needed my plaque of sufficience—I'll go hang it on my wall." These are references to *Papers, Please*, where the player receives a "plaque of sufficience" for their work, and has the option to hang it on their wall. This recycling of shared prior video game texts functioned to reframe and rekey the conversation from serious work matters between Jeff and Todd (talk about the performance review), to a non-serious, fun video game experience. This elicited laughter from Dave and me (outsiders to Jeff and Todd's shared work experience), since we had played *Papers, Please* and had equal epistemic access to it. Recycling, reframing, and rekeying in this instance shifted the conversation to a lighter key through creating an overlapping play frame. The reframing depended on correcting an epistemic imbalance in the conversation. This reframing simultaneously reinforced the shared professional identities of Jeff and Todd. It also reinforced the shared group experience playing *Papers, Please* and the nerd Millennial identities of the group.

A few weeks after this example, I observed an awkward instance where Dave attempted to recycle the exact same reference in conversation, possibly trying to spark a play frame for me to analyze. In a conversation in the dining room, where there was no epistemic or interactional dilemma, Dave randomly asked Jeff if he ever received his "plaque of sufficience" at work (note that it is also possible that Dave did not use any of the signaling mechanisms that I observed in chapter 2). Jeff seemed caught off guard and gave a minimal response of "yeah." He did not engage in the new play frame as is typical in the other examples. This failed attempt to introduce a play frame provides evidence that these video game references occur at specific points in conversation where interactional dilemmas exist, often driven by epistemic imbalances. They serve particular functions in managing group epistemics, as well as in rekeying and reframing unpleasant conversations, which ultimately serve for group identity affirmation.

The next example occurred on a Sunday evening in the shared group house, in Dave's room. Dave was sitting at his desk; I was sitting on a couch, while Jeff and Todd were standing at the door. Dave, who took responsibility for the house finances and collected everyone's rent checks each month ("getting real shit done"), had just told Jeff that his rent check was rejected at the bank because the date on the check was wrong. To negotiate this awkward interactional dilemma around rent yet again, Jeff made a game move to rekey, reframe, and adjust the epistemic territory of the conversation. He suggested that the bank acted as the video game inspection officer, saying, "I just imagine that you gave them the check and they went into 'inspection mode' and were like 'date discrepancy' and hit the 'detain button.'" To rekey and reframe the serious conversation about his rent check, Jeff used this game move to initiate an overlapping, imaginary frame that this mistake was dealt with in a game world, where the bank went into "inspection mode." He clearly shifted to a play frame, and he then embedded a frame within the overlapping play frame. He embedded a frame by using *choral dialogue* (Tannen 1989/2007), or dialogue that represents a group of people, to represent the bank. He voices the bank by saying "date discrepancy," another shared prior text lifted from the game, and describes the bank hitting the "detain button," yet another shared prior text. In this single utterance Jeff effectively reframed and rekeyed the previously serious conversation to a play frame, which was achieved by making a game move that signaled "we are living a video game," which overlapped with the real-life frame, and even created a brief embedded frame with specific prior texts from the game.

This reframing also facilitated Todd's involvement. Previous to this, Todd had not been involved in the conversation, but had been listening in while playing a game on his phone while standing in the doorway. The rent check issue did not involve Todd. It involved Dave, who managed household finances, and Jeff, who committed the rent check error. With the new reframing, however, which appealed to the prior knowledge that all three shared about *Papers, Please*, Todd was now able to participate. He quoted speech from the inspector in the game, "Maybe you should not have come," briefly constructing an embedded character frame within the overlapping play frame. Then Dave made a game move: "Wait! I can explain!" also contributing to the specific embedded frame of character speech, quoting the denied applicant in the game as they are detained. This segment then ended with the three housemates laughing, signaling that the previously serious frame about a problematic rent check has been successfully reframed through game moves consisting of *Papers, Please* references. These recycled prior texts constructed overlapping play frames and embedded frames marked by constructed character dialogue. They functioned to rekey the talk to a light-hearted and fun play frame, which all three speakers could participate in since they had equal epistemic access to it. The friends transformed this conversation to reinforce their bond as a social group, authenticating their group identity as nerdy Millennial housemate friends with the shared experience of having all played the same video game together.

One final *Papers, Please* reference came up in a conversation among Dave, Todd, and me at the house. Dave and I had been telling Todd about an unpleasant situation in which an employee at our university had reprimanded Dave for attempting to work in a certain wing of a building after business hours. Todd was not a graduate student like Dave and I, and did not know this staff member, let alone the layout of the building that we were referring to. So, upon hearing this story, Todd became involved in the talk by contributing, "And then you shouted, 'Long live Arstotzka!' and blew up the wall." This is a reference to a possible outcome of *Papers, Please,* in which a rebel group whose cause is to free Arstotzka from its corrupt leaders blows up the border wall that divides the city. Here Todd created both an overlapping and embedded frame at once by making a game move that positioned Dave as a member of a rebel group in a video game, providing him with game dialogue accompanying a possible game action. This reference to *Papers, Please* caused Dave and I to laugh in enjoyment of this reference. Here Todd overcame the epistemic imbalance in an unpleasant story about graduate student life while also shifting the frame and key of the talk by making a humorous reference to *Papers, Please,* with which all of us were familiar and could laugh about as nerdy Millennial friends who had all played the same video game.

In sum, I have shown how words, concepts, and characters from *Papers, Please* were recycled in conversation, rekeying and ultimately reframing the conversations towards non-serious game worlds. This rekeying and reframing occurred through game moves, which created overlapping play frames and embedded frames containing constructed character dialogue. This process functioned not only to rekey and reframe the conversations to be more light-hearted and fun, but, very importantly, to readjust the epistemic territory to one that all speakers have access to, allowing for group involvement and group identity affirmation as Millennial friends who had all played a recent popular video game.

The Oregon Trail in Conversation

In this section I present analysis of the use of intertextual references to the video game *The Oregon Trail*. After recording the previous example analyzed, I was fortunate enough to record another conversation at a local diner between Dave and his close childhood friend, Alan (not a housemate), and me where references to this video game were used. I demonstrate that speakers make references to *The Oregon Trail* here to rekey serious talk about an injury to a humorous key by adding an overlapping play frame of a real-life video game experience. This rekeying and reframing rely on shifting the talk from a restricted epistemic territory with which only two of the speakers can relate to the shared epistemic territory of the video game experience, allowing Alan to become more involved in the conversation as well. This equalizing of epistemic status is shown to be conducive to group identity construction.

The video game *The Oregon Trail* is a computer game originally developed in 1974, designed to teach schoolchildren about 19th-century pioneer life on the Oregon Trail. In the game, the player is a wagon leader guiding their party of settlers from Missouri to Oregon in a covered wagon in 1848. The player "experiences" various events along the trail, based on actual historical narratives. These experiences range from facing illnesses, such as dysentery, suffering injuries like a broken arm, to making choices relating to the trail, such as whether to attempt to cross a river (see Figure 5.2). The player faces potentially life-or-death consequences for choices made. In this way *The Oregon Trail* is similar to *Papers, Please* because it also provides a somewhat psychologically immersive experience. *The Oregon Trail* was also extremely successful, selling over 65 million copies. It was popular among North American elementary school students in the mid-1980s to late 1990s, as many students in the US and Canada had access to the game at school. The popularity of this game for Millennial schoolchildren during the 1990s in the US means that many students who attended school then remember playing the game, so much so that this generation is sometimes referred to as "The Oregon Trail Generation." This shared childhood media experience among Millennials means that references to this game can be used as Millennial conversational resources in the conversation I analyze here.

Figure 5.2 *The Oregon Trail*: "You are now at the Kansas river crossing"

"She will be unable to carry food for the rest of the trip": *The Oregon Trail* References in Conversation

The second recorded excerpt I analyze in this chapter is from a diner conversation with Dave, Dave's friend Alan, and me on a Friday night. This was my second time meeting Alan, and Dave and I sat in a booth facing him during our dinner meal. In the analysis, I will demonstrate how, similar to the previous examples, video game texts are recycled to rekey and reframe the conversation, as well as to shift the epistemic territory, allowing for group involvement and group identity construction. Again, we will see the emergence of an overlapping "life is a video game" frame in the construction of a game world, which also includes embedded frames. However, this conversation is different in many ways from the previous recorded excerpt that I analyzed—most notably, the overlapping and embedded frames do not completely reframe the conversation or entirely change the topic. Instead, Dave forcefully brings the conversation back to the original, serious real-life frame.

Previous to example 2a, Dave and Alan had been talking about skiing, and I was bored, since I had no experience skiing. After Alan comments on skiing with, "If you know what you're doing, it doesn't matter" (line 1) and Dave latches with "Yeah" (line 2), I begin to tell Alan about the calamitous amphibious camping trip that Dave, Todd, Paula, Aaron, and I had recently experienced (recounted in the beginning of chapter 1), which is epistemically advantageous for Dave and me, but leaves fewer ways for Alan to participate, which will eventually create the space for an epistemic frame shift.

(2a)

1	Alan	But once again, if you know what you're doing, it doesn't matter=
2	Dave	=[Yeah
3	Sylvia	=[Um-
4		We went-
5		I went kayaking and canoeing for the first time like two weeks ago.

I initiate a turn with "Um" (line 3), which Schegloff (2010) describes as a *turn-preface* when launching a new course of action. I thus seize the opportunity to change the topic to something still related to outdoor sports, but related to my own experience, with "We went- I went kayaking and canoeing for the first time like two weeks ago" (lines 4–5). Alan demonstrates uptake of my statement and Dave and I begin to tell Alan about our camping trip, which epistemically limits his opportunities to contribute to the conversation, setting up an occasion for an epistemic frame shift.

(2b)

6	Alan	How'd you like that?
7	Dave	We [went- ^camping and kayaking.
8	Sylvia	[u:h, (I didn't-)
9	Dave	So we packed all our shit into a canoe,
10		and we hopped into kayaks,
11		she hopped into a canoe.
12		[And with-
13	Sylvia	[I hopped into a kayak first.
14	Dave	Bumped your head on it.
15	Sylvia	Then I hit my head,
16	⇨	felt kind of dizz(h)y.
17	Alan	Oh(h)(h)(h)(h)!

Dave and I launch into a shared "couple's story" (Mandelbaum 1987) to which we have primary epistemic access. We explain that I "hit my head" (line 15) on the kayak and I confess that I "felt kind of dizzy" (line 16). The laughter token in "dizzy" is interesting—so far this conversation has been in a frame of telling a real-life story, and here we are talking about an injury that could have been serious, yet I laugh. Potter and Hepburn (2010) call this kind of laughter that is produced mid-word "interpolated particles of aspiration," and find that it serves to modulate the strength of an action, marking some kind of trouble in the talk. Thus, this self-conscious laughter could signal to Alan that my injury was not very serious and that laughing about this incident is acceptable, and indeed he responds with "Oh" (line 17), which, according to Schiffrin (1987) demonstrates uptake of news and change of knowledge state, and here it also indicates non-seriousness with laughter. So here we see a contrast with the talk that had been serious up to this point—now the key has already been slightly changed with our laughter, and as Chafe (2001) has remarked, laughter is "slow fading" so we see it carry into the following lines.

With the key already shifting to be more light-hearted, Alan makes his first game move by recycling a video game text, which initiates an epistemic shift and an overlapping play frame that allows him to participate in a more engaged way.

(2c)

18	Sylvia	Deci(h)ded to go(h) in the cano(h)e.
19 ⇨	Alan	Sounds like a BA:D "<u>Oregon Trail</u>" trip. [Hahaha
20	Sylvia	[And then-
21	Dave	Something [li(h)ke tha(h)t.

I continue the narrative, "Decided to go in the canoe" (line 18), again with laughter in my statement, but I omit the fact that I took Todd's spot in the canoe (this will become relevant later). Alan participates by making a game move, drawing from his epistemic repertoire with, "Sounds like a BAD Oregon Trail trip," and laughing (line 19), reframing the event as part of *The Oregon Trail* video game. I initiate another narrative clause, "And then" (line 20), but cut myself off, either due to being overlapped by Alan's laughter or perhaps because I just got the joke. Dave laughingly says, "Something like that" (line 21), showing recognition of Alan's reference to *The Oregon Trail*. In playback, I asked Alan why he brought up the video game here, and he told me that our story reminded him of the game, which he had spent so much time in childhood playing. In other words, our camping trip story involving my injury and crossing a river triggered Alan's semi-active consciousness (Chafe 1994) in recalling this childhood game, where river crossings and random injuries were common. His game move facilitated his participation in the conversation by using an intertextual video game reference that he has knowledge about, which shifted the epistemic territory of the conversation and simultaneously created an overlapping play frame of "life is like a video game we played when we were children."

Next, the speakers swiftly move into the overlapping play frame, talking about real life as a video game, where everyone can draw on their shared knowledge about the video game, thus participating with equal epistemic access, reinforcing their shared group identity as Millennial friends with shared generational experience playing *The Oregon Trail*. The overlapping play frame is again propelled by constructed dialogue in an embedded frame, with more specific epistemic orientation towards intertextual links to the video game.

(2d)

22	Alan	[S-
23	⇨	"SY:lvia knocked [her head-"
24	⇨ Dave	["SY:LVIA:..has a conCU:ssion."
25	Sylvia	*<laughing>*
26	Alan	"She will be-
27	⇨	She will be unable to collect food [for the rest of the trip,
28	Sylvia	[Hahaha.
29	Dave	[Yeah.
30	⇨ Alan	>so you can only carry 100 pounds less"<
31		*<everyone laughs>*

Here Alan and Dave recycle texts from *The Oregon Trail*, where the computer screen tells the player that someone in the game is injured or sick (see Figure 5.3 for an example), when Alan says, "SYlvia knocked her head" (line 23) and Dave repeats this structure with "SYLVIA has a conCUssion" (line 24). These game moves of constructed dialogue involve a slightly louder voice quality and vowel lengthening, which serve as contextualization cues, signaling dialogue from the game. It is also evident that the text of the game is being referenced since the speakers are talking about me in third person, even though I am present. I laugh (line 25), showing that I also "get" the jokes being made, and that I am going along with this new rekeyed play frame.

Alan further recycles text from the game in the embedded frame of "Sylvia is a character in *The Oregon Trail*," saying "She will be- She will be unable to collect food for the rest of the trip, so you can only carry 100 pounds less," (lines 27, 30). Carrying "pounds" of food is always an issue in *The Oregon Trail* (see Figure 5.4), and when someone is injured or sick in the game this affects how much food the player is able to carry. Everyone laughs (line 31) at this, showing the non-seriousness that imagining this game world has triggered.

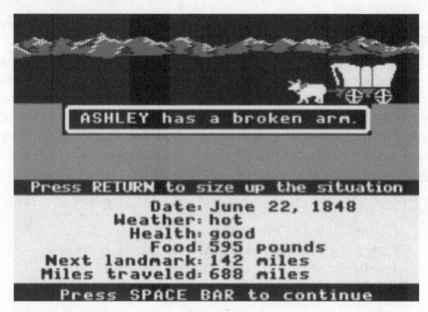

Figure 5.3 *The Oregon Trail*: "ASHLEY has a broken arm"

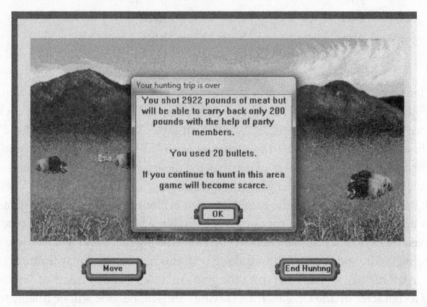

Figure 5.4 *The Oregon Trail*: "You shot 2922 pounds of meat but will be able to carry back only 200 pounds"

The constructed dialogue in this conversation, similar to the constructed dialogue of Jorji in the *Papers, Please* excerpt, again shows that an embedded frame, referring to specific texts of the video game strengthens the overlapping play frame and allows speakers to participate in a fun and equally epistemically accessible frame that discursively constructs their group identity as nerdy Millennial friends with enjoyable childhood memories of playing *The Oregon Trail*. Note that again, the embedded frame propels the overlapping play frame further away from the original topic of talk. Now instead of talking about bumping my head in a kayak in the real-life frame, we are talking about carrying pounds of food in the overlapping play frame.

As the conversation continues, the speakers make some metacomments on the play frame, and as we saw in the *Papers, Please* example, "naming the frame" breaks it:

(2e)

	32	Dave	That's absolutely correct . . .
⇨	33	Alan	Real li:fe was an "<u>Oregon Trail</u>" ga(h)me..
	34	Sylvia	[Yea:h and then-
⇨	35	Alan	["<u>Oh you broke your leg, you only made fifty dollars less today</u>."
	36	Sylvia	Haha,
	37	Dave	Well I was pissed because I realized the reason Todd didn't wanna-
	38		you know, instead of like,
	39		volunteering to kayak cause it sucks?
	40	Sylvia	Mhm?
	41	Alan	It takes more energy too, right?

Dave's metacomment, "That's absolutely correct," (line 32) is reminiscent of his earlier metacomment, "Something like that" (line 21), where he is affirming Alan's contributions to the conversation and evaluating from outside the frame, but is not as involved as he could be in maintaining the overlapping play frame. As I mentioned in the discussion of the previous conversation analyzed, Dave told me that he feels he is not good at participating in play frames—that he is more serious in conversation. This is extremely relevant for how this overlapping play frame will abruptly come to an end, instead of continuing and reframing the talk, as was the case in the first conversation analyzed. Note that I also do not participate in the overlapping play frame, but I am simply laughing in a more passive manner throughout this excerpt. I was the butt of the joke in this instance and was simply enjoying the playful teasing, but I had also become aware during this talk that this was precisely what I was looking for in my data, and it is possible that my awareness of it prevented me from becoming more involved. At the same time the teasing that occurred here can also be considered a friendly but gendered type of identity display, in which two men playfully tease a woman present through referencing a video game.

Alan next makes a metacomment, "Real life was an 'Oregon Trail' game" (line 33). Here Alan explicitly names the frame, commenting from outside the play frame about the frame itself. Perhaps interpreting his turn here as breaking the play frame, I again initiate a narrative clause with, "Yeah and then" (line 34) but cut myself short when Alan makes yet another game move with, "Oh you broke your leg, you only made fifty dollars less today" (line 35). Here Alan attempts to continue the overlapping play frame of "we are living a video game" with another embedded frame of "I am the game's narrator," marked by constructed dialogue recycled from *The Oregon Trail*.

Yet while I laugh (line 36), Dave abruptly breaks out of the overlapping play frame, moving back to the serious, real-life frame of talking about our camping experience, saying, "Well I was pissed because I realized the reason Todd didn't wanna- you know, instead of like, volunteering to kayak 'cause it sucks?" (lines 37–39). Dave's statement starts with "well" which marks a departure from expectations in the discourse that is about to come (Schiffrin 1987). Both Alan and I reorient to Dave's epistemic shift and serious rekeying (marked by his shift in emotional stance—"I was pissed") and reframing, with "mhm?" (line 40) and "It takes more energy, right?" (line 41). The conversation continues in this serious key and frame as we discuss how Dave sensed that Todd did not originally want to kayak, and was possibly annoyed when he had to kayak after I hit my head and took his spot in the canoe.

In sum, I have shown how intertextual references to *The Oregon Trail* are recycled in this conversation, rekeying epistemically limiting and serious talk by creating an equally epistemically accessible, non-serious overlapping play frame containing embedded frames that are marked by constructed dialogue. However, different from the first conversation I analyzed, the overlapping play frame in this conversation does not result in ultimately reframing the conversation. Instead, two of the speakers, Dave and I, did not fully engage in the overlapping play frame. We made several attempts, finally succeeding, to return to the serious key and epistemically limiting frame of conversation that Alan had been shifting away from. Even so, the recycling of the video game texts and the use of overlapping and embedded frames to create a game world in this excerpt still functioned to temporarily readjust the epistemic territory of the conversation, rekeying and reframing it to allow Alan to participate more. Overall then, this moment of overlapping play frames containing embedded frames of constructed dialogue, relying on shared video game texts, allowed for group identity construction as Millennial friends with shared experience playing *The Oregon Trail* as children.

"You can eat some steaks in *Minecraft*": References to Other Video Games in Conversation

Similar to my observations of many unrecorded conversations where *Papers, Please* was referenced, I also observed and noted a few unrecorded conversations where other video games were referenced. These examples provide further evidence that video game references can serve for epistemic frame shifts at interactional dilemmas, ultimately reinforcing shared group identities around knowledge of video games.

The first instance I observed of another video game reference in conversation involves *Minecraft*, a game created by Markus Persson and released in 2011. As Dave puts it, *Minecraft* is "3D Legos," or a game that allows players to build with a variety of different blocks in a 3D procedurally generated world. In survival mode of the game, players must gather resources both to build the world and to maintain health. For instance, players can acquire cattle and poultry from which they can procure steaks and chicken as food sources. *Minecraft* has received critical acclaim and has won numerous awards and accolades, and as of May 2019 it is the best-selling video game of all time. Among its millions of players were Dave and his housemates, who even ran their own multiplayer *Minecraft* server.

One Saturday night at their house, Todd was standing at the kitchen counter, putting away rice pudding that Paula and Todd had made as a dessert after their dinner and had shared with the rest of us. Jeff, Dave, Paula, and I were seated at the dining room table. After Paula had commented on how full she was, I asked her if she and Todd had made pizza for dinner. This led to Dave asking me, "What are *we* doing for dinner?" and I replied by pointing to my bowl of rice pudding. Dave then asked, "This is it?" I nodded, and Dave responded, "I'm gonna die." The topic of starving to death is unpleasant as well as epistemically isolating to the other housemates, since they had no knowledge about our dinner options or plans. Todd then became involved with our conversation by contributing, "You can eat some steaks in *Minecraft*." Here Todd created an overlapping play frame that imagines Dave and I as existing within the world of *Minecraft*, where steaks are a primary food source. Dave laughed at this video game reference. Both Jeff and Paula made onomatopoeic chewing sounds that players make when eating in Minecraft, thus temporarily speaking from an embedded character frame within the overlapping play frame. Then Dave said, "Actually I've been eating chicken lately." This utterance is spoken as if the overlapping play frame is active, but it also refers to "actually" playing the game. It has no anchors though to the real-life situation of eating dinner, and indeed Dave followed this utterance by talking extensively about his recent game play in *Minecraft*. This example shows another instance where a video game reference is used to reframe, rekey, and shift the epistemic territory of talk, ultimately functioning for shared group identity reinforcement as *Minecraft*-playing Millennials.

Two other video game references that I observed were more generic in nature in that they were not to any specific video game, but rather to role-playing games (RPGs) more generally. RPGs are a genre of game in which players assume the roles of characters in a fictional setting. While RPGs originated in tabletop games (such as *Dungeons and Dragons*), the genre has since expanded to online video games, and it is likely this latter variety that speakers are thinking of when they reference RPGs in the following two examples. The first example occurred during a long group bike ride with Dave, his friend Alan, another friend of ours, Michael, and me. During the course of our bike ride, my bike suffered a flat tire, prompting our party to stop so that Dave could repair it. After the fix was complete, our friend Michael made light of the situation by asking Dave, "How many skill points did you get for that repair?" Alan and I laughed at this RPG reference, which constructed an overlapping play frame over the real-life frame of having completed a bike repair. In RPGs, the first time a player performs a difficult action, they earn skill points. Dave responded to Michael's joke with, "Well not that much because I've done this so many times." In many RPGs, repetition of the same skilled action results in diminishing improvements to the player's abilities. So with his response, Dave was still in the overlapping play frame and the real-life frame simultaneously; he was talking as if he were a player in an RPG, but he was also referring to his real-life experience of having fixed many flat bike tires. In fact, he next went on to talk about how temporarily living in Austin, Texas, for a summer internship had required him to fix three flat bike tires in two months. The RPG reference that Michael made in this instance helped shift the frame and epistemic territory from a bike repair to a fun imaginary RPG game, helping the cyclists to laugh about the less-than-ideal situation at hand, and to bond as Millennials who were familiar enough with the concept of skill points in an RPG context.

A few weeks later, Todd, Dave, and I were circumnavigating a large building on foot while searching for the entry to a friend's wedding reception. Along the way we met other Millennial invitees looking for the entrance. Everyone was frustrated and confused about how to get in. This led to Todd rekeying and reframing the interaction by saying, "This is like an RPG where you pick up friends along the way," and everyone laughed. In many RPG games a player wanders through a world and others join in, becoming "friends" with the player. Todd's game move here constructed an overlapping play frame that imagined all of us as players within a fun RPG. This reference to an RPG functioned to reframe and rekey the situation from one of confusion and annoyance to a light-hearted and humorous one that made everyone laugh, and even made us feel like what we were doing was actually fun. Thus, all of us present were able to briefly bond over our shared confusion and our shared knowledge of RPGs as Millennials (we eventually found the entrance to the wedding reception).

I should also mention that I observed a few other instances of video game references where they did not seem to function for such clear-cut epistemic frame shifts. As with all of the references I examine in this book, sometimes references are just for fun, and at a basic level function for in-group bonding over shared knowledge around media. That is to say, they do not always function to smooth over interactional dilemmas by creating epistemic frame shifts, but they do function in this way frequently, as seen in the examples I have analyzed here.

Video Game References in Everyday Talk

This chapter has shown how different Millennial friends use video game texts as intertextual resources in their everyday conversations, for two main functions that are interrelated: (i) negotiating interactional dilemmas, by rekeying serious talk about real-life issues to humorous play frames that construct such events as part of a lived video game experience, and (ii) shifting the epistemic access required to participate in the conversation, so that different speakers can talk and demonstrate solidarity and shared "nerd" group identity.

I have analyzed reframing to show how game moves, made by recycling various bits of video game texts, construct play frames that overlap with real-life frames, allowing the participants to engage with talk about relatively serious issues (e.g., money, an injury) in a more playful way. This chapter also adds to what we know about overlapping and embedded frames in interaction. The overlapping play frames are strengthened by embedded frames that contain constructed dialogue of characters or the game text itself. Embedded frames within overlapping frames launch the speakers even further into the overlapping play frame and further away from the original real-life frame, using even more specific epistemic orientations. This process resulted in the complete reframing of the conversation in the *Papers, Please* example, but in *The Oregon Trail* example speakers cut off the video game reframing process to return to a more serious real-life frame. The two different outcomes show how speakers demonstrate varying levels of active participation in either going along with reframing, or in resisting it.

This chapter, then, has further developed how speakers are agentive in using intertextuality to manage frames. This analysis underscores the agency of speakers and the cognitive abilities they balance as they use intertextual resources to construct, overlap, embed, maintain, and switch frames. Thus this chapter contributes more broadly to our understanding of the complexity of framing in discourse as demonstrated by other scholars (e.g., Tannen & Wallat 1993; M. Goodwin 1996; Gordon 2009).

Furthermore, I have shown how epistemics play a crucial role in intertextuality, framing, and identity construction. Prior experiences of playing video games were drawn upon as epistemic resources, as video game texts were infused into conversation as an equalizing epistemic force. The epistemic shifts allowed different group members to frame shift, showing off their knowledge and participating in conversation, since they shared epistemic access to video games. In turn, this discursive work constructed their group identity as video game–playing nerds in this epistemic ecology. Gordon (2009) showed that framing and intertextuality are fundamentally interconnected, and I have built on her work to demonstrate that epistemics plays an understudied but important role in these processes.

Following Raymond and Heritage (2006), this chapter highlights the role of epistemic management in framing as well as in group social relations, further developing the field of epistemic discourse analysis. It is apparent in the examples that a shared group identity, based on shared previous experience and knowledge of shared prior texts, is being constructed—that of friends who value linking video games to real-life experiences. In addition, individuals are simultaneously negotiating their own identities within the group. For example, Dave does not participate as actively or as frequently as some other members of his friend group in the construction of game worlds. This might contribute, at these conversational moments, to his identity construction as someone more focused on "the real world." On the other hand, friends like Jeff and Paula show particular skill in creating game worlds, and I have observed throughout my data collection that Jeff is the most active of all the friends in initiating game moves to resolve interactional dilemmas, and Paula participates actively in such game worlds. So individual differences are involved, which may relate to aspects of conversational style (Tannen 1984/2005) and should be explored further.

In this chapter, I have added to the field of work that draws on the concept of intertextuality to examine interaction of a social group, with a particular focus on shared video game texts. A video game played by a group of Millennial friends in their basement resurfaces in conversations that take place in their dining room upstairs, and a video game played by Millennial children in elementary school can years later be recycled as an interactional resource in a diner. This demonstrates the fluid interplay between virtual on-screen activity (video games) and offline conversation outside of the gaming context. The connections between real life and these video games may be feasible precisely because the social realities that occur in real life, such as making long-term decisions that have lasting and undoable consequences, are reflected and reproduced in the games, and in turn this makes the games readily available resources to draw upon when interactional dilemmas arise. Additionally, when stereotypes and ideologies around things such as gender, sexuality, family, language, race, forms of governance, and nationality that are derived from our social world are embedded in video games, they also surface and are reinforced in referencing those games in interaction. In sum, while playing video games is a pastime often denigrated as being a "waste of time," this chapter has shown how Millennial friends use intertextual references to the shared experiences of playing video games to demonstrate remarkable cognitive flexibility and linguistic creativity in their conversations when confronted with epistemic imbalances and interactional dilemmas. This chapter brings together previous work on intertextuality, framing, epistemics, and identity by showing how intertextual media references are used as resources in epistemic and frame management, which ultimately contribute to shared group identity construction.

Conclusion

Frames, Epistemics, and Intertextual Identity Construction among Millennial Friends

An Interdisciplinary Approach to Knowledge and Identity

This study has situated itself primarily in the interactional sociolinguistic (IS) framework, which considers context as central to analyzing naturally occurring discourse, and to that end has examined contextualization cues, intertextuality, and framing. While IS scholars have mentioned the importance of knowledge in framing and intertextual processes (e.g., Gordon 2009; Tannen & Wallat 1993; Trester 2012), I have built on these insights by considering them in conjunction with the contemporary conceptualization of epistemics, or knowledge management in discourse, as developed in the related approach of conversation analysis. Therefore, a major contribution of this book has been to show how intertextuality and framing can be meaningfully merged with the study of epistemics; the resulting analysis has illustrated how Millennials use intertextual media references to alter frames and epistemics in everyday contexts, ultimately contributing to their shared identity construction as Millennial friends.

Building on previous IS work, I have drawn on Gumperz's (1977, 1982) work on contextualization cues. Specifically, I have illustrated how intertextual media references are signaled in everyday conversation among friends via contextualization cues, working towards the goal of better understanding intertextual processes in talk. I have shown how participants rely not only on the words spoken, but on contextualization cues to identify and interpret media references. In the process, I have uncovered that part of what makes a media text quotable is its distinctive linguistic features, such as marked phonetic features that function as a stylized performance of a particular accent, marked prosody, marked word choice, and repetition. In exploring how contextualization cues allow for conversational inference in discourse involving intertextual media references, I also analyzed another under-explored phenomenon: how listeners demonstrate engagement with

Millennials Talking Media. Sylvia Sierra, Oxford University Press. © Oxford University Press 2021.
DOI: 10.1093/oso/9780190931117.003.0006

intertextual media references they have heard in conversation. Thus I also examined how listeners responded to hearing intertextual media references, mutually engaging as members of an in-group who shared knowledge about the same media texts.

Since speakers often engaged in elaborate play frames around media references, I expanded upon my findings on the signaling of and engagement with media references by examining instances where participants used references as a way to construct overlapping and embedded play frames, engaging with the details of frame lamination as laid out in Gordon's (2002, 2008, 2009) work, where she argues that intertextuality and frames are fundamentally linked. I also expand on Tannen and Wallat's (1993) discussion of knowledge schemas, by demonstrating that specific knowledge schemas about media are precisely what drive these kinds of play frame sequences, which are ultimately conducive to shared identity construction based on referencing shared knowledge.

Intertextuality and Epistemics as Approaches to Identity

Heeding van Dijk's (2013) call for an epistemic discourse analysis, I have shown how a close analysis of discourse that engages with frames theory, intertextuality, and epistemics illuminates how intertextual references can be analyzed as epistemic resources. Intertextual media references are signaled, responded to, and called upon as resources during epistemic imbalances underlying interactional dilemmas. These intertextual references can create overlapping and embedded play frames while simultaneously managing group epistemics, which is ultimately conducive to group identity construction. I have referred to these processes as epistemic frame shifts, which capture both the epistemic and frame components of these interactions; the fact that the epistemic component consists of intertextual references to prior texts is elucidated through the analysis itself.

With this analysis, I have also found additional support for Heritage's (2012) idea that the epistemic engine does indeed drive much of talk, since the epistemic imbalances in conversation are what drives many interactional dilemmas. Media references then add fuel to the epistemic engine and reorient talk in a way that is meaningful to the participants. This can also be discussed as *enchrony* in Enfield's (2011) conceptualization of sequencing as fueled by epistemics, responsibility, and affiliation, which ultimately drive the need for restoring epistemic symmetry in interaction. Heritage (2013b) also touches on epistemics and sequence organization, suggesting that the management of epistemics may propel talk forward, is involved in topic shifts, and is implicated in the closure of sequences and topics, and these suggestions have also been born out in my analysis.

Following Heritage (2013b), I have also pushed beyond conceptualizing knowledge in a K-/K+ gradient model (Heritage 2010, 2012; Heritage & Raymond 2012), which implies that epistemics is a unidimensional phenomenon. Instead I have considered the multidimensionality of epistemic status, embracing the complexity in frame processes that results from different epistemic orientations around different epistemic resources, or intertextual media references, in this case. In answering Heritage's (2013b) call for work on epistemic ecologies, I have analyzed the discourse of specific Millennial friends with common epistemic territories showing how they draw on these territories to contribute to their shared group identity construction and reinforcement.

Intertextual Identities among Millennial Friends

In this study, I have investigated how speakers use intertextual media references as epistemic resources to manage identity construction in interaction, heeding Hamilton's (1996) call for an intertextual analysis of how people construct relatively stable social identities over time. The main finding concerning the relationship between intertextuality, frames, epistemics, and their role in identity construction can be distilled to the understanding that when faced with epistemic imbalances underlying interactional dilemmas, speakers used shared prior texts to create play frames. These play frames draw from a shared epistemic territory of talk. This balancing of the "epistemic seesaw" (Heritage 2012) is what promotes group identity construction, by promoting similarity, or *adequation* (Bucholtz & Hall 2005) among the speakers. In these conversations, the use of specific shared prior media texts as epistemic resources attests to the common experiences, memories, and interests of the speakers. This is seen when speakers reference Disney films seen in childhood, video games played in school and at home, and internet memes seen on a computer screen. These shared references encourage mutual involvement as well as group identity construction in the lives of these Millennial friends.

The analysis of media references in this study has illuminated a distinct and observable site for the construction of specific kinds of shared group identities. In many cases speakers construct shared identities through their media references, as well-educated friends with shared interests, as nerds, as digital natives, and as Millennials more broadly. In turn, my analysis begins to make clear the interplay between media consumption practices and everyday inter-action, including how cultural stereotypes in media make their way into eve-ryday conversation via the process of *enregisterment* (Agha 2007). Whether someone is voicing a stereotypical Hollywood depiction of Native Americans circulated on TV, or referencing an internet meme that draws on a stereo-type of African-American women, they are drawing on stereotypes present in the media they consume. In infusing these media stereotypes into their talk, speakers reinforce them, whether or not the intent is to mock or reject them. In doing so, they 'other' people who do not look or sound like they do, while also reinforcing the homogeneity and shared experiences of the group. The overall lack of references to explicitly LGBTQ+ media and the ideologies of gender and sexuality that made their way into conversation via media references also reinforce heteronormativity, cisgender identities, and gender normative ways of behaving in this group of friends. In turn, this others LGBTQ+ identities. By exploring stereotypes in media references, my analysis also begins to show the link between the cognitive component of identity as stored in knowledge schemas about groups of people and the categorization of identities as emer-gent, creative, and locally conceived of in everyday talk via the repetition of prior texts.

While my primary focus in the analysis of identity construction has been shared group identities as crafted through the use of shared media references, individual identities are also constructed in making media references in eve-ryday interaction. It is possible to comment on the constructed individual identities of Dave, his housemates, and me, since these are the speakers for which I have the most conversational data. For instance, I sensed that Jeff and Paula were possibly more performative in their talk when I recorded conversations in their presence. This may have had something to do with their frequent deployment of media references that often included singing or "taking on voices" (Tannen 1989/2007), and, more specifically, performing stylized accents, when I was recording. There is some evidence for this suspi-cion in how Jeff frequently addressed my digital recorder as "Recorder" and mentioned it throughout my data collection.

Regarding individual differences as presented through the analysis of media references, Jeff is the most prolific media reference-maker in the five conversations, making a total of 55 media references across just three recorded conversations that I presented here, followed by Paula with 33 references. Not only does Jeff make the most references but he also demonstrates his high-involvement conversational style (Tannen 1984/2005) by demonstrating per-sistence in repeating media references when they are not heard or responded to the first time. Jeff additionally performs far more stylized regional and foreign accents than any other speakers, and he and Paula sing more than anyone else when making references. Paula and Jeff's insights into their own upbringing provide relevant background information for interpreting their behavior in the conversations I recorded. Jeff had explained to me how he had been positioned as a "class clown" in his youth, and that his exposure to the world of improv comedy may have influenced his frequent performance of stylized accents in the conversations. Paula had also been in an improv comedy group and had performed stand-up comedy in college—so it seems plausible that both Jeff and Paula might have used the occasions of my recording their talk to practice their skills in humor. At the same time, their uses of stylized accents and singing may be part of their own acquired individual styles, whether or not they are in a performative mode.

It is also possible to compare Jeff and Paula to their housemates Todd (also Paula's partner) and Dave. Dave makes 19 media references, but in chapter 5 I analyzed how Dave resists an extended play frame around references to *The Oregon Trail,* and in playback he told me that he did not think he was good at performing accents or participating in play frames. Based on some of the references that Dave makes in this data set along with my own observations, Dave also tends to make more obscure references that people do not necessarily recognize. Todd makes only five media references in the recorded data set, but this came as a surprise to me, as well as to Paula and him, when I told them about this. While Todd is slightly more reserved in general than Paula, Jeff, and Dave, we still thought it was unusual that he only made five media references in the data set, since our general intuition was that he seems to make a lot of references. After talking with Todd about this in playback, I have surmised that on the one hand, it is likely that his high-considerateness conversational style (Tannen 1984/2005), especially in contexts where Jeff, Paula, and Dave were more performative and high-involvement, kept him from participating as actively in the conversations as he might have otherwise. To this effect, Todd related, "I guess I feel I have trouble keeping up in those situations." On the other hand, Todd said, "I do make a lot of references. However, I would say I often do not expect others to pick up on them . . . I don't speak them in a tone that suggests I am referring to something. My favorite is when quotes can be fit into normal conversation with no strain. And I just say them and see if the other notices. Occasionally if I'm really proud of it I will say it was a reference afterwards." Todd's insight on his use of references is fascinating, especially since his usage seems so different from the way other speakers in my data used references. I asked him what the pay-off is in making references at all if you don't signal them and don't even expect others to "get" them. To this, he responded, "Mainly I think I do it for my own amusement. It's fun to be able to speak the words." Todd's insights, like those of his housemates, provide additional evidence that each individual's varying usage of media references is extremely relevant to their own personality and personal identities.

As for me, I made 16 references throughout the conversations. It is possible that in everyday conversation at the time, I generally made more media references than it would seem based on the data set (like Todd) but that I was more aware of such references after I decided they would be the focus of my study. This increased consciousness possibly caused me to pull back a little in making references starting after the second conversation that I chose for analysis. However, since completing my study, I now both effortlessly *and* consciously make media references all the time, having a new understanding and appreciation for the interactional work they can do in terms of shifting epistemics and frames, creating humor, constructing identities, and facilitating social bonding.

I believe that the Millennial friends in this study often use media references as a way to cope with the growing pains that accompany early adulthood. It is widely documented that Millennials have encountered economic and related social hardships in entering adulthood, in large part due to The Great Recession, which began to erode the economy in 2007. I observed that when these Millennial friends broached issues like paying rent, being injured, introducing a new romantic partner to a nerdy group of friends, and even negotiating ownership and rights to assess newly acquired pet cats, media references functioned as a kind of escape hatch from the resulting awkwardness or mild unpleasantness of such conversations. Media references allowed speakers to shift the epistemic frame of talk in these circumstances, often making these issues into shared jokes based on shared media knowledge which infused lighthearted humor, laughter, and camaraderie into the conversation. As Grant (2012) speculates, for Millennials, "life can feel chaotic and nonsensical. To be able to laugh, then, in the face of life's absurdities relieves us and gives us hope for the future." While I observed this phenomenon in my data of Millennial friends' conversations specifically, I am certain that media references are and can be used by many kinds of people of all different backgrounds and generations for similar social functions.

Thus, while the analysis of media references in this study has provided a clear focus as well as precise evidence for the construction of specific kinds of individual as well as shared Millennial group identities, it is important to point out that at the same time, media references are an analytical means to approaching a more over-arching theoretical end. I chose to study them because they appeared to provide a clear and unique site for examining the complex interaction of intertextual, epistemic, and frame-related phenomena that contribute to group identity construction more broadly. As a researcher, I was both surprised and impressed by the wide array of old and new media that the Millennial friends in my study incorporated into their everyday talk. While the oldest generations in the US initially had printed text media to draw on for infusion into their talk, and this gradually came to include radio and motion picture media such as film and TV, Millennials are unique in being the first generation to grow up with a wide array of electronic media such as video games, YouTube videos, and internet memes, which they also incorporate into their everyday conversation. It is likely that the next generation will continue consuming and drawing on some old "classic" media in their discourse, while gradually moving up dates of relevant media and also continuing to update their media lexicon with newer media references. Thus, while my focus has been on friends of a particular generation, a crucial takeaway from my study is that any type of shared prior texts that are referenced by a group of people can be analyzed in order to understand the intertextual identity construction of any epistemic ecology.

Closing Remarks

Researchers, teachers, and students frequently desire practical takeaways from studies in linguistics and communication. How can we apply knowledge about making media references to our everyday lives? Is it possible to use media references conscientiously or even strategically to smooth over awkward moments, bring everyone together on the same page, and build relationships? How can we avoid excluding others when we make media references to texts that are not shared among our interlocutors? And how can we become more conscious of the kinds of media we consume and quote in our everyday talk, and more critical of media stereotypes?

As a result of my research on media references, I am more aware than ever about both the fun and functions that media references bring to conversation. Making media references often produces shared laughter, affiliation, and a feeling of ease and comfort with those around you. I have even, on occasion, used media references with intention when I have faced awkward interactional moments with family members and friends. I have also used media references more consciously to reinforce old friendships and to make new friends. As Glenn (2003) observes, the shared laughter that media references often provoke can help us deal with difficult situations, help us to feel good, and bring people closer together in relationships. I have even taken a few improv comedy classes as a way to learn how to incorporate more media references and humor more generally in my everyday life, as well as in my teaching. In addition, I also now playfully sing references to songs more than I used to in interaction, realizing through my research how fun it can be and the kind of desirable identities it can construct, such as being humorous and playful. To practice singing, I have learned to enjoy doing Karaoke with friends, which also provides a fun media bonding experience which can later be referenced for group affiliation. Another way I have translated my research on media references into an everyday application is by appreciating the fun in using media references in other contexts, such as in computer-mediated communication like emails, text messages, group chats, and social media sites like Twitter. Incorporating new media such as GIFs (a digital image format that features silently looping images) and YouTube videos in these contexts is another way to have fun while building relationships with others based around shared references.

At the same time, I have made observations about exactly what types of media lend themselves to deployment in everyday interaction. First, the media texts that speakers quoted in this study often had distinctive linguistic features, including marked phonetic features that function as a stylized performance of a particular accent, marked prosody, marked word choice, and repetition. These marked features in media texts seem to explain why we enjoy quoting them, often repeating the prosody and accents that are sometimes paired with unusual word choice and repetition. In addition, it seems that media such as films, TV shows, and video games with robustly built communities of characters that engage with each other and the audience in meaningful dialogue about a moral and ethical world modeled on our reality are useful in everyday talk. The more such media draws on plausible real-life situations, the more likely that consumers will then call upon that media during their everyday interactions, potentially using media in creative ways to overcome interactional hurdles and moments of difficulty, ultimately constructing affiliation and shared identities. This finding has implications for media content creators who hope that their content will spread in a meaningful way across audiences. In addition, shared group experiences involving engagement with media also facilitate the entry of such media into everyday talk. This suggests that it might be beneficial to create shared media consumption opportunities for team-building exercises, whether it's in the classroom, in the workplace, or in other kinds of organizations.

While media references can bring people together, it's important to be aware that they can also leave others out when the same media experiences are not shared among conversationalists. In this kind of scenario, media references can be a source of exclusion (Duff 2002; Kelley 2013). In the same vein, media references can also other individuals and entire groups of people who are or are not present, since much of the media we consume and later reference contains harmful stereotypes and ideologies about gender, sexuality, race, social class, age, ability, and so on. These stereotypes and ideologies can be so subtle and insidious in media that people can unthinkingly reinforce them when they reference such media. Still, I am optimistic and hopeful about this issue. I showed in chapter 4 and have seen elsewhere in talk how once an individual's awareness of the problem of performing media stereotypes is raised, the individual will often either refuse to perform, hesitate, or at the very least consciously comment on such performances after the fact. The importance that media plays in our lives means that it is important to critically examine the media we consume, as well as to appreciate the crucial role of accurate representation in media.

Media representations are increasingly being given the attention and criticism they merit. More and more, TV shows and films incorporate storylines of characters with marginalized backgrounds and experiences of the kind that traditionally have not been represented in this medium. Groundbreaking TV shows and films increasingly feature characters from geographic regions and cultural backgrounds that have typically lacked accurate representation on screen, and such media continue to broaden the representation of historically marginalized people and their experiences. Articles, tweets, and Instagram posts currently circulate online about digital blackface in gifs, and pressure is increasing for characters in film and TV to be represented by actors who share the same identity expressions as the characters they play.

This book contributes to these discussions by demonstrating how media representations make their way into our conversations. The findings indicate the need to raise consciousness in ourselves and our communities about issues of media representations, stereotyping in media, language mocking, and related topics. As I have shown, this can make a difference even in metadiscursive conversations about our media references with our friends and others. This is important work for us as a society, and is at the same time just one small component of dismantling white supremacy, linguistic dominance, and discrimination. All this to say that representation matters, not only for those who have historically not been represented, but for all of us who consume media and who will inevitably end up infusing that media into our everyday talk to shift frames, epistemics, and to construct shared identities and shared worldviews.

Postscript

More than five years have passed since I experienced, recorded, and made notes about the conversations in this book, which occurred primarily at my partner Dave's house where he lived with Jeff, Paula, and Todd. The participants are all older now, although they will always be members of the Millennial generation; we cannot escape. Some of them have married and have had children, others have finished their graduate studies, and all of their lives have changed in different ways.

Jeff was the first to move out of the house where I recorded most of these conversations. He took a job abroad, where he met his future wife. Soon after I stopped recording conversations at the house, Paula and Todd got engaged, and then married. Jeff made the trip back to the US with his soon-to-be fiancé to attend Paula and Todd's wedding, and Dave, a reverend of the Universal Life Church, officiated their marriage. A couple of years later, the housemates and I attended Jeff's US wedding, where he made just as many media references as ever. Jeff and his wife then moved back overseas where they had a baby. Paula and Todd continued to live in the same house with Dave for a few more years along with the now fully grown cats, Hydra and Liam, and with two successive housemates who moved into Jeff's old room, along. Paula and Todd eventually moved out during the COVID-19 pandemic, and they recently had a child together.

Paula, Dave, and I all finished our doctoral studies in linguistics. I left the DC area upon accepting a position at Syracuse University in New York state, maintaining a long-distance relationship with Dave while he continued his graduate studies. He eventually accepted a full-time position at a small start-up in Northern Virginia as a computational linguist, and soon after, finished his PhD. Paula also found a nearby research job. During the COVID-19 pandemic, Dave was able to work remotely and re-located to live with me in New York state.

As Millennials, the friends continue making media references to all kinds of media, perhaps with a bit of additional conscientiousness about doing so due to my research. We continue to play video games, enjoy internet memes, watch both old and new films and TV shows, read, and listen to music, all of which leads to constantly evolving media references and inside jokes. On a

Millennials Talking Media. Sylvia Sierra, Oxford University Press. © Oxford University Press 2021.
DOI: 10.1093/oso/9780190931117.003.0007

recent July 4th before the publication of this book, Paula, Todd, and Dave went on another camping trip with "long hair, don't care" Aaron from chapters 1 and 4, and some other friends and family members. I was admittedly relieved to already have made other plans, having experienced enough kayaking and tent-yacking on the earlier camping trip described in chapter 1 that launched the study presented in this book.

Transcription Conventions

Punctuation reflects intonation, not grammar
? indicates rising intonation at the end of a unit
. indicates falling intonation
, indicates continuing intonation
.. two dots indicate a noticeable pause
... three dots indicate a significant pause
/ / / indicates rhythmic speech
= equal sign indicates latching (second voice begins without perceptible pause)
[brackets indicate overlap (two voices heard at the same time)
(??) indicates inaudible utterance
(h) indicates laughter during a word
(words) indicates uncertain transcription
<*sound*> gives details about speech or non-speech sounds
[detail] gives details for clarification
∧ indicates emphatic stress
CAPS indicates speech spoken loudly
: colon following a vowel indicates elongated vowel sound
:word: indicates creaky voice
- indicates an abrupt stop in speech; a truncated word or syllable
⇨ significant line of transcript
→line continues
"<u>word</u>" indicates a media reference

References

Adegoju, Adeyemi, and Oluwabunmi Oyebode. 2015. "Humour as Discursive Practice in Nigeria's 2015 Presidential Election Online Campaign Discourse." *Discourse Studies* 17(6): 643–62.

Agha, A. 2007. *Language and Social Relations*. Cambridge, UK: Cambridge University Press.

Aguilar, Gabrielle K., Heidi A. Campbell, Mariah Stanley, and Ellen Taylor. 2017. "Communicating Mixed Messages about Religion through Internet Memes." *Information, Communication & Society* 20(10): 1498–1520.

Alim, H. Samy, and Geneva Smitherman. 2012. *Articulate While Black: Barack Obama, Language, and Race in the US*. Oxford: Oxford University Press.

Al Zidjaly, Najma. 2017. "Memes as Reasonably Hostile Laments: A Discourse Analysis of Political Dissent in Oman." *Discourse & Society* 28(6): 573–94.

Albada, Kelly Fudge, and Linda C. Godbold. 2001. "Media-Derived Personal Idioms: The Talk of a New Generation." *Electronic Journal of Communication* 11(1).

Apperley, Thomas. 2010. "What Games Studies Can Teach Us about Videogames in the English and Literacy Classroom." *The Australian Journal of Language and Literacy* 33(1): 12–23.

Ariel, Mira. 2014 [1990]. *Accessing Noun-Phrase Antecedents*. London: Routledge.

Azios, Jamie H., and Brent Archer. 2018. "Singing Behaviour in a Client with Traumatic Brain Injury: A Conversation Analysis Investigation." *Aphasiology* 32(8): 944–66.

Bakhtin, Mikhail M. 1981. *The Dialogic Imagination: Four Essays*. Edited by Michael Holquist. Translated by Caryl Emerson and Michael Holquist. Austin: University of Texas Press.

Bakhtin, Mikhail M. 1984. *Problems of Dostoevsky's Poetics*. Edited by Caryl Emerson. Theory and History of Literature. Minneapolis: University of Minnesota Press.

Bakhtin, Mikhail M. 1986. *Speech Genres and Other Late Essays*. Edited by Caryl Emerson and Michael Holquist. Translated by Vern W. McGee. Austin, Texas: University of Texas Press.

Bamberg, Michael. 2011. "Who Am I? Narration and Its Contribution to Self and Identity." *Theory & Psychology* 21(1): 3–24.

Bateson, Gregory. 1972. *Steps to an Ecology of Mind*. San Francisco: Chandler Publishing Company.

Bauman, Richard, and Charles L. Briggs. 1990. "Poetics and Performance as Critical Perspectives on Language and Social Life." *Annual Review of Anthropology* 19(59): 88.

Bayerl, Petra Saskia, and Lachezar Stoynov. 2016. "Revenge by Photoshop: Memefying Police Acts in the Public Dialogue about Injustice." *New Media & Society* 18(6): 1006–26.

Becker, Alton L. 1994. "Repetition and Otherness: An Essay." In *Repetition in Discourse: Interdisciplinary Perspectives*, edited by Barbara Johnstone, 2:162–75. Advances in Discourse Processes 47. Norwood, New Jersey: Ablex Publishing.

Becker, Alton L. 1995. *Beyond Translation: Essays Towards a Modern Philology*. Ann Arbor: University of Michigan Press.

Becker, Ron. 2006. "Gay-Themed Television and the Slumpy Class: The Affordable, Multicultural Politics of the Gay Nineties." *Television & New Media* 7(2): 184–215.

Beers Fägersten, Kristy. 2012. "Intertextual Quotation: References to Media in Family Interaction." In *The Appropriation of Media in Everyday Life: What People Do with Media*, edited by Ruth Ayaß and Cornelia Gerhardt, 79–104. Amsterdam: John Benjamins Publishing Company.

Bendix, Regina. 1987. "Marmot, Memet, and Marmoset: Further Research on the Folklore of Dyads." *Western Folklore* 46(3): 171–91.

Berger, Richard, and Julian McDougall. 2013. "Reading Videogames as (Authorless) Literature." *Literacy* 47(3): 142–49.

Biber, Douglas, and Finegan, Edward. 1989. "Styles of Stance in English: Lexical and Grammatical Marking of Evidentiality and Affect. *Text—Interdisciplinary Journal for the Study of Discourse* 9(1): 93–124.

Blackwell, Natalia L., Marcus Perlman, and Jean E. Fox Tree. 2015. "Quotation as a Multimodal Construction." *Journal of Pragmatics* 81: 1–7.

Blommaert, Jan. 2017. "Durkheim and the Internet: On Sociolinguistics and the Sociological Imagination." *Tilburg Papers in Culture Studies* 173.

Blommaert, Jan, and Anna De Fina. 2017. "Chronotopic Identities: Identities on the Timespace Organization of Who We Are." *Georgetown University Round Table on Languages and Linguistics*, 1–15. Washington, D.C.: Georgetown University Press.

Blommaert, Jan, and Pia Varis. 2015. "Enoughness, Accent and Light Communities: Essays on Contemporary Identities." *Tilburg Papers in Culture Studies*, paper 139.

Blume, Carolyn. 2019. "Playing by Their Rules: Why Issues of Capital (Should) Influence Digital Game-Based Language Learning in Schools." *CALICO Journal* 36(1): 19–38.

Blyth, Carl, Sigrid Recktenwald, and Jenny Wang. 1990. "I'm Like, 'Say What?!': A New Quotative in American Oral Narrative." *American Speech* 65(3): 215–227.

Bogaers, Iris E. W. M. 1993. "Gender in Job Interviews: Some Implications of Verbal Interactions of Women and Men." *Working Papers in Language, Gender and Sexism* 3(1): 53–82.

Bowman, John R. 1978. "The Organization of Spontaneous Adult Social Play." In *Play, Anthropological Perspectives: 1977 Proceedings of the Association for the Anthropological Study of Play*, edited by Michael A. Salter, 239–50. West Point: Leisure Press.

Brown, Penelope, and Stephen C. Levinson. 1987. *Politeness: Some Universals in Language Usage*. Cambridge: Cambridge University Press.

Bryant, J. Alison. 2001. *Television and the American Family*. New York, New York: Routledge.

Bryce, Jennifer, and Hope Jensen Leichter. 1983. "The Family and Television: Forms of Mediation." *Journal of Family Issues* 4(2): 309–28.

Bucholtz, Mary. 1999. "'Why Be Normal?': Language and Identity Practices in a Community of Nerd Girls." *Language in Society* 28(2): 203–23.

Bucholtz, Mary. 2009. "From Stance to Style: Gender, Interaction, and Indexicality in Mexican Immigrant Youth Slang." In *Stance: Sociolinguistic Perspectives*, edited by Alexandra Jaffe, 146–70. Oxford Studies in Sociolinguistics. Oxford: Oxford University Press.

Bucholtz, Mary. 2011. "Race and the Re-Embodied Voice in Hollywood Film." *Language & Communication* 31(3): 255–65.

Bucholtz, Mary, and Kira Hall. 2004. "Language and Identity." In *A Companion to Linguistic Anthropology*, edited by Alessandro Duranti, 369–94. Oxford: Blackwell.

Bucholtz, Mary, and Kira Hall. 2005. "Identity and Interaction: A Sociocultural Linguistic Approach." *Discourse Studies* 7(4–5): 585–614.

Bucholtz, Mary, and Qiuana Lopez. 2011. "Performing Blackness, Forming Whiteness: Linguistic Minstrelsy in Hollywood Film." *Journal of Sociolinguistics* 15(5): 680–706.

Buchstaller, Isabelle. 2008. "The Localization of Global Linguistic Variants." *English World-Wide* 29(1): 15–44.

Buchstaller, Isabelle, and Alexandra D'Arcy. 2009. "Localized Globalization: A Multi-local, Multivariate Investigation of Quotative *Be Like*." *Journal of Sociolinguistics* 13(3): 291–331.

Burgess, Jean, Alice Marwick, and Thomas Poell. 2017. *The SAGE Handbook of Social Media*. Thousand Oaks: SAGE.

Carter, Ronald. 2015. *Language and Creativity: The Art of Common Talk*. London: Routledge.

Chafe, Wallace. 1994. *Discourse, Consciousness, and Time: The Flow and Displacement of Conscious Experience in Speaking and Writing*. Chicago: University of Chicago Press.

Chafe, Wallace. 2001. "Laughing While Talking." In *Georgetown University Round Table on Languages and Linguistics (GURT) 2001: Linguistics, Language, and the Real World: Discourse and Beyond*, edited by Deborah Tannen and James Alatis, 36–49. Washington D.C.: Georgetown University Press.

Choe, Hanwool. 2018. "Type Your Listenership: An Exploration of Listenership in Instant Messages." *Discourse Studies* 20(6): 703–25.

Chun, Elaine W. 2004. "Ideologies of Legitimate Mockery." *Pragmatics* 14(2–3): 263–89.

Clark, Herbert H, and Richard J Gerrig. 1990. "Quotations as Demonstrations." *Language* 66(4): 764–805.

Coates, Jennifer. 1989. "Gossip Revisited: Language in All-Female Groups." In *Women in Their Speech Communities*, edited by Jennifer Coates and Deborah Cameron, 94–122. London: Longman.

Coates, Jennifer. 1993. *Women, Men and Language: A Sociolinguistic Account of Sex Differences in Language*. 2nd ed. London: Longman.

Coates, Jennifer. 1996. *Women Talk: Conversation between Women Friends*. Oxford: Blackwell Publishers.

Coates, Jennifer. 1997. "Women's Friendships, Women's Talk." In *Gender and Discourse*, edited by Ruth Wodak, 245–62. London: Sage.

Coates, Jennifer. 1998. "'Thank God I'm a Woman': The Construction of Differing Femininities." In *The Feminist Critique of Language*, edited by Ruth Wodak, 2nd ed., 295–320. London: Routledge.

Condor, Susan. 2006. "Public Prejudice as Collaborative Accomplishment: Towards a Dialogic Social Psychology of Racism." *Journal of Community & Applied Social Psychology* 16(1): 1–8.

Cook, Guy. 2000. *Language Play, Language Learning*. Oxford, UK: Oxford University Press.

Couper-Kuhlen, Elizabeth. 1996. "The Prosody of Repetition: On Quoting and Mimicry." In *Prosody in Conversation: Interactional Studies*, edited by Elizabeth Couper-Kuhlen and Margret Selting, 366–405. Cambridge: Cambridge University Press.

Couper-Kuhlen, Elizabeth. 1999. "Coherent Voicing: On Prosody in Conversational Reported Speech." In *Coherence in Spoken and Written Discourse*, edited by Wolfram Bublitz, Uta Lenk, and Eija Ventola, 11–34. Amsterdam: John Benjamins Publishing Company.

Couper-Kuhlen, Elizabeth, and Margret Selting. 2018. *Interactional Linguistics: Studying Language in Social Interaction*. Cambridge: Cambridge University Press.

Coupland, Justine, and Nikolas Coupland. 2009. "Attributing Stance in Discourses of Body Shape and Weight loss." In *Stance: Sociolinguistic Perspectives*, edited by Alexandra Jaffe, 227–249. New York: Oxford University Press.

Crystal, David. 1998. *Language Play*. Harmondsworth: Penguin.

D'Arcy, Alexandra. 2012. "The Diachrony of Quotation: Evidence from New Zealand English." *Language Variation and Change* 24(3): 343–369.

D'Arcy, Alexandra. 2017. *Discourse-Pragmatic Variation in Context: Eight Hundred Years of LIKE*. Amsterdam: John Benjamins Publishing Company.

Davis, Corey B., Mark Glantz, and David R. Novak. 2016. "'You Can't Run Your SUV on Cute. Let's Go!': Internet Memes as Delegitimizing Discourse." *Environmental Communication* 10(1): 62–83.

Davison, Patrick. 2012. "The Language of Internet Memes." In *The Social Media Reader*, edited by Michael Mandiberg, 120–34. New York: New York University Press.

Dawkins, Richard. 1976. *The Selfish Gene*. Oxford: Oxford University Press.

De Decker, Paul. 2013. "Phonetic Shifting across Narrative and Quoted Speech Styles." In *Proceedings of Meetings on Acoustics 166ASA*. ASA.

Dobson, Kathy, and Irena Knezevic. 2017. "'Liking and Sharing' the Stigmatization of Poverty and Social Welfare: Representations of Poverty and Welfare through Internet Memes on Social Media." *TripleC: Communication, Capitalism & Critique. Open Access Journal for a Global Sustainable Information Society* 15(2): 777–95.

Dobrow, Julia R., and Calvin L. Gidney. 1998. "The Good, the Bad, and the Foreign: The Use of Dialect in Children's Animated Television." *The Annals of the American Academy of Political and Social Science* 557(1):105–119.

Dragojevic, Marko, Dana Mastro, Howard Giles, and Alexander Sink. 2016. "Silencing Nonstandard Speakers: A Content Analysis of Accent Portrayals on American Primetime Television." *Language in Society* 45(1): 59–85.

Dreher, W. 1982. Gesprächsanalyse: Macht als Kategorie männlichen Interacktionsverhältens. Sprecherwechsel und Lachen Master's thesis, Berlin.

Du Bois, John W. 2007. "The Stance Triangle." In *Stancetaking in Discourse: Subjectivity, Evaluation, Interaction*, 139–82. Pragmatics & Beyond New Series 164. Amsterdam: John Benjamins Publishing Company.

Duff, Patricia A. 2002. "Pop Culture and ESL Students: Intertextuality, Identity, and Participation in Classroom Discussions." *Journal of Adolescent & Adult Literacy* 45(6): 482–87.

Duncan, Starkey, and Donald W. Fiske. 1977. *Face-to-Face Interaction: Research, Methods, and Theory*. Hillsdale, New Jersey: L. Erlbaum Associates.

Duran, Chatwara Suwannamai. 2017. "'You Not Die yet': Karenni Refugee Children's Language Socialization in a Video Gaming Community." *Linguistics and Education* 42: 1–9.

Duranti, Alessandro. 1986. "The Audience as Co-Author: An Introduction." *Text & Talk — An Interdisciplinary Journal of Language, Discourse Communication Studies* 6(3): 239–47.

Dynel, Marta. 2016. "I Has Seen Image Macros! Advice Animals Memes as Visual-Verbal Jokes." *International Journal of Communication* 10: 660–88.

Dyson, Anne Haas. 2003. *The Brothers and Sisters Learn to Write: Popular Literacies in Childhood and School Culture*. New York: Teachers College Press.

Earis, Helen, and Kearsy Cormier. 2013. "Point of View in British Sign Language and Spoken English Narrative Discourse: The Example of 'The Tortoise and the Hare'." *Language and Cognition* 5(4): 313–43.

Easton, Anita. 1994. "Talk and Laughter in New Zealand Women's and Men's Speech." *Wellington Working Papers in Linguistics* 6: 1–25.

Ebrahimzadeh, Mohsen, and Sepideh Alavi. 2017. "Digital Video Games: E-Learning Enjoyment as a Predictor of Vocabulary Learning." *Electronic Journal of Foreign Language Teaching; Singapore* 14(2): 145–58.

Edelsky, Carole. 1976. "Subjective Reactions to Sex-Linked Language." *The Journal of Social Psychology* 99(1): 97–104.

Enfield, Nick J. 2011. "Sources of Asymmetry in Human Interaction: Enchrony, Status, Knowledge and Agency." In *The Morality of Knowledge in Conversation*, edited by Tanya Stivers, Lorenza Mondada, and Jakob Steensig, 285–312. Cambridge, UK: Cambridge University Press.

Enfield, Nick J. 2012. "Reference in conversation." In *The Handbook of Conversation Analysis*, edited by Jack Sidnell & Tanya Stivers, 433–54. Malden, MA: Blackwell.

Englebretson, Robert, ed. 2007. "Stancetaking in Discourse: An Introduction." In *Stancetaking in Discourse*, 1–25. Pragmatics & Beyond New Series 164. Amsterdam: John Benjamins Publishing Company.

Erickson, Frederick. 1986. "Qualitative Research." In *The Handbook of Research on Teaching*, edited by M Wittrockk, 3rd ed., 119–61. New York: MacMillan.

Erickson, Frederick. 2004. *Talk and Social Theory*. Cambridge, UK: PolityPress.

Erickson, Frederick. 2015. "Oral Discourse as a Semiotic Ecology: The Co-Construction of Speaking, Listening, and Looking." In *The Handbook of Discourse Analysis*, edited by

Deborah Tannen, Heide E Hamilton, and Deborah Schiffrin, 422–46. Hoboken: Wiley Blackwell.

Eschler, Jordan, and Amanda Menking. 2018. "No Prejudice Here: Examining Social Identity Work in Starter Pack Memes." *Social Media+ Society* 4(2).

Fellegy, Anna M. 1995. "Patterns and Functions of Minimal Response." *American Speech* 70(2): 186–99.

Finke, Erinn H., Benjamin D. Hickerson, and Jennifer M. D. Kremkow. 2018. "'To Be Quite Honest, if It Wasn't for Videogames I Wouldn't Have a Social Life at All': Motivations of Young Adults with Autism Spectrum Disorder for Playing Videogames as Leisure." *American Journal of Speech — Language Pathology* (Online); *Rockville* 27(2): 672–89.

Fischer, John L. 1958. "Social Influence on the Choice of a Linguistic Variant." *Word* 14(1): 47–56.

Fletcher, Janet. 2005. "Exploring the Phonetics of Spoken Narratives in Australian Indigenous Languages." In *A Figure of Speech: A Festschrift for John Laver*. Mahwah: Lawrence Erlbaum.

Flores, Nelson, and Jonathan Rosa. 2015. "Undoing Appropriateness: Raciolinguistic Ideologies and Language Diversity in Education." *Harvard Educational Review* 85(2): 149–71.

Folkins, John Wm, Tim Brackenbury, Miriam Krause, and Allison Haviland. 2016. "Enhancing the Therapy Experience Using Principles of Video Game Design." *American Journal of Speech-Language Pathology* 25(1): 111–21.

Formosa, Paul, Malcolm Ryan, and Dan Staines. 2016. "Papers, Please and the Systemic Approach to Engaging Ethical Expertise in Videogames." *Ethics and Information Technology; Dordrecht* 18(3): 211–25.

Frick, Maria. 2013. "Singing and Codeswitching in Sequence Closings." *Pragmatics. Quarterly Publication of the International Pragmatics Association* 23(2): 243–73.

Fuica González, Carlos. 2013. "El Discurso Político de Resistencia En Las Redes Sociales: El Caso de Los Memes Desde Una Perspectiva Crítica y Multimodal." *Contextos: Estudios de Humanidades y Ciencias Sociales* 30: 37–48.

Furukawa, Toshiaki. 2015. "Localizing Humor through Parodying White Voice in Hawai'i Stand-up Comedy." *Text & Talk — An Interdisciplinary Journal of Language, Discourse Communication Studies* 35(6): 845–69.

Gal, Noam, Limor Shifman, and Zohar Kampf. 2016. "'It Gets Better': Internet Memes and the Construction of Collective Identity." *New Media & Society* 18(8): 1698–1714.

Geertz, Clifford. 1973. *The Interpretation of Cultures: Selected Essays*. New York, New York: Basic Books.

Georgakopoulou, Alexandra, and Tereza Spilioti. 2015. *The Routledge Handbook of Language and Digital Communication*. London: Routledge.

Gerhardt, Cornelia. 2012. "Overview of the Volume." In *The Appropriation of Media in Everyday Life*, edited by Ruth Ayaß and Cornelia Gerhardt, 17–22. Amsterdam: John Benjamins Publishing Company.

Glenn, Phillip J. 2003. *Laughter in Interaction*. Cambridge, UK: Cambridge University Press.

Glenn, Phillip J., and Mark L. Knapp. 1987. "The Interactive Framing of Play in Adult Conversations." *Communication Quarterly* 35(1): 48–66.

Goffman, Erving. 1959. *The Presentaiton of Self in Everyday Life*. New York, New York: Anchor Books.

Goffman, Erving. 1961. "Fun in Games." In *Encounters: Two Studies in the Sociology of Interaction*, 17–81. Indianapolis, IN: Bobbs-Merrill.

Goffman, Erving. 1974. *Frame Analysis: An Essay on the Organization of Experience*. Cambridge, MA: Harvard University Press.

Goffman, Erving. 1976. "Gender Display." In *Gender Advertisements*, 1–9. Springer.

Goffman, Erving. 1977. "The Arrangement between the Sexes." *Theory and Society* 4(3): 301–31.

Goffman, Erving. 1981. *Forms of Talk*. Philadelphia, Pennsylvania: University of Pennsylvania Press.

González Espinosa, F., E. Herrera Vargas, and A. Vargas Franco. 2015. "Ánálisis Crítico Del Discurso de Los 'Memes' Alusivos al Debate Sobre Paramilitarismo Del Congreso de La República de Colombia." 2014. *Revista Nexus Comunicación* 18: 70–93.

Goodwin, Charles. 1986. "Audience Diversity, Participation, and Interpretation." *Text* 6(3): 283–316.

Goodwin, Charles. 1987. "Forgetfulness as an Interactive Resource." *Social Psychology Quarterly*, 115–30.

Goodwin, Marjorie H. 1996. "Shifting Frame." In *Social Interaction, Social Context, and Language: Essays in Honor of Susan Ervin-Tripp*, edited by Dan Isaac Slobin, Julie Gerhardt, Amy Kyratzis, and Jiansheng Guo, 71–82. New York, New York: Psychology Press.

Goodwin, Marjorie H. 2006. "Participation, Affect, and Trajectory in Family Directive/ Response Sequences." *Text & Talk — An Interdisciplinary Journal of Language, Discourse Communication Studies* 26(4–5): 515–43.

Gordon, Cynthia. 2002. "'I'm Mommy and You're Natalie': Role-Reversal and Embedded Frames in Mother-Child Discourse." *Language in Society* 31(5): 679–720.

Gordon, Cynthia. 2006. "Reshaping Prior Text, Reshaping Identities." *Text & Talk — An Interdisciplinary Journal of Language, Discourse Communication Studies* 26(4–5): 545–71.

Gordon, Cynthia. 2007. "I Just Feel Horribly Embarrassed When She Does That": Constituting a Mother's Identity. In *Family Talk: Discourse and Identity in Four American Families*, edited by Deborah Tannen, Shari Kendall, and Cynthia Gordon, 71–101. Oxford: Oxford University Press.

Gordon, Cynthia. 2008. "A(p)parent Play: Blending Frames and Reframing in Family Talk." *Language in Society* 37(3): 319–49.

Gordon, Cynthia. 2009. *Making Meanings, Creating Family: Intertextuality and Framing in Family Interaction*. Oxford: Oxford University Press.

Gordon, Cynthia. 2013. "Beyond the Observer's Paradox: The Audio-Recorder as a Resource forthe Display of Identity." *Qualitative Research* 13(3): 299–317.

Grant, Elizabeth Charlotte. 2012. "Make 'Em Laugh: Sitcom Humor for Millennials." PopMatters. November 27, 2012. https://www.popmatters.com/164601-make-em-laugh-sitcom-humor-for-millennials-2495804313.html.

Gratch, Lyndsay Michalik. 2017. *Adaptation Online: Creating Memes, Sweding Movies, and Other Digital Performances*. Lexington Books.

Green, Lisa J. 2002. *African American English: A Linguistic Introduction*. Cambridge, UK: Cambridge University Press.

Grundlingh, L. 2018. "Memes as Speech Acts." *Social Semiotics* 28(2): 147–68.

Gumperz, John J. 1977. "The Sociolinguistic Significance of Conversational Code-Switching." *RELC Journal* 8(2): 1–34.

Gumperz, John J. 1982. *Discourse Strategies*. Vol. 1. Cambridge, UK: Cambridge University Press.

Gumperz, John J. 1992. "Contextualization Revisited." In *The Contextualization of Language*, edited by Peter Auer and Aldo Di Luzio, 39–53. Amsterdam: John Benjamins Publishing Company.

Günther, Susanne. 1999. "Polyphony and the 'Layering of Voices' in Reported Dialogues: An Analysis of the Use of Prosodic Devices in Everyday Reported Speech." *Journal of Pragmatics* 31(5): 685–708.

Hamilton, Heidi E. 1994. *Conversations with an Alzheimer's Patient: An Interactional Sociolinguistic Study*. Cambridge, UK: Cambridge University Press.

Hamilton, Heidi E. 1996. "Intratextuality, Intertextuality, and the Construction of Identity as Patient in Alzheimer's Disease." *Text & Talk — Interdisciplinary Journal for the Study of Discourse* 16(1): 61–90.

Hamilton, Heidi E. 2005. *Conversations with an Alzheimer's Patient: An Interactional Sociolinguistic Study*. Cambridge, UK: Cambridge University Press.

Harris-Perry, Melissa V. 2011. *Sister Citizen: Shame, Stereotypes, and Black Women in America*. London: Yale University Press.

Harvey, Lauren, and Emily Palese. 2018. "#NeverthelessMemesPersisted: Building Critical Memetic Literacy in the Classroom." *Journal of Adolescent & Adult Literacy* 62(3): 259–70.

Heritage, John. 1984. "A Change-of-State Token and Aspects of Its Sequential Placement." In *Structure of Social Action: Studies in Conversation Analysis*, edited by J. M. Atkinson and John Heritage, 299–345. Cambridge, UK: Cambridge University Press.

Heritage, John. 2010. "Questioning in Medicine." In *Why Do You Ask? The Functions of Questions in Institutional Discourse*, edited by Alice Freed and Susan Ehrlich, 42–68. Oxford: Oxford University Press.

Heritage, John. 2012. "The Epistemic Engine: Sequence Organization and Territories of Knowledge." *Research on Language & Social Interaction* 45(1): 30–52.

Heritage, John. 2013. "Epistemics in Conversation." In *The Handbook of Conversation Analysis*, edited by Jack Sidnell and Tanya Stivers, 370–94. Hoboken: John Wiley & Sons.

Heritage, John, and Geoffrey Raymond. 2012. "Navigating Epistemic Landscapes: Acquiescence, Agency and Resistance in Response to Polar Questions." In *Questions: Formal, Functional and Interacitonal Perspectives*, edited by Jan P. de Ruiter, 179–92. Cambridge, UK: Cambridge University Press.

Hewitt, Roger. 1986. *White Talk Black Talk: Inter-Racial Friendship and Communication amongst Adolescents*. Cambridge, UK: Cambridge University Press.

Hill, Jane H. 1995. "Junk Spanish, Covert Racism, and the (Leaky) Boundary between Public and Private Spheres." *Pragmatics* 5(2): 197–212.

Hill, Jane H. 1998. "Language, Race, and White Public Space." *American Anthropologist* 100(3): 680–89.

Hills, Rachel. 2006. "Adult Themes: Rewriting the Rules of Adulthood." *The Age*. November 25, 2006.

Hirschberg, Julia, and Barbara Grosz. 1992. "Intonational Features of Local and Global Discourse Structure." In *Proceedings of the DARPA workshop on Spoken Language Systems. Association for Computational Linguistics*, 1992.

Hitosugi, Claire Ikumi, Matthew Schmidt, and Kentaro Hayashi. 2014. "Digital Game-Based Learning (DGBL) in the L2 Classroom: The Impact of the UN's Off-the-Shelf Videogame, Food Force, on Learner Affect and Vocabulary Retention." *CALICO Journal* 31(1): 19–39.

Howe, Neil, and William Strauss. 2000. *Millennials Rising: The Next Great Generation*. New York: Vintage Books.

Hoyle, Susan M. 1993. "Participation Frameworks in Sportscasting Play: Imaginary and Literal Footings." In *Framing in Discourse*, edited by Deborah Tannen, 114–45. Oxford: Oxford University Press.

Hunt, Sally. 2005. "Some (More) Features of Conversation amongst Women Friends." *Southern African Linguistics and Applied Language Studies* 23(4): 445–58.

Huntington, Heidi E. 2016. "Pepper Spray Cop and the American Dream: Using Synecdoche and Metaphor to Unlock Internet Memes' Visual Political Rhetoric." *Communication Studies* 67(1): 77–93.

Husband, Charles, 1977. "The Mass Media and the Functions of Ethnic Humour in a Racist Society." In *It's a Funny Thing, Humor: Proceedings of the International Conference on Humour and Laughter 1976*, edited by Anthony J. Chapman and Hugh C. Foot, 267–72. Elmsford, NY: Pergamon.

Iaia, Pietro Luigi. 2016. *Analysing English as a Lingua Franca in Video Games: Linguistic Features, Experiential and Functional Dimensions of Online and Scripted Interactions*. Linguistic Insights: Studies in Language and Communication 220. Bern: Peter Lang.

Ilbury, Christian. 2019. " 'Sassy Queens': Stylistic orthographic variation in Twitter and the enregisterment of AAVE." *Journal of Sociolinguistics*. 24(2): 245–264.

Jaffe, Alexandra. 2009. *Stance, Sociolingustic Perspectives*. Oxford, UK: Oxford University Press.

Janebi Enayat, Mostafa, and Mohsen Haghighatpasand. 2019. "Exploiting Adventure Video Games for Second Language Vocabulary Recall: A Mixed-Methods Study." *Innovation in Language Learning and Teaching* 13(1): 61–75.

Jansen, Wouter, Michelle L. Gregory, and Jason M. Brenier. 2001. "Prosodic Correlates of Directly Reported Speech: Evidence from Conversational Speech." In *ISCA Tutorial and Research Workshop (ITRW) on Prosody in Speech Recognition and Understanding*.

Jones, Rodney H. 2012. "Introduction: Discourse and Creativity." In *Discourse and Creativity*, edited by Rodney H Jones, 1–13. London: Pearson.

Jones, Rodney H. 2016. "Creativity and Discourse Analysis." In *Routledge Handbook of Language and Creativity*, edited by Rodney H Jones, 61–77. London: Routledge.

Jones, Taylor. 2016. "AAE Talmbout: An Overlooked Verb of Quotation." *University of Pennsylvania Working Papers in Linguistics* 22(2): 11.

Kaklamanidou, Betty, and Margaret Tally, eds. 2014. *The Millennials on Film and Television: Essays on the Politics of Popular Culture*. Jefferson, North Carolina: McFarland & Company, Inc., Publishers.

Kanai, Akane. 2016. "Sociality and classification: Reading Gender, Race, and Class in a Humorous Meme." *Social Media+ Society*, 2(4):1–12.

Kärkkäinen, Elise. 2007. "Stance Taking in Conversation: From Subjectivity to Intersubjectivity." *Text & Talk — An Interdisciplinary Journal of Language, Discourse Communication Studies* 26(6): 699–731.

Karpowitz, Christopher F., and Tali Mendelberg. 2014. *The Silent Sex: Gender, Deliberation, and Institutions*. Princeton, New Jersey: Princeton University Press.

Kelley, Jeremy Carl. 2013. *Queering Conversation: An Ethnographic Exploration of The Functional Properties of Camp-Based Language Use in US Gay Men's Interactions*. Doctoral Dissertation, University of California, Los Angeles.

Kelly, Matthew. 2018. "The Game of Politics: Examining the Role of Work, Play, and Subjectivity Formation in *Papers, Please*." *Games and Culture* 13(5): 459–78.

Kiesling, Scott F. 2019. "The 'Gay Voice' and 'Brospeak': Towards a Systemic Model of Stance." In *The Oxford Handbook of Language and Sexuality*, edited by Kira Hall and Rusty Barrett. Oxford: Oxford University Press.

Kiesling, Scott Fabius. 2005. "Homosocial Desire in Men's Talk: Balancing and Re-Creating Cultural Discourses of Masculinity." *Language in Society* 34(5): 695–726.

Klerk, Vivian de. 1992. "How Taboo Are Taboo Words for Girls?" *Language in Society* 21(2): 277–89.

Klerk, Vivian de. 1997. "The Role of Expletives in the Construction of Masculinity." In *Language and Masculinity*, edited by S. Johnson and U. H. Meinhof, 144–58. Oxford: Blackwell.

Kligler-Vilenchik, Neta, and Kjerstin Thorson. 2016. "Good Citizenship as a Frame Contest: Kony2012, Memes, and Critiques of the Networked Citizen." *New Media & Society* 18(9): 1993–2011.

Kurylo, Anastacia. 2013. *The Communicated Stereotype: From Celebrity Vilification to Everyday Talk*. Lanham, MD: Lexington Books.

Kotthoff, Helga. 2006. "Gender and Humor: The State of the Art." *Journal of Pragmatics* 38(1), 4–25.

Kristeva, Julia. 1980. *Desire in Language: A Semiotic Approach to Literature and Art*. Edited by Leon S. Roudiez. Translated by Thomas Gora and Alice A. Jardine. New York: Columbia University Press.

Kristeva, Julia. 1986. *The Kristeva Reader*. New York: Columbia University Press.

Labov, William. 1972. *Sociolinguistic Patterns*. Philadelphia, Pennsylvania: University of Pennsylvania Press.

Labov, William, and David Fanshel. 1977. *Therapeutic Discourse: Psychotherapy as Conversation*. New York: Academic Press.

Labrador, Roderick N. 2004. "'We Can Laugh at Ourselves': Hawai'i Ethnic Humor, Local Identity and the Myth of Multiculturalism." *Pragmatics* 14(2–3), 291–316.

Lacasa, Pilar, Rut Martínez, and Laura Méndez. 2008. "Developing New Literacies Using Commercial Videogames as Educational Tools." *Linguistics and Education* 19(2): 85–106.

Laineste, Liisi, and Piret Voolaid. 2017. "Laughing across Borders: Intertextuality of Internet Memes." *The European Journal of Humour Research* 4(4): 26–49.

Lankshear, Colin, and Michele Knobel. 2007. *A New Literacies Sampler*. New York: Peter Lang.

Lim, Sung-joo, and Lori L. Holt. 2011. "Learning Foreign Sounds in an Alien World: Videogame Training Improves Non-Native Speech Categorization." *Cognitive Science* 35(7): 1390–1405.

Lippi-Green, Rosina. 2012. *English with an Accent: Language, Ideology and Discrimination in the United States*. London: Routledge.

Lohmeyer, Eddie. 2017. "Papers, Please as Critical Making: A Review." *Press Start* 4(1): 11–16.

Lopez, Qiuana, and Lars Hinrichs. 2017. "'C'mon, Get Happy': The Commodification of Linguistic Stereotypes in a Volkswagen Super Bowl Commercial." *Journal of English Linguistics* 45(2): 130–56.

Lull, James. 1990. *Inside Family Viewing: Ethnographic Research on Television Audiences*. London: Routledge.

Lytra, Vally. 2007. *Play Frames and Social Identities: Contact Encounters in a Greek Primary School*. Amsterdam: John Benjamins Publishing.

Makri-Tsilipakou, Marianthi. 1994. "Laughing Their Way: Gender and Conversational Mirth." *Working Papers in Language, Gender and Sexism* 4(1): 15–50.

Mandelbaum, Jennifer. 1987. "Couples Sharing Stories." *Communication Quarterly* 35(2): 144–70.

Mannell, Roger C. 1977. "Vicarious Superiority, Injustice, and Aggression in Humor: The Role of the Playful Judgmental Set." In *It's a Funny Thing, Humor: Proceedings of the International Conference on Humour and Laughter 1976*, edited by Anthony J. Chapman and Hugh C. Foot, 273–6. Elmsford, NY: Pergamon.

Martínez-Rolán, Xabier, and Teresa Piñeiro-Otero. 2016. "The Use of Memes in the Discourse of Political Parties on Twitter: Analysing the 2015 State of the Nation Debate." *Communication & Society* 29(1): 145–59.

Mathis, Terrie, and George Yule. 1994. "Zero Quotatives." *Discourse Processes* 18(1): 63–76.

Maybin, Janet. 2003. "Voices, Intertextuality and Induction into Schooling." In *Language, Literacy and Education: A Reader*, edited by Sharon Goodman, Theresa Lillis, Janet Maybin, and Neil Mercer, 159–70. London: Trentham.

McCulloch, Richard. 2011. "'Most People Bring Their Own Spoons': THE ROOM's Participatory Audiences as Comedy Mediators." *Participations: Journal of Audience & Reception Studies* 8(2): 189–218.

Meek, Barbra A. 2006. "And the Injun Goes 'How!': Representations of American Indian English in White Public Space." *Language in Society* 35(1): 93–128.

Mendoza-Denton, Norma. 2008. *Homegirls: Language and Cultural Practice among Latina Youth Gangs*. New Directions in Ethnography 2. Malden, MA: Blackwell.

Meyer, John C. 2015. *Understanding Humor through Communication: Why Be Funny, Anyway?* Lexington Books.

Milner, Ryan M. 2013a. "Hacking the Social: Internet Memes, Identity Antagonism, and the Logic of Lulz." *The Fiber Culture Journal* 22.

Milner, Ryan M. 2013b. "Pop Polyvocality: Internet Memes, Public Participation, and the Occupy Wall Street Movement." *International Journal of Communication* 7: 2357–90.

Milner, Ryan M. 2016. *The World Made Meme: Public Conversations and Participatory Media.* Cambridge, MA: MIT Press.

Mirzoeff, Nicholas. 1999. "Transculture: From Kongo to the Congo." In *An Introduction to Visual Culture*, 129–61. London: Routledge.

Mondada, Lorenza. 2012. "Coordinating Action and Talk-in-Interaction in and out of Video Games." In *The Appropriation of Media in Everyday Life*, edited by Ruth Ayaß and Cornelia Gerhardt, 231–70. Amsterdam: John Benjamins Publishing.

Morgan, Marcyliena. 1999. "No Woman No Cry: Claiming African American Women's Place." In *Reinventing Identities: The Gendered Self in Discourse*, edited by Mary Bucholtz, A. C. Liang, and Laurel A. Sutton, 27–45. Oxford: Oxford University Press.

Nakamura, Lisa. 2002. *Cybertypes: Race, Ethnicity, and Identity on the Internet.* London: Routledge.

Norrick, Neal R. 1989. "Intertextuality in Humor." *Humor — International Journal of Humor Research* 2(2): 117–40.

Norrick, Neal R. 1994. "Involvement and Joking in Conversation." *Journal of Pragmatics* 22(3–4): 409–30.

Norrick, Neal R., and Alice Spitz. 2010. "The Interplay of Humor and Conflict in Conversation and Scripted Humorous Performance." *Humor — International Journal of Humor Research* 23(1): 83–111.

Ochs, Elinor. 1993. "Constructing Social Identity: A Language Socialization Perspective." *Research on Language and Social Interaction* 26(3): 287–306.

O'Donnell-Trujillo, Nick, and Katherine Adams. 1983. "Heheh in conversation: Some Coordinating Accomplishments of Laughter." *Western Journal of Speech Communication* 47(2): 175–91.

Palmer, Kimberly. 2007. "The New Parent Trap: More Boomers Help Adult Kids Out Financially." *US News & World Report.* December 12, 2007. https://money.usnews.com/money/personal-finance/articles/2007/12/12/the-new-parent-trap.

Park, Yujong. 2009. "Interaction between Grammar and Multimodal Resources: Quoting Different Characters in Korean Multiparty Conversation." *Discourse Studies* 11(1): 79–104.

Pérez, Raúl. 2013. "Learning to Make Racism Funny in the 'Color-blind' Era: Stand-up Comedy Students, Performance Strategies, and the (re) Production of Racist Jokes in Public." *Discourse & Society* 24(4): 478–503.

Phillips, Whitney, and Ryan M. Milner. 2017. *The Ambivalent Internet: Mischief, Oddity, and Antagonism Online.* Cambridge, UK: Polity Press.

Piirainen-Marsh, Arja. 2012. "Organising Participation in Video Gaming Activities." In *The Appropriation of Media in Everyday Life*, edited by Ruth Ayaß and Cornelia Gerhardt, 195–230. Amsterdam: John Benjamins Publishing.

Pitarch, Ricardo Casañ. 2018. "An Approach to Digital Game-Based Learning: Video-Games Principles and Applications in Foreign Language Learning." *Journal of Language Teaching and Research* 9(6): 1147–59.

Pope, Lucas. 2013. *Papers, Please.* Japan: 3909 LLC.

Potter, Jonathan, and Alexa Hepburn. 2010. "Putting Aspiration into Words: 'Laugh Particles,' Managing Descriptive Trouble and Modulating Action." *Journal of Pragmatics*, Laughter in Interaction 42(6): 1543–55.

Poveda, David. 2011. "Performance and Interaction during 'Reading Hour' in a Spanish Secondary School." *Linguistics and Education* 22(1): 79–92.

Prensky, Mark. 2001. *Digital Game-Based Learning.* New York: McGraw-Hill.

Rampton, Ben. 1995. *Crossing: Language and Ethnicity among Adolescents.* London: Routledge.

Rampton, Ben. 2006. *Language in Late Modernity: Interaction in an Urban School.* Cambridge, UK: Cambridge University Press.

Rawitsch, David, Bill Heinemann, and Paul Dillenberger. 1985. *The Oregon Trail*. Apple II. Brooklyn Center, Minnesota: Minnesota Educational Computer Consortium.

Raymond, Geoffrey, and John Heritage. 2006. "The Epistemics of Social Relations: Owning Grandchildren." *Language in Society* 35(5): 677–705.

Reale, Steven Beverburg. 2012. "A Sheep in Wolf's Corset: Timbral and Vocal Signifiers of Masculinity in The Rocky Horror Picture/Glee Show." *Music, Sound, and the Moving Image* 6(2): 137.

Rintel, Sean. 2013. "Video Calling in Long-Distance Relationships: The Opportunistic Use of Audio/Video Distortions as a Relational Resource." *The Electronic Journal of Communication* 23(1 & 2).

Robles, Jessica. 2015. "Extreme Case (re) Formulation as a Practice for Making Hearably Racist Talk Repairable." *Journal of Language and Social Psychology* 34(4), 390–409.

Robles, Jessica. 2019. "Building Up by Tearing Down." *Journal of Language and Social Psychology* 38(1): 85–105.

Robles, Jessica, and Anastacia Kurylo. 2017. "'Let's Have the Men Clean Up': Interpersonally Communicated Stereotypes as a Resource for Resisting Gender-role Prescribed Activities." *Discourse Studies* 19(6): 673–93.

Romaine, Suzanne, and Deborah Lange. 1991. "The Use of *like* as a Marker of Reported Speech and Thought: A Case of Grammaticalization in Process." *American Speech* 66(3): 227–79.

Ronkin, Maggie, and Helen E. Karn. 1999. "Mock Ebonics: Linguistic Racism in Parodies of Ebonics on the Internet." *Journal of Sociolinguistics* 3(3): 360–80.

Ross, Andrew S., and Damian J. Rivers. 2017. "Digital Cultures of Political Participation: Internet Memes and the Discursive Delegitimization of the 2016 US Presidential Candidates." *Discourse, Context & Media* 16: 1–11.

Sacks, Harvey. 1992. *Lectures on Conversation: Two Volumes*. Edited by Gail Jefferson and Emanuel A. Schegloff. Oxford: Blackwell.

Sacks, Harvey. 1999. "Everybody Has to Lie." In *Discourse Reader*, edited by Adam Jaworski and Nikolas Coupland, 252–62. London: Routledge.

Schegloff, Emanuel A. 1989. "An Introduction/Memoir for Harvey Sacks-Lectures." *Human Studies* 12(3): 185–209.

Schegloff, Emanuel A. 2010. "Some Other 'Uh(m)'s." *Discourse Processes* 47(2): 130–74.

Schiffrin, Deborah. 1987. *Discourse Markers*. Cambridge, UK: Cambridge University Press.

Schiffrin, Deborah. 1993. "'Speaking for Another' in Sociolinguistics Interviews: Alignments, Identities, and Frames." In *Framing in Discourse*, edited by Deborah Tannen, 231–55. Oxford: Oxford University Press.

Schiffrin, Deborah. 1996. "Narrative as Self-portrait: Sociolinguistic Constructions of Identity." *Language in Society* 25(2): 167–203.

Schilling, Natalie. 2013. *Sociolinguistic Fieldwork*. Cambridge, UK: Cambridge University Press.

Schlobinski, Peter. 1995. "Jugendsprachen: Speech Styles of Youth Subcultures." In *The German Language and the Real World: Sociolinguistic, Cultural, and Pragmatic Perspectives on Contemporary German*. Oxford: Oxford University Press.

Scholz, Kyle. 2017. "Encouraging Free Play: Extramural Digital Game-Based Language Learning as a Complex Adaptive System." *CALICO Journal* 34(1): 39–57.

Schütz, Alfred. 1946. "The Well-Informed Citizen: An Essay on the Social Distribution of Knowledge." *Social Research* 13(4): 463–78.

Scollo, Michelle. 2007. *Mass Media Appropriations: Communication, Culture, and Everyday Social Life*. Doctoral Dissertation, University of Massachusetts Amherst.

Segev, Elad, Asaf Nissenbaum, Nathan Stolero, and Limor Shifman. 2015. "Families and Networks of Internet Memes: The Relationship Between Cohesiveness, Uniqueness, and Quiddity Concreteness." *Journal of Computer-Mediated Communication* 20(4) 417–33.

Sestero, Greg, and Tom Bissell. 2013. *The Disaster Artist: My Life inside The Room the Greatest Bad Movie Ever Made*. New York: Simon & Schuster.

Shankar, Shalina. 2004. "Reel to Real: Desi Teens' Linguistic Engagement with Bollywood." *Pragmatics* 14(2/3): 317–35.

Shaputis, Kathleen. 2004. *The Crowded Nest Syndrome: Surviving the Return of Adult Children*. Olympia, Washington, D.C.: Clutter Fairy Publishing.

Sherzer, Joel. 2002. *Speech Play and Verbal Art*. Austin: University of Texas Press.

Shifman, Limor. 2012. "An anatomy of a YouTube meme." *New Media & Society* 14(2): 187–203.

Shifman, Limor. 2013. "Memes in a Digital World: Reconciling with a Conceptual Troublemaker." *Journal of Computer-Mediated Communication* 18(3): 362–77.

Shifman, Limor. 2014. *Memes in Digital Culture*. Cambridge, MA: The MIT Press.

Shirazi, Mahshid, Seyyed Dariush Ahmadi, and Ali Gholami Mehrdad. 2016. "The Effect of Using Video Games on EFL Learners' Acquisition of Speech Acts of Apology and Request." *Theory and Practice in Language Studies* 6(5): 1019–26.

Sierra, Sylvia. 2016. "Playing Out Loud: Videogame References as Resources in Friend Interaction for Managing Frames, Epistemics, and Group Identity." *Language in Society* 45(2): 217–45.

Sierra, Sylvia. 2019. "Linguistic and Ethnic Media Stereotypes in Everyday Talk: Humor and Identity Construction among Friends." *Journal of Pragmatics* 152:186–89.

Slobe, Tyanna. 2018. "Style, Stance, and Social Meaning in Mock White Girl." *Language in Society* 47(4): 541–67.

Smith, Christopher A. 2019. "Weaponized Iconoclasm in Internet Memes Featuring the Expression 'Fake News.'" *Discourse & Communication* 13(3): 303–19.

Søndergaard, Bent. 1991. "Switching between Seven Codes within One Family—a Linguistic Resource." *Journal of Multilingual and Multicultural Development* 12(1–2): 85–92.

Spigel, Lynn. 1992. *Make Room for TV: Television and the Family Ideal in Postwar America*. Chicago: University of Chicago Press.

Spigel, Lynn. 2001. *Welcome to the Dreamhouse: Popular Media and Postwar Suburbs*. Console-Ing Passions. Durham, North Carolina: Duke University Press.

Spilioti, Tereza. 2015. "Digital Discourse: A Critical Perspective." In *The Routledge Handbook of Language and Digital Communication*, edited by Alexandra Georgakopoulou and Tereza Spillioti, 133–45. London: Routledge.

Spitulnik, Debra. 1996. "The Social Circulation of Media Discourse and the Mediation of Communities." *Journal of Linguistic Anthropology* 6(2): 161–87.

Stec, Kashmiri, Mike Huiskes, and Gisela Redeker. 2015. "Multimodal Analysis of Quotation in Oral Narratives." *Open Linguistics* 1(1).

Stevanovic, Melisa, and Maria Frick. 2014. "Singing in Interaction." *Social Semiotics* 24(4): 495–513.

Stivers, Tanya, and Federico Rossano. 2010. "Mobilizing Response." *Research on Language and Social Interaction* 43(1): 3–31.

Stokoe, Elizabeth. 2003. "Mothers, Single Women and Sluts: Gender, Morality and Membership Categorization in Neighbor Disputes." *Feminism & Psychology* 13(3): 317–44.

Stokoe, Elizabeth. 2009. "Doing actions with Identity Categories: Complaints and Denials in neighbor disputes." *Text & Talk — An Interdisciplinary Journal of Language, DiscourseCommunication Studies* 29(1): 75–97.

Stokoe, Ellizabeth, and Derek Edwards. 2014. "Mundane Morality: Gender, Categories and Complaints in Familial Neighbour Disputes." *Journal of Applied Linguistics and Professional Practice* 9(2): 165–92.

Straehle, Carolyn A. 1993. "'Samuel?' 'Yes, Dear?': Teasing and Conversational Rapport." In *Framing in Discourse*, edited by Deborah Tannen, 210–30. Oxford: Oxford University Press.

Strauss, William, and Neil Howe. 1991. *Generations: The History of America's Future, 1584 to 2069*. New York: William Morrow & Co.

Streeck, Jürgen. 2002. "Grammars, Words, and Embodied Meanings: On the Uses and Evolution of so and Like." *Journal of Communication* 52(3): 581–96.

Sykes, Julie M. 2018. "Digital Games and Language Teaching and Learning." *Foreign Language Annals* 51(1): 219–24.

Tally, Margaret. 2014. "'Comedy Natives': Generations, Humor and the Question of Why Smart + Funny Is the New Rock and Roll." In *The Millennials on Film and Television: Essays on the Politics of Popular Culture*, edited by Betty Kaklamanidou and Margaret Tally. Jefferson: McFarland.

Tannen, Deborah. 1986 [2011]. "Introducing Constructed Dialogue in Greek and American Conversational and Literary Narrative." In *Direct and Indirect Speech*, edited by Florian Coulmas, 311–32. Berlin: Mouton de Gruyter.

Tannen, Deborah. 1993. "What's in a Frame? Surface Evidence for Underlying Expectations." In *Framing in Discourse*, edited by Deborah Tannen, 14–56. Oxford: Oxford University Press.

Tannen, Deborah. 1996. "Researching Gender-Related Patterns in Classroom Discourse." *TESOL Quarterly* 30(2): 341–44.

Tannen, Deborah. 2005 [1984]. *Conversational Style: Analyzing Talk Among Friends*. Oxford: Oxford University Press.

Tannen, Deborah. 2006. "Intertextuality in Interaction: Reframing Family Arguments in Public and Private." *Text & Talk-An Interdisciplinary Journal of Language, Discourse Communication Studies* 26(4–5): 597–617.

Tannen, Deborah. 2007 [1989]. *Talking Voices: Repetition, Dialogue, and Imagery in Conversational Discourse*. Vol. 26. Cambridge, UK: Cambridge University Press.

Tannen, Deborah. 2011 [1986]. *That's Not What I Meant! How Conversational Style Makes or Breaks Your Relations with Others*. New York: Morrow.

Tannen, Deborah. 2017. You're the only one I can tell: Inside the language of women's friendships. New York: Ballantine Books.

Tannen, Deborah, and Cynthia Wallat. 1993. "Interactive Frames and Knowledge Schemas in Interaction: Examples from a Medical Examination/Interview." In *Framing in Discourse*, edited by Deborah Tannen, 57–76. Oxford: Oxford University Press.

Tartter, Vivien C., and David Braun. 1994. "Hearing Smiles and Frowns in Normal and Whisper Registers." *The Journal of the Acoustical Society of America* 96(4): 2101–7.

Thompson, Sandra A, and Ryoko Suzuki. 2014. "Reenactments in Conversation: Gaze and Recipiency." *Discourse Studies* 16(6): 816–46.

Thornborrow, Joanna. 1997. "Playing Power: Gendered Discourses in a Computer Games Magazine." *Language and Literature* 6(1): 43–55.

Thurlow, Crispin. 2012. "Determined Creativity: Language Play in New Media Discourse." In *Discourse and Creativity*, edited by Rodney Jones, 169–290. London: Routledge.

Thurlow, Crispin, and Kristine Mroczek. 2011. *Digital Discourse: Language in the New Media*. Oxford: Oxford University Press.

Toolan, Michael. 2012. "Poems: Wonderfully Repetitive." In *Discourse and Creativity*, edited by Rodney H Jones. London: Pearson. 17–34.

Tovares, Alla. 2006. "Public Medium, Private Talk: Gossip about a TV Show as 'Quotidian Hermeneutics.'" *Text & Talk-An Interdisciplinary Journal of Language, Discourse Communication Studies* 26(4–5): 463–91.

Tovares, Alla. 2007. "Family Members Interacting While Watching TV." In *Family Talk: Discourse and Identity in Four American Families*, edited by Deborah Tannen, Shari Kendall, and Cynthia Gordon, 283–309. Oxford: Oxford University Press.

Tovares, Alla. 2012. "Watching Out Loud: A Television Quiz Show as a Resource in Family Interaction." In *The Appropriation of Media in Everyday Life*, edited by Ruth Ayaß and Cornelia Gerhardt, 105–30. Amsterdam: John Benjamins Publishing Company.

Trester, Anna Marie. 2012. "Framing Entextualization in Improv: Intertextuality as an Interactional Resource." *Language in Society* 41(2): 237–58.

van Dijk, Teun A. 1992. "Discourse and the Denial of Racism." *Discourse & Society* 3(1): 87–118.

van Dijk, Teun A. 2013. "The Field of Epistemic Discourse Analysis." *Discourse Studies* 15(5): 497–99.

van Dijk, Teun A. 2014. *Discourse and Knowledge: A Sociocognitive Approach.* Cambridge, UK: Cambridge University Press.

Varenne, Hervé, Gillian Andrews, Aaron Chia Yuan Hung, and Sarah Wessler. 2013. "Polities and Politics of Ongoing Assessments: Evidence from Video-Gaming and Blogging." In *Discourse 2.0.: Language and New Media*, edited by Deborah Tannen and Anna Marie Trester. Washington, D.C.: Georgetown University Press.

Vásquez, Camilla, and Samantha Creel. 2017. "Conviviality through Creativity: Appealing to the Reblog in Tumblr Chat Posts." *Discourse, Context & Media* 20: 59–69.

Wachau, Susanne. 1989. "Nicht so Verschlüsselt Und Verschleimt!-Über Einstellungen Gegenüber Jugendsprache." *Osnabrücker Beiträge Zur Sprachtheorie*, 69–97.

Wagener, Albin. 2018. "Russophobia in DotA 2: A Critical Discursive Analysis of Online Discrimination." *International Review of Pragmatics* 10(1): 57–75.

Wahl, Alexander. 2010. "The global Metastereotyping of Hollywood 'Dudes': African Reality Television Parodies of Mediatized California Style." *Pragmatics and Society* 1(2): 209–33.

Warnock, Roy Melissa Gideon Loftus Warnock Foster. (2015). *Dementia and Singing: A Conversation Analysis Case Study of Signing in Everyday Interaction.* Doctoral Dissertation, University of Colorado, Boulder.

Watkins, S. Craig. 2018. "The Mobile Paradox: Understanding the Mobile Lives of Latino and Black Youth." In *The Digital Edge: How Black and Latino Youth Navigate Digital Inequality*, edited by S. Craig Watkins, 50–77. New York: New York University Press.

Wiggins, Bradley E., and G. Bret Bowers. 2015. "Memes as Genre: A Structurational Analysis of the Memescape." *New Media & Society* 17(11): 1886–1906.

Wolfers, Solvejg, Kieran File, and Stephanie Schnurr. 2017. "'Just Because He's Black': Identity Construction and Racial Humour in a German U-19 Football Team." *Journal of Pragmatics* 112: 83–96.

Yang, Siyue. 2017. "An Analysis of Factors Influencing Transmission of Internet Memes of English-Speaking Origin in Chinese Online Communities." *Journal of Language Teaching and Research* 8(5): 969–77.

Yoon, InJeong. 2016. "Why Is It Not Just a Joke? Analysis of Internet Memes Associated with Racism and Hidden Ideology of colorblindness." *Journal of Cultural Research in Art Education* 33: 92–123.

Yule, George, and Terrie Mathis. 1992. "The Role of Staging and Constructed Dialogue in Establishing Speaker's Topic." *Linguistics* 30(1): 199–215.

Zappavigna, Michele. 2012. *Discourse of Twitter and Social Media: How We Use Language to Create Affiliation on the Web.* London: A&C Black.

Zivony, Alon, and Tamar Saguy. 2018. "Stereotype Deduction about Bisexual Women." *The Journal of Sex Research* 55: 4–5, 666–78.

Zsiga, Elizabeth C. 2012. *The Sounds of Language: An Introduction to Phonetics and Phonology.* Hoboken: John Wiley & Sons.

Index